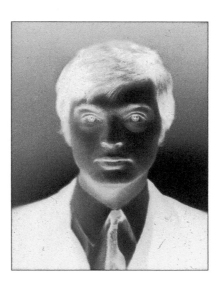

the anonymity of an
in-house designer

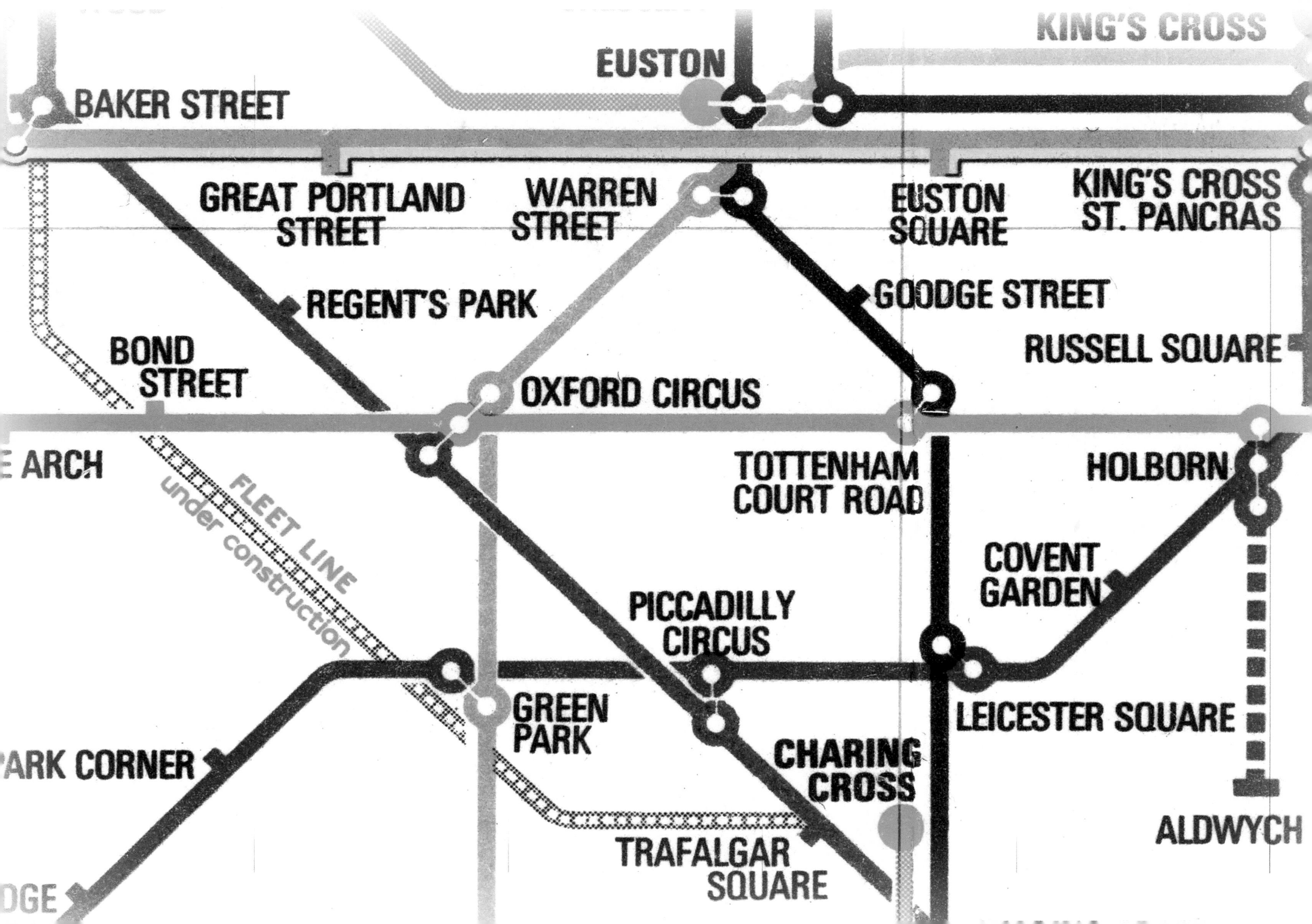

KING'S CROSS

EUSTON

BAKER STREET

GREAT PORTLAND STREET

WARREN STREET

EUSTON SQUARE

KING'S CROSS ST. PANCRAS

REGENT'S PARK

GOODGE STREET

BOND STREET

RUSSELL SQUARE

OXFORD CIRCUS

E ARCH

TOTTENHAM COURT ROAD

HOLBORN

FLEET LINE under construction

COVENT GARDEN

PICCADILLY CIRCUS

GREEN PARK

LEICESTER SQUARE

ARK CORNER

CHARING CROSS

TRAFALGAR SQUARE

ALDWYCH

DGE

the anonymity of an in-house designer

Tim Demuth

Grafica Muti

Published by:
GraficaMuti,
248 Gosbrook Road,
Caversham, Reading,
RG4 8EA

Designed by:
Tim Demuth

Printed digitally by:
CPI Group (UK) Ltd,
Croydon, CR04YY

Acknowledgments

My thanks and appreciation
must go to all the people who
facilitated my advancements to
the position inwhich I find myself
now: my parents and my sister,
teachers, employers, printers,
colleagues and friends.

I also extend my thanks to
Val and Stan Friedman who read
the text in its earliest stage and
encouraged me to persevere.

To numerous friends and
acquaintances who reminded,
or corrected, me of past
happenings.

Some photographs originate from
the Transport for London archives
now housed at the London
Transport Museum at London's
Covent Garden to whom I extend
my thanks.

Typeset in:

text: 8.6/11pt Zapf Elyptical
        initial chapter characters
        54pt English 111 Adagio

captions:6.5/7.5pt Helvetica
        condened and roman

chapter titles:
        52pt Helvetica thin

Contents

Twenty years separates these two publications, both written by the author of this volume.

The top illustrates pages of the thesis written, produced and bound for submission to the Diploma in Art and Design course in 1960. It discusses some reasons why the Courage brewery adopted a cockerel to symbolise its products.

Just two spreads are shown on the right illustrating an article which appeared in two parts in the LONDON BUS MAGAZINE in 1980. It traces the use of Johnston lettering on signs, vehicles and publications throughout the London bus network.

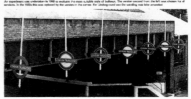

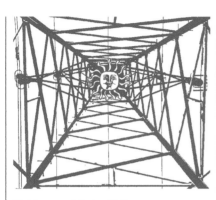

Christmas card design 1963.

*I*n most walks of life we make use of and consume objects without considering that there was one or more persons who created and developed them. It is sometimes only during unsatisfactory experiences with objects that the consumer demands to know who invented or built them.

The profession in which the author spent his working life was as a graphic designer, sometimes described by the uninitiated as an 'artist'. But artists – whether they be painters, sculptors or potters – usually conceive and produce their own work to their own briefs and initially stand or fall by the perceived success of their work culminating in 'making a name for themselves'. By contrast, a graphic designer is the facilitator to project the attitudes and messages of his client – the client's 'image'. The designer might be used to enhance an environment within a building, in association with an interior designer or architect. Or his ideas may help to convey safety or directional messages on signs, or facilitate the readability of books, magazines and newspapers with page layouts and typography. By far the most graphic designers lend their talents to aid the great capitalist merry-go-round in the form of making products more attractive or imperative to be bought, be they artworkers, typographers, painters or film makers within the advertising industry.

This book aims to describe the experiences of a graphic designer who worked within the former category, aiming to simplify the visual display of information to the individual reader. The project started as a reaction to seeing works captioned as being designed anonymously or credited with incorrect or fictitious names, sometimes erroneously confusing the designers' and printers' names. The stock of printed work in the author's possession stirred memories of the birth and growing pains of many of these projects – some sprang from an idea to the final item as a smooth flow; most were the result of a journey over hurdles, styles, hill climbing and reversing.

To broaden the picture, much of the author's background and personal thoughts intertwine and shadow the story, since the two were often emotionally connected to, or sometimes in conflict with, each other. So the book can be described as a treatise on informational graphic design, or the autobiography of a person who drifted into graphic design. Whichever way the text is approached, it was the graphic design that gave the author sanctuary when domestic and political pressures sometimes became too complicated to be resolved on their own. He has described himself as being, fairly uniquely, lucky in his adult life as his work developed into his hobby.

The title of the book, *the anonymity of an in-house designer*, could be said to be contradictory, since the author's name did occasionally appear on graphic works designed by him. But the few works on which his superiors demanded his name be recognised were considered by them to be 'commendable works of art', thus showing the blurred line separating art and graphic design.

Hopefully this book will be of use to graphic design students as an introduction to the types of projects that may still be encountered in their field, even if today's methods of production and reproduction differ in almost every respect to those employed in the twentieth century. But the initial approach to analysis and logical problem solving remains the same.

One might bemoan the time when type was set in metal by journeymen compositors and artwork was drawn on cardboard and sent to engravers to be turned into halftones and line blocks. Nowadays, with the aid of a camera, scanner and computer, the entire work can be accomplished by one person up to printing stage in one small room, as was this work.

During development, this project was shown to a number of people, all who looked forward to its completion. Non more so than Stan and Val Friedman, to whom I offer my sincere thanks for their encouragement.

Tim Demuth
Reading RG4 8EA

June 2012

Tim aged 3 with his sister
Bridgett, 18 months older, at the
front door of 4 Oakshade Road in
Oxshott in 1945.

Father and mother, when they
still lived in Boscombe in the mid
1930s.

My first recollection of an existence on this planet was my mother's reprimand when I spilt my tomato soup. My clumsiness was excusable since, instead of sitting at the dining room table, I was crouched under it for protection, together with my mother and sister, Bridgett, as sirens wailed a warning of a possible attack from the air. As it transpired to me later, these 'attacks' which we regularly sheltered from were by enemy planes unloading excess bombs following raids on London, to make themselves lighter and allow their limited fuel to return them to their own friendly airstrips on the continent of Europe.

The year would have been 1944. The location was a small village south of London in Surrey, called Oxshott, between Esher and Leatherhead. The exact address was in the unmade up and pot holed Oakshade Road, at number 4, which was a semi-detached house rented from the local builder, H. G. & A. Osman Ltd of Steels Lane, the other half being occupied by the postman, Mr Furley and his wife, who were both very old. On the other side or our home was a separate house behind a high fence and hedge, in which the Robinsons resided. I only knew of them, since I cannot visualise the adults and am not aware of any children. Because the houses along our side of the road were set back our front garden, and I think the Furley's next door, had been converted to the

cultivation of food. Ours contained vegetables neatly planted in rows and a menagerie of chickens and ducks. The chickens were Rode Island Reds and small and noisy Bantams, which laid rich small eggs. This was during the Second World War, when food was in short supply and much of it rationed. But the conditions were something of a gift to my father, who enjoyed gardening, and to my mother who loved animals.

On the other side of the road was a field that could just be seen through a thorn hedge. Traffic was minimal – I remember Prewett's horse drawn daily milk delivery wagon grinding and lurching over boulders and into valleys, the bottles chiming in unison.

My parents had met in Boscombe, a suburb of Bournemouth, when they were in their early twenties. It was when my future father was bathing with a party of young ladies, that his glass eye was washed out of its socket by a wave – some years earlier a fall on the pavement had caused a lens of his glasses to splinter, resulting in the loss of one eye. So the girl that he would later marry, my future mother, stayed in the water, while the others went home, diving and re-diving to the sea bed until she repatriated the submerged staring china globe.

Claud Frederick Demuth and Rosemarie Pearl Thompson were married in Christchurch Priory in Hampshire. They then moved to London, where Claud (nicknamed Tim within his family) took up a job as a copywriter in Barkers advertising agency in Kensington High Street. Claud and Rosemary moved into a top floor flat at Holland Park on the unforgettable evening, for those who were there, that the Crystal Palace burned to the ground. Father and mother told me that they spent much of the night gazing from the flat at the glowing sky – a portent of further night time glows two years later. They would have moved to Oakshade Road in Oxshott just before the War started, since Bridgett was born on 20 June 1939 in a nursing home a few miles away at Cobham, a village that we would move to in 1948. When war broke out in August 1939, father's

limited sight made him ineligible for national service. His contribution to the war effort was spent at nights on the roof of Vickers Weybridge aircraft factory, spotting and giving warning of enemy aircraft. His remaining eye answered the call admirably!

I was born on 24 January 1942, a month earlier than expected, possibly as a result of my mother's fall down the stairs at our home the night before. Thick snow meant that not only could my mother not be moved to a nursing home, but the district nurse was unable to attend my birth at number 4 Oakshade Road. The broken stair bannister served as a reminder to me of my abrupt entry to this world since it was not repaired as long as I lived at that address.

Father commuted to London on weekdays (and Saturday mornings) and tended his vegetables in our garden at the weekends, while mother looked after the livestock, Bridgett and me and took us shopping in the little village. This was the routine that I was brought up in. We also went for walks amongst the pine trees and sandy soil of Oxshott Woods, situated to the west of the railway line.

I quite vividly recollect my second encounter with the War extending to our tranquil village, when I ran down the garden path towards the front gate pointing at a cigar shaped sausage in the sky emitting a slow farting noise. It was my mother' concern which probably caused my mind to retain

It all began with a doodlebug

St.Andrew's Church in Oxshott as it looked in the 1940s.

this image, since she led me smartly back into our home to the safety of under the dining room table. The noise, of course, belonged to a V1 rocket, what was colloquially referred to as a doodlebug, heading for London.

Breaks from daily routine meant that I spent some time on the other side of the Furleys, at the bungalow called Potterscroft of the Wrens. Denise and her adult daughter Rosemary ran a pottery from a shed in their front garden producing pots and plates on the wheel and firing them in a kiln on the premises. Mother often visited the Wrens in their workshop where she continued with her hobby of making pottery animals that she had started when living in Boscombe. Since moving to Oxshott she started attending evening classes at Guildford Art School, which was easy to get to by train. The Wrens used to hold fancy dress parties in their bungalow. Bridgett and I would be put to sleep in Jenny's bed – on the floor were their goats sleeping on beds of straw.

We often visited the Hutchinson family, who lived in The Ridgeway, a turning off Oakshade Road with a smooth concrete surface, in contrast

to our unkempt rutted road. They lived in a 1930s-built detached house, in which the rooms had ceilings without cracks across them which I considered to lack character. Barbara and her husband Martin Hutchinson's eldest daughter, Jillian who was about the same age as Bridgett were good friends. Their other children were Mathiew who was slightly older than me and Katherine who was a bit younger but who I was more friendly with. During this time, mother was toying with getting closer to God. There was St.Andrew's, a little church at the end of Oakshade Road, in which I had been Christened, but which I considered to be rather inferior since it had merely a bell hanging from an extension above the roof line, instead of a spire or tower. I think a reason for Barbara's friendliness with mother was to try to get her to join the Catholic Church. Even at such a young age, I was very aware that the Hutchinsons were not the same as us because they belonged to a different religion (later, when I re-met and was going out with Katherine, I witnessed the fanatical side of Barbara that converts to the Vatican faith often possess, as she treated me as a harmful alien once I made known my new found association with the Young Communist League).

Two aunts used to visit our family, both related to mother. They were Theo, who lived in Dorking and Dodo from London, who performed

conjuring tricks with thimbles going through articles of her clothing.

When the War finished, I was three and a half, but I think that it was before then that mother began taking Bridgett and me by bus on regular visits to Esher, which was the closest shopping centre. Once on the bus, I liked to go upstairs which meant climbing the steep winding staircase at the back and open to the elements. Mother usually stayed downstairs (or inside as the conductor described it). The conductor would shout "ole tay', before ringing the bell twice for the bus to move off from each stop. At Esher we often visited the Embassy cinema, either to see a film or just to have tea and cakes in the cinema café. We also shopped in MacFisheries – fish were not rationed and would last for a couple of days at home on the cold marble shelf in the larder (there were no fridges then) before being converted, usually, into fish pies.

We went for occasional visits to London, meeting father in the foyer of the Regent Palace Hotel at Piccadilly Circus. During one of the journeys on the Bakerloo Line, on leaving Charing Cross (now Embankment) father told me that we were about to travel under the River Thames. After a short distance, the train stopped and the lights went out, except the lamps right at the ends of the car that continued to glow dimly. I remember sobbing (probably embarrassingly screaming) with fear at the thought

that we may be swamped if the river was breached, which is why I think that the War must still have been in progress. The red coloured Tubes stuck me as being far sleeker than the elderly green Southern Electric trains that had carried us to Waterloo, with their grinding clicking break cylinders when stationary, their clanking chains when travelling and their leather straps, like father's belt, to hold the windows in the doors open at different levels. In contrast the Tube trains would screech into stations with their break cylinders whining; people on the platform waited until all those had alighting through the wide sliding doorways – both groups being chivied along by the platform staff shouting "let em off first", "mind the gap" and "mind the doors", before the doors closed and train sped on to the next station. These Bakerloo Line trains were the youngest on the Underground – the 1938 design classics. I also remember the 'follow the lights' illuminated signs as we made for the top of the escalator to take us into the bowels of the system – we usually followed the brown sign directing towards Paddington, on our usual journey from Waterloo to Piccadilly Circus, although some trips would take us on the Northern Line, with their 'follow the lights' to Euston.

Another memory of rides on public transport, was when mum, Bridgett and I made occasional visits to the dentist, Mr Mellish.

These trips entailed a train ride from Oxshott to Surbiton, where we then caught a trolleybus from opposite the modernistic station, which took us up St.Mark's Hill and then a short distance along Ewell Road. In those days the trolleybuses were the famous *diddlers*, which looked very similar to normal double decker buses, except that the radiator front was filled in and painted red with a large central headlamp set into it, echoing the large single upper deck front window. The inside also displayed subtle differences, one being the use of blue paint for items that appeared in green inside their motor bus counterparts. And then, of course, the drumming on the upper deck ceiling, especially when we went under junctions in the wiring when returning to the station. Once back on the station platform awaiting our local train, we were usually there long enough to witness a few expresses, both steam and electric, roaring through the station and violently vibrating the platform and bench we were sitting on – a truly exhilarating and exciting mode of travel that I had not yet experienced.

Once the War ended, we regularly

visited Aunt Theo at Dorking. For this journey, we caught the bus 416 from Oxshott to Leatherhead and then the Green Line coach 714, which was a TF-type single decker with the usual separate driver's cab, but a void where the engine would normally have been beside the driver at the front. This slightly incongruous arrangement gave these vehicles a very modern appearance. The entrance door was slightly set back from the front, giving space for two seats right at the front, looking onto the engineless void (the engine was somewhere under the floor). Theo lived in a first floor flat and had the use of a garden containing high hedges and flowers, surrounded by a very tall brick wall. Within the garden was a two story summer house, the lower floor containing a number of large wooden toys, one being an old open top bus that was large enough for me to sit astride and ride upon. I don't remember Bridgett ever being there, or even travelling with us. I used to spend hours on my own in that 'secret' garden until I became fearful that I might not be the only person in it.

Our family summer holidays took us to the Isle of Wight. The railway

company would collect our suitcases a day or two before our departure and deliver them to our holiday boarding house in time for our arrival. We took the local train to Guildford where we changed onto an electric express to Portsmouth Harbour. When stationary in stations, these trains emitted a high pitched whine similar to the '38-stock Bakerloo Line trains making them sound very powerful, in contrast to the clanking of the local trains that I was used to, as well as a different internal aroma too. We could walk the entire length inside, from

carriage to carriage – some with side corridors, others with central gaps between each set of seats, past toilets, guards vans and even a kitchen and restaurant. When seen from the line side and travelling at speed, the front corridor connection of these trains swayed from side to side stirring a feeling of unexplained fascination. From Portsmouth a ship with paddles either side took us to the island. Father used to take me to the engine room where huge black painted iron beams pumped amid brightly polished brass and copper handles and pipes.

1950   Seaview Isle of Wight

Viewing the mainland, or perhaps an ocean liner.

Mum, Bridgett and me posing on the rocks, photographed by father,

Writing post cards from the island. In the background is the graceful suspension pier at Seaview, which would only last until the end of 1950 when it was washed away by a storm.

We stayed at Seaview, a journey from Ryde by a bus painted red and green in clashing similar tones. The Albion Guest House had window glass tinted in various colours, vivid blue and red, in the front door and in the window half way up the staircase.

Seaview pier was constructed of suspension spans which gave it a very distinctive look with its dipping sections between towers. It had been closed to the public as long as I could remember, so I was surprised when father climbed the locked gates and lifted me over. We walked with care, avoiding missing floorboards, to the pier's extreme end. I'm glad father risked our lives since the pier was later destroyed by a winter storm.

We travelling to Shanklin, Ventnor and Bonchurch, this final place upsetting me as it contained a number of buildings destroyed, I was told, by bombing. Father bought a ticket enabling us to travel over the entire island rail network, which we did – it took us all day – on an island about 22 miles wide and 11 miles deep! The trains and their engines were always immaculately clean and the drivers and firemen treated me as part of their families. Between Brading Junction and Bembridge I rode in the cab of the engine, getting scorched by the fire and not seeing very much from the cramped little cab, while father rode in the front carriage – there wasn't room for him as well on the engine!

In 1948 my family moved about five miles to Cobham, into a large, rambling very old house next to the church in Church Street. I was six years old and found it fascinating and scary. I would only fleetingly enter some rooms, mainly at the front of the house which was oldest. These were the attics, staircases … and, scariest of all, the cellar. The garden was also large, containing a formal garden and an adjoining part behind a high privet

Timothy – seaview
august 1947

hedge. In this secluded section there was a corrugated iron clad building once used as a chapel, numerous sheds and a greenhouse. The chapel was perhaps the main reason for the move, which was converted into a pottery studio for mother.

I was sent to a primary school called Brooklands, which was a short bus ride from Cobham village towards Cobham & Stoke d'Abernon Station. I travelled in the mornings with father, who continued to the station to catch the train to London. Later, when he bought a Frances Barnet autocycle, father took me on the back as far as the turning for school. When school broke up in the afternoons I often walked home, which meant that I could spend the bus fare saved on a bun when I got back to Cobham. Brooklands was not a happy time for me. I didn't seem to get on with some of the teachers (most of whom appeared to be volunteers and rather fat) who frequently accused me of pranks which had been perpetrated by other kids.

Boarding

However, this routine existence was nothing compared to the shock of being taken to a boarding school in far away Hampshire where I was left by my parents without even a good-bye.

That was in the summer of 1950 when I was aged 8 years, and the school was Dunhurst, about a mile outside Petersfield in Hampshire. Bridgett had already been there for two years, so she went off to greet her friends while I was left to fend for myself. Because I had started at the summer term instead of the previous autumn, the colleagues that I shared a dormitory and lessons with had already established their own friendships. So it probably took me longer than normal to make friends – in fact most of my acquaintances

were with the girl friends of Bridgett. Over time I gradually lost touch with my Cobham friends since I was away from them during term times, which meant that I spent more and more of the holidays on my own.

The head mistress at Dunhurst was Amy Clarke (Tarky) who was a spinster in her late fifties, with a frail body and manners like a distant aunt who could only be spoken to if she addressed me. But the visual force running the school was Miss (Mary) Cocker, aged about the same as Tarky, but powerfully built with a strong voice. I respected Tarky and Miss Cocker for the ways that they presented themselves – they counterbalanced each other perfectly.

The class rooms were in a wooden building off a shallow staircase that followed the hill side down from the

main school. In a room at the bottom of the hill was the art studio, with Miss Hunt in charge. It was at wood working where I excelled. Run by Mr Messingham (EAM), his separate barn shaped entirely timber building housed the woodworking workshop as well as, in a partitioned off corner, his sleeping quarters which he shared with his wife Miss Cocker (apparently they came into the main school bathrooms for a wash when all of us were asleep at night). Messingham, as he was called, supervised and taught the timber construction of sledges, carved out model boats and stilts. I also made two toy buses, both about a metre long, a double decker painted red and a single decker Green Line constructed to scale from drawings in the COMMERCIAL MOTOR. The wheels on both were turned in wood on one of two lathes within the workshop, one electrically driven and the other by foot treadle. I also turned wooden bowls and dishes on the lathes. Messingham insisted that all workings and joints were implemented correctly. He taught the sharpening of plains and chisels

on emery stones, how to resharpen saws by filing their teeth and setting each in alternate alignments to prevent sticking when in use. On the construction side he taught the correct way to plain timber in the direction of the grain. Also mortise and tenon joints, dovetail joints and tongued and grooved joining of planks using rebate plains. All this was learned between the ages of 8 and 11 years – one of my final projects was the construction of a small rectangular oak coffee table.

I unintentionally received extra tuition when Miss Hunt, the art teacher, heard me swearing. The automatic penalty was a mouth wash with carbolic soap and water, performed by Messingham. He first gave me further advice for about an hour on working with different tools and the suitability of different types of timber, followed by an apology that he would have to go ahead with the mouth wash. It wasn't that bad – not bad enough to stop me swearing, especially if the prize was personal tuition at my favourite subject!

Assembly was taken every morning after breakfast in the quad which

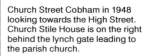

Dunhurst School. The boys' dormitories were on the top floor and the girls' dormitories on the floor below. In the central section of the ground floor was the dining room, whilst classrooms and the library were on the left.

Church Street Cobham in 1948 looking towards the High Street. Church Stile House is on the right behind the lynch gate leading to the parish church.

I fell out of a tree and broke my left arm when I was ten years old, which I managed to repeat 44 years later. Behind me is the bicycle shed, next to the climbing frame. This was the spot where I uttered the swear word that landed me in so much trouble – and private tuition!

doubled up as gymnasium and theatre. Well into each term each of us had to stand up and tell the rest of the school an aspect of what we did during the holidays. At some point in most peoples' descriptions was "and we mucked around" to cover for a shortage of recollection, which was always corrected by Miss Cocker as being not grammatical and should be replaced with "manured around".

On the last night of each month we wrote down the names of the girls that we fancied (and the girls wrote the names of their favourite boys) on slips of paper that were stowed under our pillows ready to be drawn the next morning, when the person drawn would be sought to be given a kiss. Also, on the first of each month, we would come down stairs to the main school with our eyes closed – the first person physically contacted also receiving a kiss, when eyes could be opened. One first of the month's blind contact resulted in me kissing Miss

Cocker who scolded me and banned the practice in future.

The dining room had about eight tables arranged around the edge, each accommodating about 10 people, around the top table in the centre of the room, at which Tarky would host at lunch times with selected teachers. There was strictly no talking until grace had been said by Tarky, and then only after permission had been given. Any breaking of the silence rule was punished by the offending person having to remain silent for the rest of the meal. Naturally, noises were made during the silence period to attempt to incriminate other people. Breakfast had other senior teachers heading the top table, usually Miss Cocker, but sometimes the army trained Mr Vine. The evening meal, which was at 5:30 in the afternoon, was supervised by Messingham standing at the corner of the shoulder high crockery trolley parked by the dining room door.

Food was rationed at this time, which was most noticeable at breakfast with a pat of butter divided into 10 portions per table, each about the size of a sugar lump. Hot porridge was alternated daily with 'Swiss' porridge which was normal oats with raisins soaked overnight in water – it was delicious and very filling.

Whist we were kept in glorious isolation from the outside world, one special announcement that Tarky made, standing behind her chair at the top table in the dining room, was

that King George VI had died during the night, to which we all replied with "Ahhhh …". That would have been on Tuesday morning 5 February 1952. The following year, on 6 March 1953, another announcement was made from the top table, but this time by Mr Vine. He broke the news of the death of Josef Stalin with, I thought even then, very politically biassed overtones such as 'good riddance' and 'scoundrel'. I don't remember our reply. Of course, at that time we were all catching the fever of Queen Elizabeth's Coronation, symbolising as it did the continuing respect for wealth and the holders of it.

The transition to Bedales was made somewhat gradually. Once a week, during my final year at Dunhurst, I went to the Bedales wood working shop to be taught how to make wooden joints – mortise and tenon, dovetail and mitre – all were made in the abstract and the exercises continued into GCE O-level. I had already practised all of these joints on actual jobs that I had constructed under the guidance of EAM in his workshop at Dunhurst. However, it was at metal working that I really shone. I was taught to make copper dishes from flat discs of the metal, by pounding the material into recesses with wooden mallets followed by, once in rough shape, constant 'planishing' over metal 'mushrooms' with metal hammers. All this bashing made the metal very hard, so it was put in the

furnace and heated to red hot with a gas fired blow torch to soften it ready for the next planishing session. The master was 'Biff' Barker who I grew to like and respect more and more . He helped me construct a model steam locomotive from brass, copper and tinplate. Some of the parts, such as the chimney and smokebox door, were made on the lathe where two chisels, each controlled by handles gradually cut into the metal object to shape it. I think I was one of his best pupils while I was there and we bade each other a genuinely sad farewell when I left in 1959 – particularly since he was retiring at the same time.

The other master who had a lasting effect on me was, surprisingly, the maths teacher Anthony Gillingham. Maths was definitely not my forté. Algebra left me cold and mental arithmetic stretched my prowess unless I could use my fingers for assistance. The maths classroom was illuminated by tungsten lamps hanging from the ceiling, each with glass bell shaped shades which rang a peal when tapped. Mr Gillingham would tap the lampshades with a 3-foot wooden ruler to acknowledge correct, or otherwise, answers to his mental arithmetic quick fire questions. My mental calculations were so far off the mark that, on one occasion, his frustration led him to shatter one of the shades with the ruler, such was the force that he struck it. Other occasions were on the rugby field where he scolded my ineptitude by tackling me for no reason, usually when I was not even holding the ball. Fate decreed that he would become my house master for one year. Every teacher was allotted a number of pupils for a school year and would entertain them every Sunday early evening at the teacher's own living quarters. Mr Gillingham entertained his quota, which included me, at his Edward Barnsley designed timber framed house in Steep village, where he played long play records of his choice of classical music. However, it was not one work per evening, but a small section of a work. At intervals he explained the build up and construction of the music being demonstrated. He sometimes brought in parts of other works for comparison and played demonstrations of different instruments to illustrate their effect for particular occasions. He analysed the Second Symphony and Violin Concerto, both composed by the Finnish composer Sibelius, in weekly sections spanning one school term, resulting in my subsequent understanding giving me a closeness to the works that I would never have had it not been for his tuition. He did invite me to join in the school choir after hearing me singing during the regular Sunday evening service, which I declined since I was devoting a lot of my spare time to metalwork or painting in the studio and cycling.

Because of my complete inability

Bedales School in the foreground, with the Ernest Gimson designed Lupton Hall of 1911 and Memorial Library completed in 1921 further to the left. The building of both was supervised by Edward Barnsley. Behind, amongst the trees, is Steephurst where the girls slept. The boys slept on the top floor of the main school building, the two floors below being occupied by classrooms. The dining hall occupied the central largest of the three wings on the right of the building, being two and a half stories high, with a dormitory, with balcony above it.

to learn lines I had to refuse an offer from the drama teacher, Rachael Cary Field, to become a permanent actor, following my performing a number of non-speaking parts in a school production of Hamlet.

When I started at Bedales in 1954, it still owned a farm which it practised in the surrounding fields. Machinery was hired for harvesting, including steam driven traction engines to provide power through their fly wheels and belts, to threshing machines and bailers. There was also a dairy which I used to help in, from washing cows' backsides to the fitting of milking teats, to the cooling of milk to its bottling and fitting of cardboard stoppers. I also assisted in the maternity section, washing mothers and calves, hand milking the mothers after their calves had filled themselves to keep mum's supplies continuing.

At running and swimming I was good enough to participate in sports days and occasionally even won!

Although I was mediocre at football I often found myself keeping goal in matches against Churchers College, the grammar school in Petersfield, where we usually lost.

I tried every way to avoid cricket, but when I failed grabbed a long stop position when fielding, gradually making my way to the boundary. On one occasion the ball landed on my back before running down it and settling on the grass. I could have caught it easily had I been concentrating on the match. But instead, my attention was fully absorbed by the girls on the nearby tennis courts who had removed their tops to allow themselves greater freedom of movement on that hot sunny afternoon. I was later banished to the pavilion where I became adept at recording cricket scores and overs in a thick specially ruled book. That became my rôle at inter-school matches and actually enjoyed it. The Portsmouth Grammar School cricket

ground had a tuck shop at which I was given special preference at half time, together with the players, since we had to consume all that we could afford to buy before the start of the second half. The approach to Portsmouth in those days was along a wide boulevade as the coach majestically crossed over the bridge from Cosham onto Portsea Island, with views of the masts and funnels of ships in the background.

I also sporadically helped with the mowing of the playing fields, sitting at the controls of massive articulated petrol driven machines.

Cycling accounted for much of my spare time, which was on Wednesday and Saturday afternoons and Sundays. I had two bikes, a little gearless one that I had grown out of but still used for negotiating muddy and flint strewn dirt tracks – called a 'siff-bike' – and a racing bike with dropped handlebars and *déraillier* gears for long distance tours. Much engineering was devoted

Bedales is about a mile and a half uphill from Petersfield in the village of Steep. The Aldershot & District ran its single and double decker buses, painted in a livery of two shades of green separated by black edged cream lines, on an hourly service to Steep crossroads, marked by the Cricketers Inn on one side and the blacksmith and petrol station opposite. Little Wonder provided a less frequent service with its little Bedford OB coaches to the same point at Steep, continuing up Stonor Hill to Froxfield.

The majestic Ernest Gimson designed the timber framed library at Bedales, where talking was banned and shoes had to be removed inside the front door to maintain the tranquillity, despite most floorboards creaking when walked over. Every pupil was allocated a bay in which to read, study and express themselves.

1957   Alton – Fareham railway

The semi-derelict Privett Station viewed from under the Alton – Fareham road bridge as I would have encountered it when cycling along the track bed.

South end of the 1,000yd (910m) long curving Privett tunnel during the last weeks before the line closed on 7 February 1955.

to both: dismantling, cleaning, tyre changing on the two free afternoons, while the cycle trips were made on Sundays. There was a circuit on public roads of about 12 miles, starting with a continuous climb of some 3 miles up Stoner Hill to Froxfield and then in the direction of Fareham to the crossroads with the Winchester road and back towards Petersfield, finally ascending the steep Bell Hill returning to school. On one occasion I cycled along the disused trackbed of the Alton to Fareham railway line, passing Privett Station and then came across a tunnel. I had to dismount and walk since it became utterly pitch dark and cold as it curved round cutting out all natural light. On nearing the exit I was made aware of life forms such as insects and birds, such had been the utter quiet and solitude in that tunnel – I later saw it advertised for sale as an ideal place to grow mushrooms: I wonder if I have eaten any of its produce.

One of my dormitory bosses was Jonathan Wheatcroft whose family was famous for breeding roses. He invited me to accompany him one night to Steephurst, the separate building where the girls slept, where he wished to surprise his girlfriend. In those days the only activity performed was some sort of innocent proof that the visit had occurred, although if caught, the offender could face expulsion from the school. While Jon spent time looking for his girlfriend, I occupied myself by collecting all the bras I could find from the chairs next to the girls' beds which I took back to the main school quadrangle. The quad formed the centre of the school, with classrooms around two sides of it and squash courts at one end. It had a glass double pitched roof supported in the centre by steel columns, similar to a rail terminal station. I found a ladder and after hooking the bras together I formed them into a chain spanning the entire length of the quad. The bras were surprisingly heavy to hitch up to the ceiling (although not as heavy as when they were being used for the purpose they had been designed for). I took the risk, once I witnessed the amusement of my fellow pupils and staff alike, and owned up and suffered little punishment!

Rosamund Brereton of my school year, who I didn't know particularly well, suggested that we should try some sex to see what it was all about. We arranged to meet at a hay barn a short walk across the fields from the school at about 5 o'clock on a Sunday morning. Before the event I knocked on the back door of *The Harrow Inn* and negotiated a bottle of brown ale for me and one of cider for Rosamund. We met on the appointed Sunday as the sun was rising and siped our beverages to relieve our nervousness. But the bitterness showed in our distorted faces and we agreed not to consume any more – and returned to our separate dormitories and beds. Many years later, when I was in my twenties, I was walking with my girl friend of that time through one of the connecting foot tunnels at Trafalgar Square Tube Station, when Rosamund with her boyfriend appeared walking towards us. We giggled at each other and walked on without exchanging any words – my girl friend asked for an explanation and I am sure Rosamund's boyfriend asked the same!

I had – and still have – a particular friend, Philip Fleming, who was a year ahead of me and had a dry wit which suited my own sense of humour. We visited each other at our homes during the holidays – Philip lived in north London at Ranulf Road, a bus ride up Finchley Road from the station. At school, one of our social activities was occasionally to go for a second Sunday lunch – to supplement the meagre school ration – at the *Blue Peter Café* near Petersfield Station, where bacon, egg and chips would be leisurely consumed accompanied by a browse through the Sunday papers.

We heard that some Soviet battle ships were visiting the docks at Portsmouth. They were there in April 1956 as part of a state visit by Nikita Khrushchev, who was first secretary of the Communist Party of the USSR, and who I had already seen gazing through a Pullman carriage window as his train steamed through Petersfield Station taking him and politburo member, Marshal Bulganin, to London. Later in 1956, Khrushchev assumed supreme power when he became prime minister also. This was the visit given infamy when the British Naval diver Commander Buster Crabb disappeared and whose body was found 15 month later.

Philip and I took the train to Portsmouth Harbour and walked to the quayside where the Soviet cruiser *Ordzhonikidze* was moored. On going aboard we were greeted by Soviet sailors who indicated that they were willing to trade their hammer and sickle within gold edged red star cap badges. On discovering that they would take sugar in exchange, we made for a quayside grocery shop and returned to the destroyer with packets

of sugar lumps which we successfully bartered. We signed our names (and addresses!) in one of the visitors books that were on a table on the open deck (once back on the quayside I noticed a rating throwing a, presumably, full visitors book overboard as he replaced it with a fresh one).

There were two social activities which I took part in which I felt were more important than being a prefect. I joined the school fire wardens from quite an early age. The glossy side was to help supervise practice evacuations, almost always timed at meal times, of the entire school population on to a variety of outside sites. Behind the scenes the local fire brigade visited to give instructions into the correct handling and directing of hoses and their maintenance. Later, the room doers voted me onto their team. Our job was to move school trunks between lorries and dormitories at the start and end of every term. Also to clear the dining hall of tables and re-arrange the chairs for school dances twice or three times a term.

Mr Prain, the chemistry master, a shy and dry Scotsman, selected me to be his assistant for film shows projected in the Lupton Hall. This entailed lowering the screen from the ceiling of the stage before shows and replacing it after performances quietly during prayers. He showed me how to thread the film through the projector and the repair of broken films – sometimes making for acrobatics during performances when I had to rapidly leave my chosen companion, climb over members of the audience and run to the back in darkness to assist with running repairs.

In November 1956 mother finally gave up after a long and painful fight against cancer. I was relieved for her as I watched her frustration as diminishing strength left her barely able to control the pencil as she did her final sketches from her bed – dear mother, she remains my inspiration.

Mother would have come with us the following year for our first trip abroad, had she lived. Father drove Bridgett and me, with Aunt Theo, across France to north west Spain. The French main roads were long and straight and usually tree lined. Traffic was scarce, usually tractors and grey painted Citroen *Deux Cheveux*. I guided father through towns using the street plans in the *Guide Michelin*, which was also invaluable for finding the best restaurants he had chosen. Indeed, our routes and schedules were planned around the locations of suitable high quality eating places.

Whereas France had certain similarities to Britain, Spain had few – I viewed it as being beyond Europe – it was during Franco's hold on that country. Bridgett and I were arrested on the beach at Lequeitio – the village we were staying at along the coast from San Sebastian – for wearing skimpy bathing costumes. We also visited the ruins of Guernica which was not shown on any maps.

The following year we travelled to Italy, staying in the coastal village of Bonassola north of La Spezia. Our hotel bedroom looked out to sea across the railway which was built on a viaduct spanning the cove.

I did not have enough 'O'-level passes to consider studying for any 'A'-levels, let alone going on to university. But art schools, which in those days were not part of the university system, would take anyone they considered had a talent to develop. The Principal, Mr Brill, considered that I had, so I left Bedales in July 1959 and prepared myself for the next three years at Kingston-on-Thames School of Art.

1969   Alfred Marks Bureau Limited

Printer   Burrup Mathieson, London

The illustration from the cover of the company's annual report and accounts.

Alfred Marks was a job centre specialising in the placement of office support staff, an almost exclusively female occupation in those far off days, which is why the illustration features a girl – the model was a secretary in the company's head office.

This is a mezzotint taken from a photograph.

*I*t was on Tuesday 30 March 1971 that I embarked on a career in the Publicity Office of London Transport that would last for exactly a quarter of a century – to the day. On that first day I was made more aware than ever that I was part of the establishment that had not only invented corporate identity but had always had faith that utilising good design was an integral part of providing and generating loyalty to its service. For me, it was the culmination of a process of gaining experience that had begun eight years earlier when I commenced my first job after leaving college.

At Kingston Art School I was to become an un-spectacular student, when I embarked on a basic design course in July 1959 lasting one year, followed by a further two years specialising in an aspect of design if I was deemed to be up to the required standard. That initial year studying basic design was to provide me with the visual awareness of what has been the foundation of my thinking to this day. It consisted of exercises followed by more exercises – exercises in line, colour, composition, texture, drawing and lettering. Each course approached each of the visual senses in the abstract and each was inter-related with the others. Line exercises consisted of drawing lines using different materials: pen, hard pencil, soft pencil, carpenters pencil, crayon, paintbrush, scratched and embossed; first in monochrome, later

A PIONEERING VEHICLE

Grandparents would be quite accustomed to this mode of travel, but the changing conditions of today have made necessary continual improvements in our public transport system.

Gone are the days of the tramcar and horsedrawn bus. Now the trolleybus, the vehicle that replaced the tram a generation ago, is itself being usurped by a type of vehicle which is as revolutionary today as the electric tramcar was at the beginning of the century.

The Routemaster
by London Transport

in colour once the colour exercises had been embarked upon. Equally, the composition exercises were commenced using a collection of different sized and shaped black cards positioned in various ways on a piece of white card to achieve a visual balance. This was developed into coloured shapes, followed by textured shapes and then with lines added. Additional exercises were conducted in three dimensions using wood, wire and plaster of paris. The only study in representational art during this first year was in the form of still life and life drawings. Here also, the applications were dominated by the use of texture provided by the pencil and composition provided by the lighting and position of the artist in relation to the objects being drawn. The construction of the letters of the alphabet was also taught; again, each letter was considered as an abstract balanced shape, as were the shapes made between adjoining letters.

The next two years at Kingston were spent on a specialist course in graphic design, or Commercial Design as the Ministry of Education described it. Initially, I had difficulty connecting the previous year's intensive abstract exercises with the representational briefs that I received from the various graphics instructors. One student who interpreted the briefs perfectly was Roger Bristow, who became a great friend; surprisingly (but in hindsight perhaps not) since he and I had been

Social engineering

A self portrait drawn with a wax litho crayon straight onto a zinc lithographic plate and then printed.

1962   Young Communist League Membership Card

The first of a number of cards that I was issued with. I joined on my 20th birthday. Inside were 52 spaces where stamps were fixed to prove that weekly dues had been paid.

The TD-type bus on which I rode from Cobham to Kingston and back. It had a maximum speed of about 25 miles per hour!

An identical model to the little 1931 2-seater Morris Minor that I acquired towards the end of my time at art school. I wrote it off in a skid having passed it through an MOT test on the same day!

reared at opposite ends of the social extreme – Roger, having attending Tiffin's boys Grammar School in Kingston and living above the grocer's shop that his dad managed in Surbiton's Victoria Road and me, having boarded at an independent private co-educational school in the Hampshire countryside and living in a big house in Cobham. Roger was an example of the relevance to society of a state education system, which had harnessed his natural intelligence in a way that the social order that I had been brought up in believed to be humanly impossible (and undesirable). He was responsible for providing some order to the restless frustration and confusion that was surging through me to find a direction to provide some fairness to our society. We later went on to join others to discuss the path to a more equitable society, as were many like minded people during this period in the early 1960s of the Beatles, the Stones and the Animals, Campaign for Nuclear Disarmament (CND) and Swiss graphic design.

I was already aware that the Labour Party was vulnerable to a take over by its right wing, thus becoming a party supporting capitalism but with a social conscious, as apposed to a party promoting socialism. This was at the time when Hugh Gaitskell had gained leadership of the Labour Party and was taking it down a moderate path that was allowing the right of the party to exert an increasing influence, a situation that had existed in the 1930s and would again 70 years later. Roger invited me to join with him at the Kingston branch of the Young Communist League (YCL). Whilst communism seemed to be rather extreme for someone with my background, the prospect of an MP in the House of Commons seemed a good way to keep the Labour Party faithful to their manifesto. About 10 of us met regularly in the living room of the branch secretary's Chessington home.

In the YCL we discussed articles that we had read in CHALLENGE, the fortnightly YCL newspaper, and DAILY WORKER. We also listened to speakers from the adult party who enlightened us with their experiences, often in the Spanish Civil War and also in the Soviet Union in the 1930s. Some of our guests preferred the informality of conducting our discussions in pubs, which suited most of us very well. Croydon District office, whose area our branch came within, sent Bob Garvy to steer us back to the correct path. Bob was a serious comrade who

dressed unfashionably, usually in a crumpled suit under a crumpled macintosh – he occasionally laughed with a nervous giggle – the ultimate grey trouble shooter sent from district headquarters! The result was a compromise – we brought out what existed of the human side of Bob – indeed, he lured a girl from me who I was attempting to woo – while he induced us to take the political project more seriously, with a wider book list to read, mainly translations of Lenin's pamphlets and speeches. But the 3-volume *Dialectical Materialism* by Maurice Cornforth encapsulated my future society in the easiest language for me to understand. His works were given life by a visit to our branch by Pat Sloan who was the author of a number books explaining socialism and was also the president of the National Secular Society – the two really go hand in hand. He was like an uncle – I felt I had always known him. In an hour he spelt out the advantages to all of a socialist society – it was all so easy, if only the population of the world could see it as I then did.

A few years later, in about 1964

and after my YCL membership had lapsed, Bob phoned me proposing that we met. When we did Bob had lost his nervousness and appeared with an assurance that I had never before credited him with. He told me he had met someone in London's Hyde Park and a casual conversation had developed, with the result that they had become regular partners – perhaps they still are. It wasn't until 1967 that homosexuality in England punishable with a prison sentence would be decriminalised, indicating the belief Bob must have had in me as a confidante at that time.

The Surrey County Council reimbursed me for my student half fare bus travel for the 30 minute ride from Cobham to Kingston, without requiring any proof that I had actually ridden in a bus. The half fare pass also allowed me to travel anywhere on any London bus 'on student business'. I sometimes cycled from home to the art school, which took about the same travelling time as by bus, or walked the eight miles which took two hours.

There were two fellow students

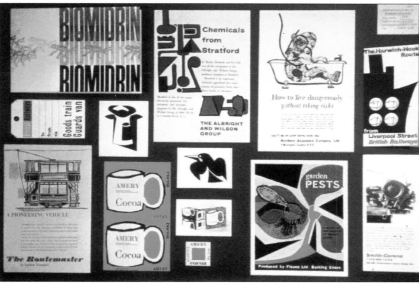

who made the same bus journeys as me. The girl was a fashion design student in my year and frequently joined me on the bus at Tartar Hill in the mornings. The boy lived in Ripley and we sat at the back of the bus going home as far as Cobham where I got off, and he continued to end of the route. I don't remember the girl's name but I do remember that the boy was called Eric Clapton. He was in the year below me but I often encountered him during the day sitting on a locker playing his acoustic guitar. Having completed the basic design year he left to play lead guitar in the *Yardbirds* rhythm and blues band. Also leaving at the same time was Keith Relf to become their vocalist. I frequently chatted with Keith, since we were both in the same year on the graphic design course. He told me before he left, through a throaty asthmatic cough, that he was joining the band to bring some money in to his family since his dad, who was a builder, was out of work. I later saw quite a lot of the band performing at venues in Richmond and central London.

A totally different character to open my mind was another student at Kingston Art School. I think Bill Wilson would have been happier in the fine art department, combining his encyclopaedic mind on artists as well as classical music composers. I listened to his logical and convincing opinions on the works of Matisse, Modigliani, Georges Braque, Chopin and Lizt. He would countenance any artist or movement and was completely unprejudiced.

And there was Ralph Moore-Maurice who, being commercially minded to a rather basic garish degree, was probably the best equipped amongst the small group of students I got to know at college to develop the learning gained there into the sort of career that companies wanted. When I started my first job in an office building on London's Horseferry Road, I would walk over Millbank Bridge to the south side of the River Thames to see Ralph, who was then art director in the record sleeve department of Decca Records. He spent night times at Ronnie Scott's club listening and grooving to modern jazz.

Having left Kingston Art School in July 1962 I scanned the jobs advertised in CAMPAIGN and ADVERTISERS WEEKLY. I didn't want to work in an advertising agency, as a result of work experience I had taken during my final term at Erwin Wasey, Ruthrauff & Ryan, an agency in Eastbourne Terrace, Paddington. There, I sketched roughs for adaptations to the different sizes and proportions of the same Hovis bread advertisement required for the range of newspapers and magazines placing it. But I wasn't sure what I did want to do. I regularly met up with Roger who was also having difficulty finding a suitable job, eventually taking a position designing displays for army recruitment offices.

I took a break and went to stay with Clare, a fellow student who's bed sitter in Kingston I had often visited. She was on holiday in Devon with her mother who took an instant dislike to me and made me sleep on my own in a caravan about a mile away on the edge of Dartmoor. It was a depressing time, being unwanted in Devon and unable to find a worthwhile job. One night, having returning to Cobham, on preparing for bed with a lingering headache and reaching for the aspirins I thought of one of my friends who had swallowed about one hundred, only to bring them up about an hour later. There were about 60 in the jar so I swallowed them all with water and went to bed. At this point the story could have ended. Instead, I awoke the next morning in such a sweat the bedclothes were soaking. It was a Sunday and the church bells were ringing and echoing through my head: ding-g-g-g dong-g-g-g. Echoes lasted all day, even the sounds of my movements being multiplied. Roger phoned so I met him in Kingston, felt very fragile, but didn't mention what I had attempted the night before.

1962   Kingston Art School National Diploma in Design

One of the submissions to the Ministry of Education, the others being a thesis and print design.

Ralph and Bill on the steps of St. Peter's in Rome's Vatican City in 1962.

Singer Keith Relf and guitarist Eric Clapton shortly after the formation of the *Yardbirds*.

1964 **EFTA Markets**
Size: 245 × 165 mm
Printer: Kynoch Press, Birmingham

When the European Common Market was established Britain chose, at first, to stay out, instead becoming a member of the European Free Trade Association, which was a looser association with six other nations. This was the cover of a booklet explaining the advantages of membership.

The diesel powered Birmingham Pullman departing from London Paddington on its non-stop journey to Birmingham Snow Hill.

1963 **ICI Magazine**
Printer: Kynoch Press, Birmingham

A regular article appeared in each issue: The Signatory Trade Unions. That featuring the Amalgamated Engineering Union carried illustrations of past leaders which were submitted by me as printers guides but were considered to be of a quality that could be printed in their own right.

Kynoch

Towards the end of 1962, after writing more job applications and attending many more interviews, two companies offered me employment with them on the same day. The better one was as a junior assistant in the London studio of the Kynoch Press, a Birmingham based printer belonging to Imperial Chemical Industries in London's Millbank. The Kynoch Press, although always owned by a larger company, was considered in the 1930s to be a member of that select group of, what were termed, private printers. These printers, while taking on any work that they were capable of producing economically, also indulged in a certain amount of publishing, commissioned typographers to design alphabets and ornaments and employed typographic designers to aid their composing room in the laying out of printed matter. The London studio, managed by John Slee-Smith, was situated in Horseferry Road, just along the Embankment from the Houses of Parliament and a short walk from Waterloo Station where I had commuted from Cobham. The winter of 1962–3 turned into the coldest since 1947. I remember the condensation that built up on the inside of the carriage windows when the train was stationary becoming frozen once it was moving. Just as I also recall every morning walking gingerly over frozen snow and ice on the pavement

outside the Houses of Parliament, in Parliament Square, well into March.

In those early days at the Kynoch Press I was not yet ready to be a designer. I laid out the pages of ICI's various house magazines and others, pasting down galley proofs of columns that had been typeset in Birmingham onto layout grids of the pages. Photographs had also to be scaled in a projector onto tracing paper where a sketch was made for the engraving company to make copper or zinc plates to the required size. Tony Streak was the cool, quiet and patient qualified designer at Kynoch's London office. One of the stepping stones he gifted to me was over production schedules. The pasted-up magazine proofs, with their pictures, had to be returned to the composing room at Birmingham by the required date or risk the entire job missing its booked time for printing, binding and despatch. He also told me about gathering pictures with the same enlargement or reduction together to save production times and costs. Gradually, Tony allowed me to design small and fairly non-urgent jobs. It was a long

process, conducted amongst hours of discussion.

But the sales team at the London Office was unable to generate enough work to keep Tony and me fully employed, so I was offered the chance to extend my experience in the Birmingham design studio. I had already made a number of visits to the Birmingham factory. Type styles were sometimes required that neither the Birmingham works or their local trade typesetters possessed. Metal type was then set on the keyboard, usually by Monotyping Services in the City of London, so I combined a visit to the factory with carrying a weighty parcel of type to the Black Country by train from London to Snow Hill Station at Birmingham. On one occasion I took the newly introduced blue Pullman diesel-electric train from Paddington. Squeezing into the limited second class section in the end of the car carrying the massive diesel engine at the other end, I was buffeted from side to side for the entire journey. Having paid the supplementary fare, my finances did not extend to any refreshments which, had I indulged,

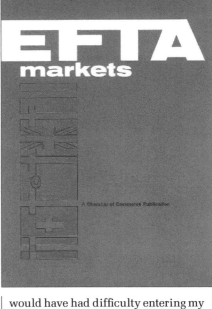

would have had difficulty entering my mouth.

Also moving to the Birmingham headquarters was George, the London-based estimator. He had bought a house in the suburb of Yardley, in Vera Road, and offered me a room to stay in. So I became a commuter on the Outer Circle number 11 bus to Kynoch Works at Witton. The printing works was situated in a corner of the huge complex of Imperial Metal Industries, which was formerly ICI Metals Division. I learned that it was safer to be early rather than late, when I arrived 15 minutes after the normal start of work at 8:30 in the morning to find the factory gates closed and locked. I had to wait until 11:00 for them to open with a consequent loss of pay. I spent some lunch times wandering around the vast aircraft hanger sized smelting shops, where normally dim doorways and windows were intermittently flash-lit by the copper ore. This, I thought, was where

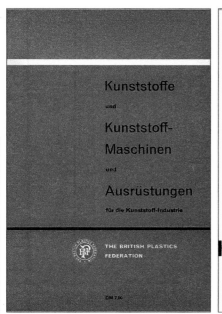

the real work was done.

The studio was run by Roger Denning, with the very capable assistance of Len Harvey, a born and bred local *brummie*. Together with the managing directorship of Wallis Heath, a very strong design team existed to tackle the large number

of engineering based brochures and booklets that the Birmingham sales team procured from the heavy industry that then abounded in the west midlands. I was now right next to and rubbing shoulders with the typesetting keyboard operators, the compositors, the machine minders

and the tranquillity of the readers. Nearly all typesetting was produced on Monotype keyboards, leading to machine set hot metal type and I learned the economics of utilising this method of setting rather than hand setting in the composing room. Although Kynoch possessed no film

setting equipment, jobs that were set in the newly acquired Univers hot metal series sometimes required the related Univers condensed for tabular work which was available filmset from outside suppliers. I drew the layouts to be followed so accurately that they themselves could almost have been used as artwork, such was my fear of misinterpretation caused by my own clumsiness leading to increased costs.

My southern upbringing generated some attention. In those far off days people generally stayed in the same area all their lives. Cars weren't built to travel many miles in a day and trains were too slow to carry people for long distances without overnight stays. Branches of shops were usually confined to their own areas

1965 **British Plastics Federation**
Size: 210 × 148 mm
Printer: Kynoch Press, Birmingham

A purely typographic catalogue of plastics manufacturers in Great Britain. It is called Kunststoffe und Kunststiff-Maschinen und Ausrüstungen für die Kntstoff-Industrie. Set throughout in Monotype Grotesque 215 medium and 216 bold and printed letterpress.

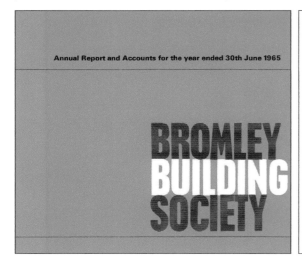

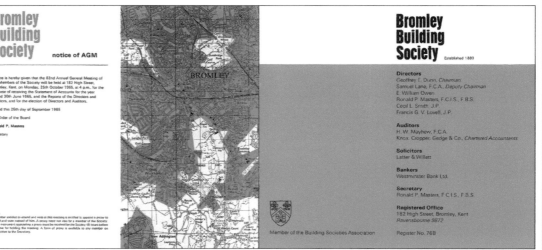

1965 **Bromley Building Society**
Size: 192 × 216 mm
Printer: Kynoch Press, Birmingham

A very short annual report consisting of a 4-page cover and 8-page text section only.

CRABTREE NEWS BULLETIN

New issue Number 12/1964

New Zealand   **France**

The Crabtree activities "down under" continue to flourish. Our photograph shows the recently installed 'Courtene' press at the Auckland, New Zealand, works of United Empire Box Ltd. Mr. Ewell, Willis, Printing Manager of U.E.B., is on the right of the picture, Mr. Frank Ewell, a Director of our New Zealand agents Messrs. Morrison and Morrison Ltd., is on the left of the picture and Mr. Ralph Kent, a Director of R. W. Crabtree & Sons (Australasia) Pty. Ltd., is in the centre.

The Crabtree 'Marquess' metal decorating press is pre-eminent in its field. The continuous development programme carried out on this press, the considerable increase in the volume and variety of decorated metal articles, and the advances made in metal decorating techniques are all factors which have contributed to the considerable success of the 'Marquess' press throughout the world.

The above photograph shows two 'Marquess' presses installed in France at the works of Société Française d'Emballages Métalliques.

The 'Marquess' single and tandem Quick-ing two colours at each closing) presses have a maximum mechanical speed of 6000 sheets per hour and are available in five maximum sheet sizes as follows: 36 in. × 26¼ in. (914 mm × 673 mm), 36 in. × 29 in. (914 mm × 736 mm), 36 in. × 34 in. (914 mm × 864 mm), 40 in. × 34 in. (1016 mm × 864 mm) and 40 in. × 36 in. (1143 mm × 914 mm).

13

1964   R. Hoe & Crabtree
Size: 210 ×148 mm
Printer: Kynoch Press, Birmingham

The house magazine for a printing equipment manufacturer based in Lambeth. The magazine was printed litho on one of their machines from letterpress typeset repros.

In Birmingham, the buses only showed the outer route terminals on their single line destination displays. So the only indication of the direction of travel was on the quaint, by London standards, bus stops.

1964   Design essay inserts
Size: 297 × 210 mm
Printer: Kynoch Press, Birmingham

A series of design essays were published in conjunction with the Designers and Art Directors Association, in which leading designers were given free expression of their work within an A4 size booklet or folder.

and fashions were self contained, without too much visual influence to inform the different regions about each other. So my appearance in Birmingham wearing trousers that stretched around my, then, trim little bum and hugging my thighs down to my knees, then splaying slightly on their way down to my ankles, was a mile away from the usual baggy trousers or overalls. On my feet were boots with zips up the sides, raised on tapering heals about 30 to 40 millimetres high and at the front diminishing to a fairly sharply pointed toe – the legendary Cuban heals. At the apex my hair was considerably longer than the closely cut, creamed and sideways combed with a parting favoured by the locals and my dad's generation. If that wasn't shocking enough for the *brummies*, when I opened my mouth the listener to my speech perceived a delivery that had only been witnessed electronically – over the wireless or fledgling television or in the cinema – and not really believed to actually exist. Not surprisingly, with all these handicaps any approaches to the local girls with an offer of my company in the evening was rebuffed with the

excuse that "I was very sweet but I didn't really need to offer" – most of the girls thought that it wasn't girls that I really fancied!

At weekends I often went to the local pubs in Yardley. All were quite large 1930s buildings and many ran bingo sessions in the evenings. Mild ale was generally the local drink and was usually supplied by Mitchells & Butlers or Ansells, the two largest

Birmingham brewers.

By the time I had spent a total of 18 months at the Kynoch Press, nine of them in Birmingham, I developed the first of a regular bout of itchy feet. The designers at Kynoch had given me invaluable advice and experience. What hastened my move was seeing a job advertised with Ernest Hoch, one of the legendary European designers who had settled in this country after the war. Just as others had devised the DIN standardised sizes of stationary and envelopes which are now in universal use, his aspiration was in the standardisation of the size and position of windows within envelopes, which are not in universal use anywhere. The Ernest Hoch

design consultancy was situated in two upper story rooms of his house in London's Highgate near the Archway. Hoch employed Derek Hodgkinson, who described himself as an inventor rather than a designer, which left him unfettered by fashions and traditions. Derek had already developed and marketed a cardboard sheet in which the surface was pre-scored at intervals vertically and horizontally, making bending and turning into boxes very easy. This was being sold in stationary shops. When I joined the consultancy he was working on a range of crockery for British Railways for use in their dining cars. The common aspect of the design was the hump rising in the centre of the interior base of

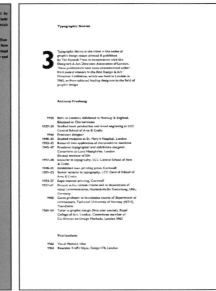

plates, bowls, cups and saucers. These humps broke the waves that would normally develop in liquids as the train swayed and jolted. He developed this as a common style which, with plates, aided stacking and within saucers led the liquid to the edge away from the base of the cup. While the railways rejected the very stylish looking set, we suspected that it was because they didn't want to admit that their trains swayed enough to warrant such remedial crockery. This was also at a time when the riding of newly built vehicles was generally worse than those being replaced – something that I could vouch for on my rides on the diesel electric Pullman trains to Birmingham although no subtle shapes inside soup bowls would provide protection from their lurching. Derek's next project was a sprung egg box in which the six eggs were held in suspension from each other and within an outer frame. All was constructed from strips of thin card and clipped together by a combination of folds and cuts in the strips of card – a skill now called cardboard engineering. For testing, I bought eggs (in the traditional boxes) from a corner shop near Highgate Station. We would keep each set of eggs for about three days and took turns to take them home to be eaten while they were still fresh. Mrs Hoch believed that we were taking the eggs from her refrigerator since ours had the same number stamped on them

as did hers. Our explanation that the same number was accounted for by them having all been supplied from the same egg packing station was not believed by her or Mr Hoch. So Derek left – I think he was relieved that this excuse had developed for him to go. The following day Mrs Hoch turned her attack towards me, which prompted me to leave. So in a space of two months I had decended to the bottom of the ladder of success.

Holiday brochures

I never claimed unemployment pay, having saved enough to keep me going for a few months if I was careful. Also, I didn't want the next employer to see my situation. In fact I had enough put by to be able to afford to move from Cobham to a terraced house behind and above a hairdresser in King's Road, Kingston, close to the Kingston Gate of Richmond Park. Roger from the art college wanted to move from his home and Tony who had been in the fine art department was also looking for somewhere to live. It was a fairly short time that an interview with the travel agent Thos Cook & Son (now known as Thomas Cook) at their headquarters in London's Berkeley Street produced the offer of a job that I wasn't really in a position to refuse. I viewed it as somewhere to learn a little more while I searched for a more stimulating job. Cooks, which was the world's first travel agent, had merged

in the late 1920s with the Brussels based *Companie International des Wagons-Lits et du Grand Express Europeans* to become its travel agency arm. But, as Belgium was over run by the Nazis in 1940 the CIWL and Thos Cook found themselves within enemy territory. So Cooks and its branches in Great Britain was compulsorily bought from its parent company, Cook/Wagon Lit by the British government for £5. For the duration of World War II Cooks was vested with the London Midland & Scottish Railway, the intention being to return it to CIWL when the war was over (assuming Britain won). However, when peace returned and Labour formed the post war government Cooks remained with the LMS and so was duly nationalised with it in 1948, along with the main line railways and London Transport to become executives of the British Transport Commission. Later that year Thomas Tilling sold its bus and coach interests to the BTC, in that brave new period when the prime utilities of the nation were to be owned by and run for the benefit of the entire population, which they did admirably until destroyed in the 1980s and '90s. Thos Cook & Son, together with Pickfords and Dean & Dawson therefore became the agents for leisure and business travel provided by the socially owned rail and road transport organisations.

I worked in the studio laying out a vast array of brochures describing

How did it feel to be Cleopatra?

Cruise down the Nile this winter and see the sights she saw. Cooks have chartered the m.s. Oonas specially for you to visit Edfo, Dendera and Thebes and stay at Aswan, Luxor and Cairo. It will be a warm and leisurely holiday combining the mysterious fascination of the past and the excitement of the present in Egypt.
For details get a copy of Cooks

WINTER SUNSHINE

holiday destinations in all parts of the world. In most cases there were existing styles to be followed based on hot metal typesetting and squared-up black and white halftone blocks, which meant that there was very little design input required – it was mainly copy fitting using the vast range of Monotype Times New Roman founts. Occasionally one of the British Transport companies felt that they needed the Cooks expertise and this was where I applied and built on my limited skills and learned a little more layout and typography by doing so.

My desk was positioned opposite that occupied by Marion, the staff photographer. She was middle aged and unattached, which left her free to travel with Cooks coach tours around Europe, taking pictures for publication in the following season's brochures. Superficially it appeared to be a carefree and exciting job, like a succession of holidays. But the details that she related to me during her brief spells in the office showed the job to be unenviable and tiring. She had to keep her eyes focused for entire journeys to anticipate sites to stop the coach for picture taking, especially when travelling through mountains. Often the driver couldn't stop because

1965 **Press advertisement**

The Cooks Nile cruises were legendary and popular. The publicity management of Cooks were very impressed with a series of press advertisements, of which this is one, set in Egyptian style typefaces and borders. This attention to typography giving a mood to a campaign was new to Cooks, who generally used Times New Roman and standard centred layouts.

However, shortly before her first cruise following a refit, a mishap befell MV Oonas causing her to sink, so the advertisements never appeared in the press!

Torquay

Holiday RB19 8 days' *Private Hotel* £19 0s

Holiday RB20 15 days' *Private Hotel* £31 0s

Including coach fare from and to London

Torquay's exotic gardens

Everyone knows Torquay is a marvellous place. You can have an eight or fifteen days' holiday here, in this world-famous international resort; be wise and book early. You will love the red cliffs and exotic flowers of Torquay; the eight beaches, the warm sun, the regattas and unending amusements; the little village of Cockington with its thatched inn and blacksmith's forge.

Sightseeing Excursions

1 Whole-day motor coach drive over Dartmoor to Princetown and Plymouth (including table d'hôte luncheon).
2 River Dart circular motor coach and steamer excursion (morning or afternoon, according to tide).
3 Afternoon motor coach drive to Buckfast Abbey.

Early Season Reduction £1 1s weekly for holidays completed by May 29.

Cost excluding travel tickets
8 days £15 12s 6d
15 days £27 11s 6d
Single rooms, if available, 12s 6d extra weekly.
Travel by coach from other centres—details on request.
For what the charges include see introduction.
Recommended departure times (Saturdays): From London 9.15 a.m. To London 9.45 a.m.

Penzance

Holiday RB27 8 days' *Guest House* £19 14s
Including coach fare from and to London

Holiday RB28 8 days' *Guest House* £21 6s 6d
Including coach fare from and to London and a Steamer Excursion to the Scilly Isles, allowing four hours ashore.

Bella Vista overlooks attractive gardens

You stay at the homely BELLA VISTA, situated in a quiet private terrace standing back from the sea, but commanding magnificent views of Mounts Bay and The Lizard. The Bella Vista overlooks Penlee Gardens, with tennis courts and bowling greens. All bedrooms have hot and cold running water and there is a comfortable lounge with television. The quaint fishing centres of Newlyn and Mousehole are near at hand.

Sightseeing Drives

Monday Afternoon drive to Helford Passage and Falmouth.
Wednesday Whole-day drive to Mullion Cove and The Lizard (including table d'hôte luncheon).
Friday Afternoon drive to Coverack.

Early Season Reduction £1 2s for holidays completed by May 29.

Cost excluding travel tickets £14 10s
Single rooms, if available, 12s 0d extra.
Travel by coach from other centres—details on request.
For what the charges include see introduction.
Recommended departure times (Saturdays): From London 7.30 a.m. To London 8.30 a.m.

Bournemouth

Holiday RB1 8 days' *Guest House* £19 14s

Holiday RB2 15 days' *Guest House* £33 3s

Including coach fare from and to London

Glorious Bournemouth

You are bound to enjoy a stay in Bournemouth —especially when we are looking after you! It is one of Britain's show resorts—an evergreen valley—with miles of sands, beautiful shops, exquisite gardens and parks. Richly wooded chines lead down to the shore, and pines exhale a wonderful scent.

Sightseeing Drives

Monday Whole-day by motor coach and steamer to the Isle of Wight, with drive around the Island (including table d'hôte luncheon).
Tuesday Afternoon motor coach drive to the New Forest.
Thursday Afternoon drive to Lulworth Cove.

Early Season Reduction 12s weekly for holidays completed by April 30.

Single rooms, if available, 12s 6d extra weekly.
The charge also includes transfers between coach station and hotel at Bournemouth and gratuities to hotel servants.
Travel by coach from other centres—details on request.
Cost excluding travel tickets: 8 days £17 18s
15 days £31 7s
For what the charges include see introduction.
Recommended departure times (Saturdays): From London 9.00 a.m. To London 9.10 a.m.

Ventnor (ISLE OF WIGHT)

Holiday RB13 8 days' *Second Grade Hotel* £17 18s
Including coach fare from and to London
June 7 to August 28.

The King Charles I Hotel at Ventnor

Ventnor's sand and shingle beach by the great mass of St. Bonifac catches all the sun. There's a g sports too, and entertainment in

You stay at the historic King Ch about 12 minutes' uphill walk fr hot and cold running water in a a comfortable lounge, games roo room. Licensed.

Sightseeing Drives

Tuesday Whole-day Round the Island d'hôte luncheon).
Friday Afternoon drive to Osborne Hous

Supplementary Charges (each person weekly Twin-bedded Rooms 12s; Front Rooms £1 4s Travel by coach from other centres—details on

Early Season Reduction £1 3s for holidays co
Cost excluding travel tickets: 8 days £15 14s
For what the charges include see introduction.
Recommended departure times (Saturdays): Fro
To London 9.00 a.m.

Sandown (ISLE OF WIGHT)

Similar arrangements can be private grade Grand Hotel, Sa details on request.

1965 Royal Blue holidays
Size: 210 × 99 mm
Printer: Causton Press, Eastleigh

The running of coaches was the most profitable side of many bus companies' operations. Western and Southern National jointly owned Royal Blue, providing long distance scheduled services and holiday travel. They came to Cooks, who had the experience of designing brochures and booking hotel accommodation.

This brochure is designed on a grid, giving prominence to the important information such as length of stay, accommodation and price. Royal Blue were pleased enough that they reproduced this brochure's cover inside the ABC Coach Guide.

of dangers to other traffic or because of late running. She was usually away for about a month to six weeks at a time, transferring from one tour to others and staying in the cheapest rooms in the hotels that were booked for her.

The section that I worked in was run by Mr Faircroft. He was small and jumpy, with a goatee beard and hankered after a quiet life to prepare him for retirement. Also in the studio, was Nöel who patiently laid out never ending brochure pages while dreaming of a happier and more fulfilling life somewhere else,

while Bob Baker was a highly strung version doing the same thing to other brochures. I regularly went to lunch with Bob, which was generally at Lyons Corner House in Dover Street. We usually ordered curry, which consisted of a ring of boiled rice close to the edge of the plate in which mincemeat containing currents and curry powder flavouring was dunked in the middle. On each visit, the ring of rice became smaller and retreated from the edge of the plate as the measure of curried mince was reduced. When the portion could no

longer be reduced without becoming a saucer-sized disc, the price was increased and the portion returned to the edge of the plate, for the routine of reduction to be repeated again. Most mouthfuls were interrupted by Bob, exclaiming, "Look at that! I could give that a seeing to!" referring to one of the range of constantly changing female customers. Compared with Kynoch there was no one available with whom I could discuss graphics. If I thought Bob was basically repetitive by dreaming of his luck with the Lyons Corner House females he must

have thought me incredibly boring hankering after design.

At the far end of the office was the print buying section where a very large and loud mouthed Mr Snoswell barked at and joked with the printers that he was negotiating with my work to be printed. More personal negotiations were made quietly enough to be drowned by the constant piped music that pervaded all the offices (it was rumoured that the publicity manager had connections with the music recording company).

The office was bureaucratic to the point that I had to sign in and out to the nearest half minute (always in the company's favour) while the staff clerk watched and checked my honesty. Alternate Saturday mornings were also 'worked'. The time was generally spent by most people playing cards or dominoes, catching up with domestic chores such as sorting out bills or writing to friends (in those days phoning out was not possible since calls were still controlled by operators vetting the destinations and contents of calls). Chatting to the opposite sex also formed a productive activity to while away the time. Tweed jackets and grey trousers were worn instead of the normal weekday suits, although ties were still obligatory.

Before the move to Kingston, when I was still living in Cobham, I had a girl friend called Sylvia. She lived at Ham Common, between Kingston and Richmond. Evenings spent at Cobham would end by riding to Kingston with her on the bus, then walking her to Ham, walking back to Kingston and usually missing the last bus home, which meant walking the eight miles if I couldn't hitch a

lift. Sylvia had a lovely responsive body, but she and the late nights were sapping my strength. I eventually had to see the doctor because I was going down with every illness in circulation – he proscribed more sleep! Sylvia departed the scene, mainly because she was becoming rather preoccupied with the prospect of marriage.

To increase my mobility while still living in Cobham, which was becoming more remote by the year as the once regular bus service to Kingston was reduced in frequency, I bought a little red Fiat 600. Roger and I used this very foreign looking car (in those days) for a number of trips around southern and eastern England. Once I moved to Kingston it was used most Saturday evenings to carry small parties to London's Fulham Road which then visited the *Queen's Elm* and the 'Finches' *King's Arms* pubs. I drank tomato juice, washed down with lemon and pineapple juices, while my friends became louder and sillier (they always do when you are remaining sober) on pints of beer followed by whisky macs. I then drove them back, dropping some at their homes (at least one lived as far away as Walton-on-Thames, which usually entailed carrying him along the garden path to the front door of his home).

Things didn't really work out between Roger, Tony and me at the Kingston terraced house, as we were each developing our separate lives.

My bedroom also happened to be the ground floor living room, which made entertaining potentially new girl friends a very communal affair. Tony was always broke and relied on Roger and me to over stock the groceries during our respective weeks' housekeeping rota so that there would be enough to keep the kitchen ticking over during his housekeeping week without buying anything.

Roger decided to leave us to share a place with his girlfriend, Maggie, and I didn't want to be left sharing with and subsidising Tony. I was hankering after living in central London, which coincided with the luck of finding a bedsitter on the third floor of a house on the corner Queensbury Place and Harrington Road in South Kensington, close to the Natural History Museum.

From the age of 22 I lived in central London, SW7, and would do so for the next six years. For the first time, I was within walking distance of my places of work. My old friends ceased to visit the Fulham Road pubs on Saturday nights, possibly because they were having to make their own travel arrangements – Fulham Road was now within walking distance for me.

My Fiat 600 came with me, but found little use in London, with frequent buses and tubes to anywhere that I wanted to go. I took it for runs at the weekends just to keep the wheels from seizing up. On returning from a drive I would often have to park miles from my bedsitter and walk home,

1963   **Party**
Size: 114 × 152 mm
Printer: by Adana

1965   **Dance**
Size: 77 × 102 mm
Printer: anonymous

Doubling as invitations and entrance tickets these two items are advertising almost identical events and were designed within two years of each other. Yet they employ completely different designs and typefaces.

The party invitation was printed on an Adana letterpress office printer, from a line block of the title and swelled rule and standard founders types.

The Dance card was also printed letterpress, but from a line block made from a typesetter's repro.

having lost a nearby parking space. It had to go – and it would be the last car I ever owned. From then on I have practised my dedication to the concept of public transport.

It was while I was at Cooks that I met Gill Stern, who was the ex-girlfriend of one of the lads who worked with me. She lived a walk

1966 Pan Books publication list brochure

Size: 210 × 99 mm
Printer: Fanfare Press, London

One of a number of brochures containing different subject lists of publications.

1966 Penbritin pharmaceutical booklet

Size: 205 × 127 mm
Printer: Fanfare Press, London

Beechams Research Laboratories was a large client of London Press Exchange and LPE Design Services. It was the latter firm which was responsible for the design of 'ethical' literature.

1966 Bell Ferries

Symbol design applied to containers owned by this firm. Initiated by Frank Hall the design was developed by me to be accepted in this form by the client.
Seen here in model form on a rail wagon manufactured by Märklin and full size on a cargo vessel.

1966 Brylcreem bottle shape

The volumes of liquid and that making up the container, be it glass or plastic, would be combined and the same amount of plasticine would then be used to arrive at a possible bottle shape, including the cap. This shape would then be translated into a solid perspex prototype. All elements were designed to increase the apparent size as seen on the shelf.

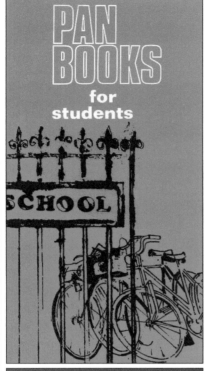

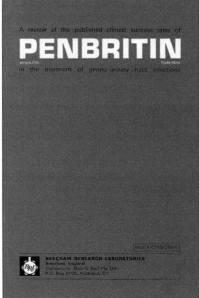

away from my bed-sit, in Earl's Court. We spent an idyllic summer living alternatively at her place then mine, whilst going to art galleries and museums during the day. I silk-screen printed a piece of material, having made the wooden screen and stapling organdie to it which I had bought from John Lewis. The stencils were cut into brown wrapping paper which I attached to the base of the screen. Using transparent ink the resulting randomly repeating designs were very colourful. Gill cut and sewed the printed fabric into a dress which she then wore when we went to a club for some dancing. But as the warm atmosphere dried out the constantly moving fabric the ink started cracking off until the floor was covered with what appeared to be coloured dandruff – I had used paper ink instead of fabric ink! Her ex- returned and re-claimed her attentions. When she re-appeared, my life had moved on, so the relationship that she tried to re-kindle floundered.

Design consultant

Buying ADVERTISERS WEEKLY led at last, after nine months, to the offer of a job in one of the studios of LPE Design Services in London's St.Martin's Lane.

LPE Design Services was wholly owned by the advertising agency London Press Exchange, which was situated at the bottom of St.Martin's Lane above Trafalgar Square Post Office. One purpose of LPE Design Services was to produce artwork from the visuals generated in the studios of the advertising agency and approved by their clients. Another activity, this time where the subsidiary worked independently of the agency, was as a design consultancy, reflecting the increasing number of independent concerns dealing with the growing need by companies for long life corporate identities, as opposed to direct marketing dealt with by advertising agencies. However, positioned as it was in the shadow of an advertising group, LPE Design Services contained a certain commercially biassed brash approach to design not possessed by the purist self contained design consultancies.

The company consisted of a number of design studios, a very large studio devoted to the production of artwork and a small airbrush section. In the midst of this complex on three disjointed floors, connected by narrow squeaking staircases, was a small room containing a restaurant where hot soup, succulent steaks, salads, sweets and fresh coffee would be prepared to order by an unflappable lady. Also forming part of the company, and a couple of doors up St.Martin's Lane, was The Fanfare Press which had once ranked among the select band of private presses in the 1930s. It was during that decade that the Fanfare Press commissioned Bertold Wolpe to design a large set of type ornaments as well as the display type face called Tempest. By the 1960s the Fanfare Press was merely an imprint as far as quantity printing was concerned and its activities were limited to setting and running out letterpress repros for use on artwork. The studio that I started working in was probably closest to that to be found in an advertising agency since it was headed by Vic Smith who was an old agency man. I worked on a number of projects that emanated from the LPE parent company. One was for the tv boards that were displayed at either ends of commercial breaks for *The Human Jungle* programme series featuring Herbert Lom. Of course, in those days of black and white transmission, the boards were produced with a combination of grey, black and white papers and paints. Another project was the design of a price list for Harvey's Bristol Cream that was shown to off licensees by representatives. By far the most time was spent in this section planing the layouts and production of artwork for the Ford Data Book – a series of loose leaf volumes distributed to garages tabling and illustrating every spare part that was available for the entire production of Ford cars, vans and trucks. It was a very boring job to maintain, but someone had to do it, and it is worth remembering when consulting a hefty catalogue, that someone has planned and produced it. As I was processing these routine

jobs, there was Vic, whose desk was opposite mine, dreaming away and reminiscing about the good old days and fun in advertising. A welcome relief from him was when the young office assistant, Mary, came to help. We got to know each other very well over the next few years, and at one stage even planned to get married.

It was while I was making no progress at all in Vic's office, that I offered to help out one of the other sections who were temporarily short

of capacity. Layouts were required for a series of booklets and brochures for the Automobile Association. Frank Hall was the section leader who had began designing a new symbol for the AA. The design for the symbol was running late, but the material that was to carry it could not be delayed since much of it was geared to initiatives aimed at gaining new members for the following summer. But the design of this material was being delayed whilst waiting for final approval of the symbol. With Frank's blessing,

I therefore approached the designs of his material as though his symbol was already being used. On approval of his symbol design, the surrounding designs would already be in existence. Frank was impressed enough with my suggested strategy that he asked his director if I could work permanently in his section, which was granted. There were two directors at LPE Design Services, Jerry Downs and Cyril Cooke. Jerry was jumpy and would think aloud while pacing up and down and around in circles, while Cyril was quiet, thoughtful and sensitive. I got on with them both in different ways, but found Cyril more open to listening to suggestions.

Frank's AA symbol was duly approved – the AA had progressively removed the small 'speed' serifs from the left side of each A. Frank had

1966   **Automobile Association promotional leaflets**
Printers   Causton Press etc
Size: 210 × 148 mm
The new symbol was introduced on leaflets aimed at recruiting new members. A keyline was only permitted to surround the symbol if yellow was the background colour. Supplementary type was standardised using the versatile Univers series.

1966   Automobile Association roadside telephone point

This studio shot appeared on the cover of the 1976/7 *Members' Handbook*, indicating that the design enjoyed a successful life. In fact this was the last new design before all call points were withdrawn in favour of members' own mobile phones.

1966   AA badge

The badge was originally manufactured using an enamelled iron panel held in place by a chromium plated frame. The frame held the fixing screws that could only be applied from the back of the radiator grill. In the days when members were still saluted by patrolmen, the AA was very concerned that their badges could not be removed from members' cars to be installed on impostors vehicles.

1966   AA roadside call box key

The diamond shape was chosen to form a contrast to any other key likely to be found in members' pockets. The 'ears' were also thought to give a little more leverage when opening stiff locks that were dirty or frozen.

already placed the symbol within a square and added a rectangle to the right of it containing the word Service. I favoured using Helvetica as the house typeface, but Frank was practical enough to opt for Univers which was more readily available as hot metal type than was Helvetica. In those days most type setting was still in the form of hot metal, either printed directly or as repros and photographed for lithographic printing.

The leaflets were changed very quickly, followed by a long series of application forms for membership, merchandise, insurance, star service, continental help . . . the list went on and the forms were badly printed by the AA's own computer. The badge needed special treatment and my suggested design of a vitreous enamel symbol enclosed within a stainless steel frame was excepted. The fixing of the badge to the radiator

was necessarily complicated since its unauthorised removal had to be almost impossible. Badges were also designed for application to uniforms – sample new uniform materials were obtained by me from visits to the rag trade in the Whitechapel area – motorcycles and vans.

I designed a new roadside phone point in the shape of an elongated mushroom, which went into production and appeared along the A40 to Oxford. The AA exercise was a useful lesson on a side of designing for which I had little experience. But once the AA work started winding down I again became itchy for a move and a job interview with the studio manager of a printer re-kindled my love of type. When Cyril Cooke offered me a larger salary to stay I reluctantly refused. Had LPE Design Services been a genuine design group I might have stayed, but its philosophy mirrored that of its parent company where an advertising design had a short life, meaning that a degree of superficiality was acceptable.

Financial typography

Burrup, Mathieson & Co Ltd had a history stretching back to its inception as a City of London printer in 1628 in St.Paul's Churchyard, next to the cathedral. During its chequered history of amalgamations and changes of premises, printing for the institutions of the City of London were its lifeblood. It had survived being taken over by one or other of its city competitors by becoming a subsidiary of the Exchange Telegraph company, whose electronic news gathering and distribution systems were prophetically close to the direction that printing was destined. When I joined Burrups in 1968, it had occupied its premises in Lavington Street, Southwark for just nine years, its first permanent address since having been blown out of 114 Southwark Street by an enemy bomb in 1940. The studio was at the back of the building on the third floor adjoining the accounts department. Facing south, natural lighting was excellent through an all-glass wall.

Southwark Street was fairly new, in that it had been driven through a web of alleyways and narrow lanes by the Metropolitan Board of Works to connect London Bridge with Southwark Bridge Road. Completed in 1864, large Romanesque and Gothic style commercial buildings were erected either side of its length. Some were triangular in shape, reflecting the diagonal crossings with former streets. One such building which I became very familiar with on my daily walk to work, bore the inscription above its uppermost windows 'facts, not opinions'. The building belonged to Mr Kirkaldy's Experimentation Works and had been erected to house the machinery which was to test the metal fatigue of the ill-fated Tay Bridge girders, the steel which would form Hammersmith Bridge, Sydney Harbour Bridge and Blackfriars Bridge amongst others, as well as research into the De Haviland Comet failures in the 1950s. Other buildings that were architecturally solid were occupied by the typefounders of Stephenson Blake

& Co and Stevens Shanks. Indeed the industrial nature of the area spurred me to comment to my colleagues that I was crossing to the 'western sector' when I was going across the river for lunch to the Strand and West End!

The studio manager was Peter Wadey, who had also interviewed me and led me to believe that I was his first choice by a fairly long stretch. He was ten years my senior and I warmed to him immediately. The firm itself might seem a strange choice for me to be working for, since its survival relied on work for the City – share option forms, share certificates, company prospectuses, company report and accounts – all ingredients that oiled

annual report and accounts 1968

1968   Lotus Cars report and accounts
Size: 210 × 297 mm
Printer: Burrup Mathieson, London

Lotus required a stylish publication to match their image and that of their chairman, Colin Chapman. The cover lettering was printed on an acetate overlay which, when lifted would display the Lotus car without any distractions. The application of illustrations on the accounts pages was not normally approved of by accountants, who preferred to see their pages devoid of any distraction to the utilitarian process of capitalism.

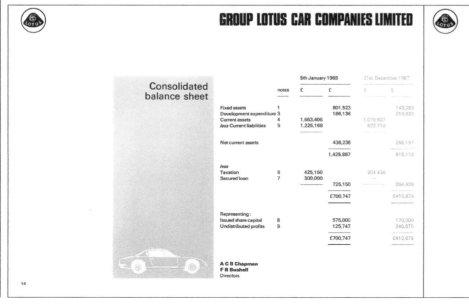

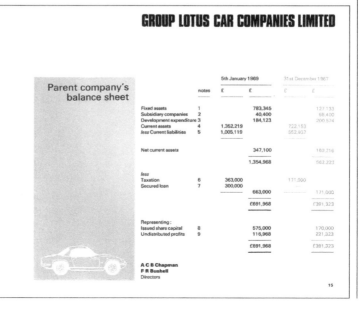

1969 **Alfred Marks Bureau Annual Report and Accounts**

Printer: Burrup Mathieson, London
Size: 297 × 210 mm

This approach would never be allowed these days, but it did reflect the company's interests in the 1960s. Alfred Marks was an employment agency, placing secretarial staff and managerial assistants, just about all of whom were in those days, female.

Parts of the same girl (who was employed by Alfred Marks as a secretary) was used as the model throughout the book, including and unusually, on the accounts pages (accounting is a serious business and accountants do not like to be distracted). The pictures were reproduced through a mezzotint screen, giving a softer effect than the bleached out tint that was used for the cover.

the inner mechanics of capitalism. However, being this close to the heart of commerce was no different from providing designs at other stages of companies' profit development. My reasoning at Burrups was first to make the projects that I work on typographically more readable – in other words, to make documents attractive enough for people at first sight to want to read them. The prevailing notion was that since some information had to be included as a legal requirement it could be compressed into a format whether it could be deciphered or not – the 'small print'. I took the view that any information that was required to be

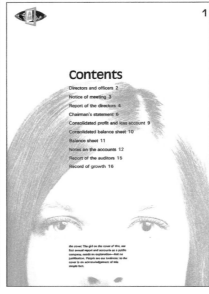

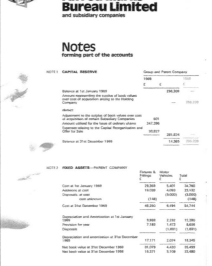

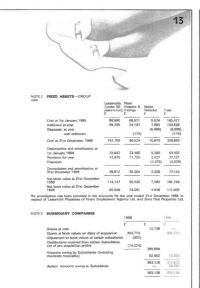

1969   **Constellation Investments Limited annual report and accounts**

Printer: Burrup Mathieson, London
Size: 297 × 210 mm

One of a number of covers designed for company annual reports. While the stars' pictures were positioned randomly, those on the back cover complained.

included deserved to be read whatever its reason for being there, even if it was just by a legal department checking that it was. In short, I was and am as against 'small print' as I am against whispering.

In planning and laying out typographic documents I learned about the intricacies of set widths of different typefaces when selecting the most suitable faces for each project. With the composing room and keyboard operators just one floor away I often picked their brains before starting particular jobs. Sometimes I pushed them to try things on their keyboards that they had thought to be impossible. One such was the setting of small blocks of type – for example a two-line company's name – with minus leading, which worked perfectly to get lines close together, as long as there were no conflicting ascenders and descenders. This simple expedient saved the expense of repros and line blocks. The litho artists also taught me the intricacies of their work, to the extent that I could help them when I did a paste-up, as they would help me by allowing me to give them instructions as they worked at the light table.

While some of the company's representatives appreciated my attention to detail others couldn't understand what I was aiming to achieve. But most jobs which required problem solving were given to me. While Burrups provided a secure

CONSTELLATION
INVESTMENTS LIMITED

Directors' Report and Accounts,

for the year ended,
30th June, 1969.

CONSTELLATION
INVESTMENTS LIMITED

Directors' Report and Accounts,

for the year ended,
30th June, 1969.

1968   **The Exchange Telegraph Company corporate identity**

Burrup Mathieson was one of a number of printers owned by Extel, the electronic information organisation. The synergy was that Extel and all of its subsidiary companies dealt in communications with the City and Stock Exchange. Extel also communicated racing results, which did not go amiss with Burrups reps when they were not scrutinising the Stock Exchange performance.

The symbol's top and bottom colours changes according to the subsidiary. It was designed to be applied to security staff uniforms, delivery vans and letterheads.

1969   **Mutual of Omaha Insurance Company**
Printer: Burrup, Mathieson, London
Size: 210 × 99 mm

This American insurance company was attempting to make inroads into the UK market. The model on the brown cover is Allan from the Burrups studio while the photographer was myself. A mezzotint screen is again used for the semi bleached out effect.

environment for accurate financial information and guaranteed delivery dates, printing quality unfortunately came last. It was for the first reason that I was given the information to produce typographic layouts to publicise company financial details and options in the national press as prospectuses. My layouts went either to the national newspapers to be set as full or half page (or even 2-page) layouts, which meant accurate casting off of the text – in those days any resetting of type would have caused the entire job to run at loss. If set in-house my layouts would go to the composing room to be set as repros which were turned into line blocks and stereos. This reduced the number of people to a minimum who could have the opportunity to see and speculate from the sensitive financial information. Traditionally, newspaper prospectus advertisements were set in serifed typefaces with headings in capitals and centred on

the layout above justified text set in such a small size that it would only be read by dedicated speculators. One of the prospectuses that I laid out was for the advertising agency, KMPH, who were wishing to raise finance. I obtained examples of their best advertising campaigns to illustrate the prospectus, while specifying a grotesque (Univers) typeface for all the typesetting which I ranged left. All of the type setting was done in-house by Burrups (if the newspapers had type set the text, their limited and differing range of Linotype faces would have been used). This was the first time, to my knowledge, that this type of work was set in a non serif type face ranged left unjustified and with illustrations to relieve the greyness.

My usefulness to produce accurate and creative layouts from confidential information came into conflict with the managing director, Sam Bartlett, when he suspected that I was fermenting the collapse of capitalism by selling the information that was passing by me to the Russians. It had come to Sam's notice, especially by way of the manager of the accounts department which occupied the same floor as the studio, that I could be a leftist troublemaker, especially since I was at the forefront of getting the studio staff into trade union membership. There was a grudging acceptance that unpaid overtime working was a condition when taking up employment with the company,

until a need emerged for a series of visuals that were required literally overnight for delivery the following morning. I was willing to work all night if I received payment. In seconds the payroll department had calculated rates for all studio staff, which unsurprisingly were the same as daytime rates – but it was a start. Sam wanted me sacked – competence is as nothing when the upholding

of the *status quo* is at risk, as many statesmen have demonstrated, or discovered, to their cost – so I insisted on seeing him myself and explained my professional philosophy, in conjunction with ridiculing the notion that the Kremlin had any interest in the information that I handled at Burrups. The subject died, probably because Sam realised that we were sailing dangerously close to

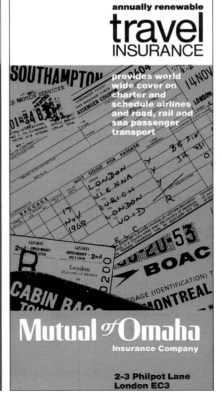

KMPH Limited

(Incorporated under the Companies Acts 1948 to 1967)

Glyn, Mills & Co.

Offer for sale

358,000 Ordinary Shares of 2s. each at 14s. per share

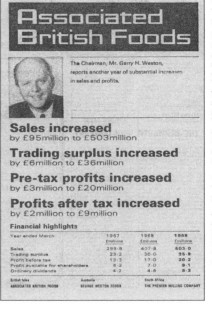

1969   Financial Times
Typesetter: Burrup Mathieson, London
Size: 600 × 417 mm

Full-page share offers appear regularly in the financial press and were traditionally set using serifed type with all headings centred above justified columns. This announcement broke with the tradition by the use of sans serif type (Univers series) text and bold headings ranged left. The inclusion of illustrations were also an innovation.
Setting was done at Burrups and stereos were supplied to the newspapers concerned.

1969   The Observer
Typesetter: Burrup Mathieson, London
Size: 220 × 150 mm

A financial advertisement for Associated British Foods, where Burrups set the type, inserted blocks and supplied stereos (zinc printing plates) to the newspapers concerned.

the interests of various individuals on the sales floor in the confidential affairs of their clients that they were supposed to be dealing with purely professionally!

I aimed to make company annual reports more attractive to be read by the small shareholders, who may own some shares in a company for emotional reasons because they liked what a company did, rather than the hard nosed accountants who were concerned wholly in profit and financial gain. Companies that produce tangible products should have them illustrated wherever possible within their annual reports.

1969 **National Westminster Bank Limited share certificate**
Printer: Burrup Mathieson, London
Size: 202 × 257 mm

The merger of the National Provincial and Westminster banks necessitated the issue of new share certificates to former shareholders reflecting the new identity. One advantage of working for a City printer was the closeness to company secretaries and therefore chairmen, which meant that work could be done and presented to them before the relevant publicity managers became aware.
On sensitive issues, outside organisations – especially those that were security based – were preferred to in-house staff who may not be able to control their tact.

I was therefore able to design the first symbol to be associated with the new company (now called NatWest) – very different from their previous identifications – when I was given the new share certificates to design. Besides the two shapes being formalised initials of the company, the W takes on the shape of castle battlements (for security) and the N fits neatly into the W (symbolising a neat merger).

1969 **The Latin Quarter Theatre Restaurant programme**
Printer: Burrup Mathieson, London
Size: 152 × 102 mm

The fact that Burrups printed this type of work probably says more about the Burrups rep than the customer! However, it was a welcome relief from finance-based typography. The typefaces used are a selection from the Burrups type list and some won't have felt the printer's ink and foller for many years.

No. of Certificate   Transfer nos.   Date   Number of Shares

National Westminster Bank Limited
Incorporated under the Companies Acts, 1948 to 1967

This is to Certify that

is/are the Registered Holder(s) of

Ordinary Shares of One Pound each ful

subject to the Memorandum and Articl

Given under the Common Seal of the Ba

on the date written above

Exd

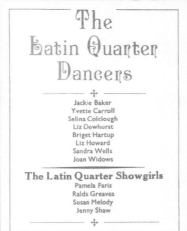

The Latin Quarter Dancers

Jackie Baker
Yvette Carroll
Selina Colclough
Liz Dewhurst
Briget Hartup
Liz Howard
Sandra Wells
Joan Widows

The Latin Quarter Showgirls
Pamela Faris
Ralda Greaves
Susan Melody
Jenny Shaw

TOLAINI'S

LATIN QUARTER

THEATRE RESTAURANT

Programme

Wardour Street
London W1
Gerrard 6001

London's Premier Theatre Restaurant

BY ARRANGEMENT WITH JAMES VERNER LTD   JOHN BARBER PRESENTS

the new Latin Quarter Show

A HIGH SPEED GLAMOUR REVUE

ORCHESTRATION AND ORIGINAL THEMES BY TED TAYLOR   STAGED BY DAVID TOGURI   DESIGNED BY HERBERT SIDON

1 NIGHTS AT THE GAIETY
Latin Quarter Showgirls & Dancers with ROGER DEE

2 Direct from Paris - First time in this country
Charlotte Opal
LA PERLE ET LA COQUILLE

3 Join us at the PALAIS
The Latin Quarter Showgirls & Dancers with ROGER DEE

4 Gilbert and Partner
LIKE FATHER - LIKE SON!

5 LIVING FOR KICKS!
The Latin Quarter Showgirls and Dancers introduce
EVE
and the Serpent

6 Psychedelic Mania
The Latin Quarter Showgirls and Dancers

7 ROGER DEE
THE COMPLETE ENTERTAINER

Costumes executed by HERBERT SIDON LTD   Lighting by HOWARD HEATH

8 FINALE   The Company bid you GOODNIGHT!

Press & public relations by PETER WHEATLEY
Musical Director BRETT DALTON

Latin Quarter Direction by Mr. JOHN TOLAINI   Restaurant Manager Mr. LORENZO
DAVID TOGURI APPEARS NIGHTLY IN "CHARLIE GIRL" AT THE ADELPHI THEATRE

Pictures are now the normal content of annual reports, but they were an innovation in the 1960s, as was typesetting in any type face other than Times New Roman or Baskerville.

While I was re-packaging capitalism with readable typography and pictures, at the same time as fermenting revolution on the streets of Westminster, I was joined in the studio by Laura Bishop who had worked in the artwork studio at LPE Design Services. Laura was blonde, tallish, slim, amply endowed and wore torso hugging cotton dresses with very high hemlines. I think her appearance, and quirky humour, took a lot of pressure off me from the ultra-conservative element of the firm trickling down from Sam through to the elderly to middle aged reps who believed that peace, flower power and free love was a threat to their monetary greed. Between us we enabled Burrups to offer extra peripheral design services, such as displays, small corporate identities and company logotypes. Since we were dealing with company secretaries, with their close proximity to their directors and chairmen, we had a degree of success in getting our work seen that could not have been achieved through the normal channels of going through publicity departments which had a habit of weeding out the best work before it got to the top because they didn't understand it – a hurdle that still exists today.

Professional suicide followed by redemption

I had been at Burrups for more than two years and was arriving at the point where they could teach me nothing more about their form of tabular work, for which I was, and still am, extremely grateful. What spurred my decision to leave was that I had seen an advertisement for

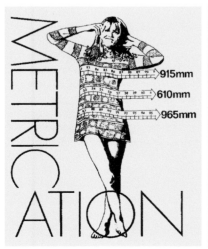

employed and the directors, both of whom I got on well with, occasionally hired part timers to help out at busy times. I laid out a monthly tabloid size newspaper for RoSPA (Royal Society for the Prevention of Accidents) and a high quality magazine for Southern Gas. The directors, one who was a copywriter and the other who was the company accountant, hid any pessimism that they might have had and viewed the dire situation as temporary. I wasn't prepared to wait for things to get better, I was on overdrive at the newsagent buying every advertising and design magazine for the vacancy pages.

There was a job advertised in London Transport's Publicity Office for a visualiser/typographer. I went for an interview at Griffith House in Old Marylebone Road in Michael Levey's office, which resulted in me starting work there in the spring of 1971. Whereas procedures were very formal the people who I met were not. On passing the first interview, I had to return to Griffith House about a month later for a medical check. Because London Transport had such a constant supply of applications for the types of operating jobs that were fitness critical, it made sense that the organisation performed medicals by its own staff instead of sending applicants to see their doctors. The results of the check were immediate, and positive, which gave me time to have a good look around the office

where I would be working – this time I was waiting until I was completely satisfied until I gave notice to my existing employer of my intention to leave. Peter and Bernie, who I was to get to know very well once I started, took me to lunch at the *Beehive* in Homer Street, where I also met some of the printers that serviced the Publicity Office. About three hours later I staggered back to the office in Holborn, wrote a very scruffy notice of my intention to leave and handed it to the copywriting director with a slurred explanation.

While I was working my notice at Holden's Press Bureau, my wife Jan, of just over a year, gave birth to Alice. By then we had moved into a cottage in Amersham's old town, which would be our home for the next 16 years.

Commuting to London was either by diesel train into Marylebone or on a Metropolitan Line A60-type electric train, which continued beyond Baker Street to the City during rush hours. At these times trains ran non-stop between Moor Park and Finchley Road and, because they were underpowered, the drivers would try to make use of the considerable downward gradients to give them momentum to help

a job at a publisher in London's High Holborn. Holden's Press Bureau had interviewed me on leaving art school but I was unsuccessful. So when they offered me a job eight years later I not only accepted it, but declined the invitation to look around the premises since I had already done so. On reporting for work a month later I immediately regretted my impetuosity – the office was devoid of people. The once-humming work force had been reduced to the two directors and a secretary. The handful of offices still contained desks, chairs and telephones but they were empty and dusty. I had enough work to keep me

Scenes in Burrups' studio: Peter Wadey is just visible amongst his plants, while I pose at the other end of the room in front of examples of bread and butter work taped to the wall.

1970 Taylor Recorder
Printer: Burrup Mathieson, London
Size: 297 × 210 mm

Illustration in a civil engineering company's house magazine explaining the conversion from imperial to metric measurement.

them up the subsequent hills. This was particularly apparent on southbound journeys from Harrow-on-the-Hill where trains gathered speed downhill to Wembley Park after which they scuttled over the points leading to Neasden Depot, followed by even more commotion with doors rattling traversing the considerably larger junction at the exit from the depot, before gradually losing speed ascending the bank towards Willesden Green. Junctions on the Underground continued to be constructed with components of the rather springy bullhead track, long after British Rail had adopted the more solid flat bottomed rails as their standard. But I'm not aware of any A60 trains actually derailing on the Neasden junctions.

However, I had experienced one of these trains' predecessors,

Chesham to Chalfont & Latimer train running on the last day of steam on 11 September 1960. The carriages of the 3-car set were by then over 60 years old, having been built in 1898, and still exist in preservation. They were painted brown in London Transport days, replacing the varnished teak livery of the Metropolitan Railway.
Since the mid-1930s engines were supplied by the LNER and later, British Railways from Neasden BR Depot.

One of the tickets issued to me marking the occasion, displaying the signature of fireman John Rowe on the reverse.

ten years earlier, when I cycled from Surrey to Chalfont & Latimer in Buckinghamshire to travel to Chesham on London Transport's last steam passenger train. At Chesham the fireman invited me to return to Chalfont on his engine, only the second time I had ridden on a footplate since being a guest on a Brading to Bembridge engine on the Isle of Wight when I was five years old in 1947.

The contrast in sizes of the organisation I had just left and that which I had joined could not have been greater. My first day at London Transport was spent in the company of other newcomers at its headquarters above St.James's Park Station taking part in, what was described as, an induction course. On this course we were told of the whereabouts of the many facilities that made London Transport a society in its own right. Within 55 Broadway were the offices of the Chairman and most of the directors and their chief officers, many of whom I would meet professionally, and some socially, during the following years. It was also there that departments concerned with different aspects of staff's moral and financial welfare were situated. There was also the lending library, the canteen and a licensed bar. Down the road from South Kensington Station was a diners' club where a better quality lunch could be obtained. We were introduced to various transport trade unions who were brought in

to describe their relevance to the different types of work performed within the organisation. At Burrups I was preparing to join a trade union – the Society of Lithographic Artists, Designers, Engravers and Process Workers (SLADE), which I pursued on joining LT. But, as the representation would have been so small they advised me to join the relevant office transport union, which was the Transport Salaried Staffs Association (TSSA). Outside the work place we were told where various staff associations could be found, ranging from all aspects of sports with their own sports fields, to clubs catering for literature, drama, opera, painting, model railways and travel.

Armed with all this information, I entered Griffith House the following day to spend the first hour with the Publicity Officer, Bryce Beaumont. His approach to running his office summed up a practicality and professionalism that had been gained from the many conflicting challenges of a vast organisation – at that time London Transport employed 60,000 people, equalling the population of York. He had prepared an itinerary for me to meet the Publicity Office departmental leaders – there were very few people joining the organisation from the outside who hadn't worked their way up from leaving school.

The office was divided into two parts, the creative side headed by Michael Levey and the display side

headed by Douglas Teague. I answered to Mr Levey and would be working in the Printing Section, headed by Frank Mussett, which looked after the production and printing of posters, maps and timetables. A similar process was performed by the copy section, headed by Ron Pigram, responsible for the production of leaflets and the publishing of books. Stan Draper ran a one-man section, producing the maps displayed in bus stop frames showing the positions of all the other bus stops in the area.

The road and the rail development sections were the two promenant parts of the display side, headed by Harry Marion and Tom See respectively. Each contained desk staff and uniformed outdoor reps responsible for the maintenance of signing and the posting of timetables and posters throughout the bus and tube systems. Another part of the display side was the photographic section which, besides housing the official LT photographic library, commissioned pictures from outside photographers on behalf of all London Transport departments. The cost of photographs came from the Publicity Office budget and all photos taken were filed in the library, thus keeping duplication of subjects to a minimum. Other sections were: Walter Harris whose staff gave film and 'magic lantern' shows to outside organisations; the shop, which sold posters, post cards and books; the staff office led by Kathy McDicken, who looked after the affairs of the entire office which amounted to about 150 people.

The design section occupied an area at the end of the open plan printing section which over looked a vista of the transition of Marylebone Road into the Westway A40 extension which had opened in July 1970. Edgware Road Station immediately below us. Doug Peacock sat at the other desk in my section and worked on customising diary Underground diagrammatic map artworks to individual clients' requirements. He also drew geographic maps and local street plans showing positions of bus stops for incorporation into leaflets informing passengers of bus routes changing to one man operation. He played the guitar which he sometimes brought into the office and had an irritating habit of whistling *Chirpy Chirpy Cheep Cheep*, the original of which was written by Lally Stott, who looked remarkably similar to Doug, and reached no.1 in the charts in 1971 as performed by *Middle of the Road*.

Doug later left to join London Country Bus Services as a Green Line coach driver and sometimes picked me up if he saw me walking along Edgware Road. His gap was filled by Kate Murphy, who had few of his artworking skills but compensated by being very good at drawing.

My section was separated from the main Printing Section office by a row of filing cabinets. Nearest to me was

the timetable section dealing with the preparation of bus stop timetables for printing and the production of leaflets explaining changes of routes or bus types from conductors taking fares to paying the drivers, as well as bus stop and bus interior informational publicity. Peter Sims, who led the section, had developed an efficient routine to handle this work, all of which had to be completed to pre-arranged schedules. He was assisted by Michael Kiersnowski who was less well organised and spent much of his day scanning the small advertisements in the POLISH PEOPLES & WORKERS DAILY with the aim of acquiring a female companion. He eventually found who he was looking for and had a short and very happy marriage until his fatal heart attack in the office ended it. Malcolm Lemmer later joined the timetable section to handle a new type of bus departure display and then left for the Central Office of Information to produce government leaflets and booklets.

Further down the open plan office was the section where the mainly type only posters that were seen all over the bus and Underground systems were laid out, preparing them for printing by one of about half a dozen printers. They also designed posters for staff recruitment as well as posters advertising performances by the LT dramatic and operatic societies. Bernie Hawes led the section. He was assisted by Una Rabbitt who would

In the background is the unimposing Griffith House in Old Marylebone Road, which would inspire some of my most creative thinking during the next ten years.

later model in different publicity schemes, and Joan Ward, who later had to go as being supernumerary.

In a separate room at the end of the printing section was Frank's own office, although he spent most of his time in the main office commenting about everything and nothing to anyone who walked past him.

The office clerical helper was Lyn Scott, who was so shy she sometimes burst into tears when confronted by brash young go getting printers' representatives. She often sat beside my desk and chatted to me about herself, sometimes continuing her monologue at the close of the working day as we caught the train together from Baker Street since she lived at Northwood, on my way home.

When Lyn left she was replaced by the much more forward (by all definitions) and very sociable Barbara

who, within a short time, developed a relationship with Bernie which led to their marriage. Completely unaware of the developing situation, Frank commented to Bernie and me " 'ave you seen the size of what that Barbara's got?" " 'ere Bernie, wouldn't you like to be givin' that a seeing to!" as he nudged Bernie with his elbow.

That was the office that I joined.

Briefs for all work from other departments would come through an official channel, which in my case was from Michael Levey, who would send me the request, having decided it was me who would do the work. I would send the completed job back through him. While I would talk to staff in other sections I would not do work for them until they had officially requested the work through Michael, or through the Publicity Officer if it was coming from another office.

Where's your momma gone
  (*Where's your momma gone*)
Little baby gone
  (*Little baby gone*)
Where's your momma gone
  (*Where's your momma gone*)
Far far away ...

1971   Bullseyes

The range of London Transport
bullseyes in regular use on
printed material until replaced by
the roundel at the end of 1971.
1 saw regular use in the 1940s but
was more or less replaced by
2, which looked particularly
refined when seen in conjunction
with fine serifed or sans serif type.
3 was used to sign off bus and
corporate information (usually
type only) posters, as was
4 which used in conjunction with
Underground posters.
5 was, since the transfer of
Green Line to the National
Bus Company, one of the few
bullseyes with a particular
specific purpose.

1971   Roundel

The grid drawn up for the
construction of the newly
proportioned roundel. In most
cases, for artworks and signing,
roundels were actually drawn
using compasses and rulers
following this grid.

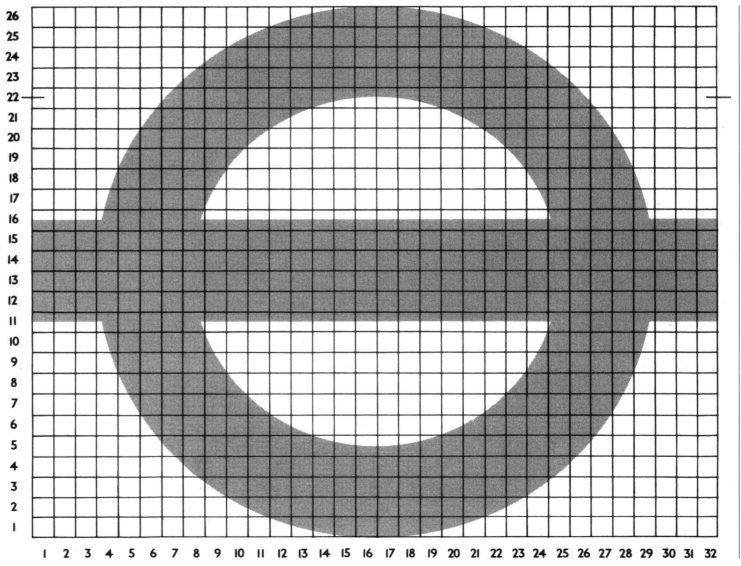

Members of the Board of London Transport, keenly aware of the organisation's design heritage, formed the London Transport Design Committee as a regular forum attended by members and Officers with interests in things visual. Other Chief Officers would be invited to attend one or other monthly meeting if an aspect of their particular business was to come under scrutiny. The Chief Public Relations Officer, together with his Publicity Officer (responsible for publicising the organisation) and Commercial Advertising Manager (who looked after the selling of space and display of other organisation's advertising material on sites throughout the system) would attend regularly, as would the respective bus and rail rolling stock Chief Officers.

The ghost of Frank Pick was very much in evidence when I arrived in 1971, and one only needed to mention his name to higher members of other departments to make them realise that design decisions ultimately resided with those in that profession. Indeed, Frank Pick enjoyed a similar reverence accorded to his name by London Transport employees as did Jesus by those of the Christian faith or to Lenin in the Soviet Union, or even John Hayden Badley, founder of Bedales school where I attended as a teenager. I was a mere village priest within the organisation, but was treated with the ore that I may possess a personal direct line to the great man

that only those in my profession could possibly hope to be blessed with.

In the mid-1960s the Design Committee endorsed the decision to reduce the size of the initial and final letters of the word Underground on signs to that of the intermediate letters. Subsequently, as a recognition that neither the Committee as a group or any of the individual members had the expertise to keep up with trends in design, they invited the Design Research Unit, under the direction of Mischa Black, to act as consultants and guide its hand. Originally DRU only commented on subjects which were on the Committee minutes for discussion. Gradually they gained the confidence of the Committee enabling them to suggest more radical developments. As London Transport's predecessor had been amongst the first to recognise corporate identity as an important marketing and (in the right hands) aesthetic device, so Design Research Unit was one of the original design groups creating well managed corporate design to market products. DRU had been formed by Milner Grey and Mischa Black during the early post World War II years, establishing themselves as leaders in the field of packaging design, with prestigious clients such as Tate & Lyle sugar and Courage brewery.

During 1970 DRU was asked to look at the corporate identity of London Transport. In an attempt to keep up with contemporary thinking, London

Transport had made some small cosmetic changes. They were to a fleet of trains whose external livery had changed from red to silver and to a fleet of buses that was rapidly losing its house character as standard manufacturers' models were bought to replace the models that had been designed and built especially to serve London. The Victoria Line trains had been delivered with Underground fleet names, replacing the familiar underlined London Transport style on their unpainted aluminium bodies, followed by a similar style on Circle Line trains. On London's red RT and RM double-decker buses, the underlining was also removed from the gold London Transport fleet name, when it adopted same size lettering (and thinner black outlining). This style of lettering, but in red, was already being applied to the grey waist bands of the new breed of single-deck MBs, SMs and SMSs introduced to replace the RF single-deckers and some double-deckers. The front entrance and centre exit DMS double-decker, being marketed as the *Londoner*, was designed as the replacement for the RT fleet. This had the linear bullseye, with London Transport across the bar, applied in white on either side and providing the only relief to the all-red livery.

DRU's first notable act as consultants to the Design Committee was to suggest a standardisation to the bullseye, where the bar would

become the same colour as the circle. The thickness of the bar would be reduced, so that both bar and circle would appear to be the same weight. No lettering would appear across the bar – they argued that there was no need, since the overall device would indicate London Transport service.

DRU's suggestion was, in fact, a development of what had been discussed following the formation of the London Passenger Transport Board in 1933 and had gained momentum in 1939 when the word Underground, applied to the bar of the bullseye, was replaced by London Transport on new stations and signing – it was really a tidying up operation. On the establishment of the LPTB, General disappeared from the sides of buses, the individual tram company names and municipal devices were removed from tramcar sides and Underground ceased to be applied to rail car sides – all to be replaced by London Transport. But Green Line survived, to distinguish their vehicles from ordinary green country buses – an exception was already creeping into the corporate decision. There would be more to come. The fleet of inter-station single-deck with raised rear section buses, in their attractive mid-blue and cream that linked the main line station terminals, gained their own fleet name in the *sedan chair* style already being applied to the new generation of Green Line coaches. The traditionally fronted T, full

The corporate image

41

1967   Bus 212 Bus stop panel
Paper size: 302 × 212 mm
Printer: The Baynard Press

The use of Johnston, for the large heading, and Gill Sans, for all the other type was the style of typesetting in use since the 1950s. The red border had been in use since that time, until stocks were exhausted in the late 1960s.

1967   Bus 103 Bus stop panel
Paper size: 302 × 212 mm
Printer: The Baynard Press

Setting throughout in Johnston ranged left with a bullseye on the right was the typical typographic layout in use from the 1950s to the 1980s. The red border is the version in use since the 1960s.

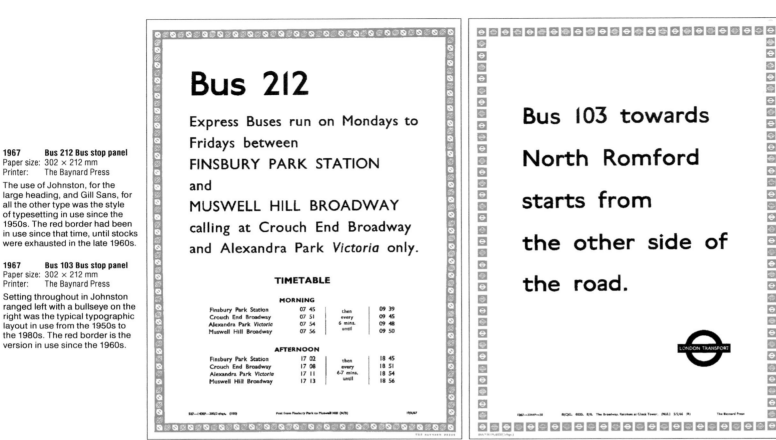

Bus 212

Express Buses run on Mondays to Fridays between
FINSBURY PARK STATION
and
MUSWELL HILL BROADWAY
calling at Crouch End Broadway
and Alexandra Park *Victoria* only.

TIMETABLE

MORNING

Finsbury Park Station	07 45	then	09 39
Crouch End Broadway	07 51	every	09 45
Alexandra Park *Victoria*	07 54	6 mins.	09 48
Muswell Hill Broadway	07 56	until	09 50

AFTERNOON

Finsbury Park Station	17 02	then	18 45
Crouch End Broadway	17 08	every	18 51
Alexandra Park *Victoria*	17 11	6-7 mins.	18 54
Muswell Hill Broadway	17 13	until	18 56

Bus 103 towards North Romford starts from the other side of the road.

fronted side engined Q and underfloor engined TF type coaches were being delivered and setting new standards of comfort and elegance. The growing trolleybus fleet gained their own style of bullseye (with a large T, with serifs, running down the middle), which was applied to vehicles as a secondary device to the standard London Transport fleet name.

It was Sir John Elliot, who had gained considerable experience and encouragement with the use of corporate identity since joining the Southern Railway as Publicity and Advertising Assistant in 1925, who, when Chairman of London Transport in the 1950s, returned

the UNDERGROUND 'logo' to the bars of bullseyes. But there still remained the illogicality of marketing trains with a proper noun but buses as a department of London Transport. I recognised this dilemma at the time that I joined London Transport and suggested that buses (which by that time were just the central area red buses) were marketed with the name of *Capital Buses*. This suggestion was rejected as being too radical (which really meant that it was not on any agenda for discussion and had probably received a frosty reception from the ultra conservative bus operating managers when floated informally) and when it was later seriously considered, the

name had been adopted by a private coach company in west London. (Another of my suggestions, that pop concerts at Wembley and other London venues could sell combined travel and entry tickets – a marketing initiative that applies these days as routine – was also rejected as being complicated, open to fraud and non traffic generative.)

The bullseye, as revised by Design Research Unit, was called the roundel and DRU supplied grids giving the number of units that would determine the circumference of the circle, its thickness, and the depth and width of the bar across the circle. When I attempted to construct a roundel from

their grid using ruler and compasses, I discovered that DRU had made a mistake with their calculation of the number of grid squares that would be required, resulting in an oval shaped circle if drawn following their instructions. I therefore increased the number of grid squares and fractionally increased the thickness of the circle to fit into at least half the width of one of the new squares – an action for which I was thanked by the Publicity Officer but not acknowledged by DRU.

Another stipulation by DRU was that the new roundel should not be applied decoratively. They were concerned at the extensive use of often repeated bullseyes as backgrounds for almost every type of message (although the ultimate, where bullseyes replaced the figures on the clocks on the Central Line post-war extension stations, had not been repeated at other venues), which included no smoking signs on tube car windows and surrounds to a great many informational posters.

It was this extensive and diverse range of posters that were to receive the first attention once the edict came from the board of London Transport that the roundel was now to be their one and only symbol. Ever since the 1920s decorative borders were seen to give some relief to posters containing type only and probably messages not written to attract or hold the attention of the reader. In the late

1940s a standard border had been devised consisting of diagonal outline bullseyes applied in white out of a coloured strip surrounding the edge of the poster or leaflet. The coloured strip border was normally printed in red but also appeared in green, for reference to country bus and Green Line subjects and blue for All-Night and other special subjects. These borders were replaced in the 1960s by similar designs but containing horizontal bullseyes in white within coloured squares, but appearing in the same variety of colours as before. Within these border frames the type was ranged left and ragged on the right, which was visually centred horizontally and vertically within the border, in much the same way that a poem is placed on the page of a book. At the base a bullseye, containing the words London Transport or Underground across the bar, was placed towards the right hand side.

So it was a replacement for this extensive series of posters that Bryce Beaumont ask me, in a casual way, if I could produce some designs. This was the first piece of corporate design that I had been asked to evolve since arriving at London Transport and I felt the full burden of responsibility since this type of work had in the past been sent to outside design consultancies. There was an advantage and ultimate success of producing this type of work from within the organisation in that I could get close to the people actually

Bus 95

to Streatham stops here on Sundays only between 10 16 and 15 04.

At other times the stop is in Upper Thames Street.

Bus 48

to WHIPPS CROSS

leaves from this stop at the following times:

Saturdays only: 09 44, 10 01, then every 15 minutes until 18 16, 18 29, 18 48, 19 12, then every 20 minutes until 23 32, 23 52^L, 00 12^L, 00 35^L.

L—To Leyton Green only.

The complete daily service runs from the stop in Kingsland Road.

1972   **Bus 95 Bus stop panel**
Paper size: 302 × 212 mm
Printer: The Baynard Press

A very early version of the new design of panel, making use of letterpress red horizontal rules and roundel. This was to make sure the arrangement really did work before thousands, in all the required sizes from three bus stop panel sizes up to double royal size, were printed and stored for use as backgrounds for later overprints.

ALTERATION TO FARES

Commencing Sunday April 9, certain fares in the Warley and Brentwood areas will be revised to co-ordinate with increased fares introduced by the Eastern National Omnibus Company Ltd.

ALTERATION TO FARES

Commencing Sunday April 9, certain fares in the Warley and Brentwood areas will be revised to co-ordinate with increased fares introduced by the Eastern National Omnibus Company Ltd.

1972   **Bus window stickers**
Paper size: 255 × 318 mm
Printer: Waterlow & Sons, London

Some posters, especially those of landscape format employed type set to a centred layout. On the new style of backs, tyle was ranged left followed the style in general use for bus stop panels and double royal posters.

1972 Bus 156 Bus stop panel
Paper size: 302 × 212 mm
Printer: The Baynard Press
1972   Bus window slip
Paper size: 140 × 731 mm
Printer: Leonard Ripley, Vauxhall

Notices were often repeated on bus stop panels and bus windows, but to different proportions. The bus window slip was position so as not to interfere with the driver's vision, which meant that it was not always in the most noticeable place to be seen by most passengers. Different colour codes were used to indicate different subjects, which were understood by the staff in the Publicity print buying office but probably nobody else. Pink warned of the conversion to driver only operation – the little silhouette indicated if a double- or single-deck bus would operate the new service, which also appeared on the leaflets which were delivered door to door along the route. The red panel was posted when major timetable changes were made to a route. These were called clock backs by the Publicity staff.

Bus 165

STARTING JUNE 16,

bus 165 will be double-deck

and one-man operated.

Please have your exact fare

ready to pay as you board.

One-man bus 246 ⊖

STARTING NOVEMBER 18, Bus 246 will be double-deck and one-man operated. Please have your exact fare ready to pay as you enter.
Please see new roadside timetable.

Bus 144   THE TIMETABLE CHANGES FROM 7 AUGUST
Please see new roadside publicity

These seats are meant for elderly and handicapped persons or for people carrying children or heavy shopping

producing the day to day work, in much the same way that I was able to pick the minds of compositors when devising typographic specifications when I was working at Burrups.

The majority of the diversity of posters were concerned with bus operations. Here, Peter Sims who ran the timetable section gave extensive help in providing samples of this vast range as well as pointing out drawbacks that could possibly be eliminated at the same time. Most importantly, he encouraged me with his own enthusiasm to want to be part of this change and make it work.

The ultimate solution appears to be very simple, but it wasn't achieved

without a certain amount of heart ache. With such varying amounts of text to be accommodated, the existing arrangement of centreing a block of left ranging text appeared to be the best solution, and one that office workers and printers were used to handling. I outlawed centred typographic layouts, except for specific categories that I authorised myself. So I kept the typographic layout much the same as it had been formerly, in that the solid ranged left title to a poster counterbalanced the roundel on the bottom right.

Poster backs were pre-printed in large numbers and distributed and held by the printers who performed

the single colour overprinting of type. Normally, the policy of introducing a new style was to exhaust the stocks of the old style first. But this meant that some lightly used versions would have lasted for a long time into the new era. Because the style that I had designed was so different to the one that it was replacing, it was desired to change all posters as quickly as possible, but this exposed the following consequences. Frank Mussett, the poster print buying manager wrote to Bryce Beaumont in November 1972 giving figures of stocks of poster backs held at printers. They amounted to 35,200 double royal and 52,580 backs of other sizes. An indication of the number of posters

which were overprinted for any reason ranged from about 500 double royals for a system wide message on the Underground, to about 30 copies for most bus stop panels concerned with a change to a route. Frank also attached a green bullseye border bus stop panel back to his letter, of which there were 2,600 copies still in store. This fairly small stock would still have taken a number of years to use up, presumably for notices concerned with Green Line coaches (by now owned and operated by London Country Bus Services) traffic notices within the LT area. Much of the old double royal stock was cut down to A4 size to be turned into note pads (the surface on the plain

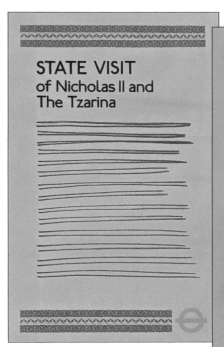

STATE VISIT
of Nicholas II and
The Tzarina

STATE VISIT OF THE
GRAND DUKE AND THE
GRAND DUCHESS OF
LUXEMBOURG

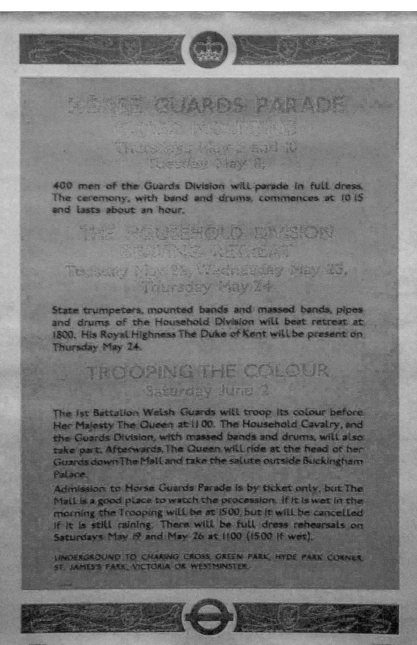

1972   State visit posters
Paper size: 25 × 40 in
Printer: various

These posters formed a special
category and needed a design
to reflect their regal character.
Initial rough layouts originally
reflected those being introduced
for the rest of the systems, but
with ornamental embellishments.
However an entirely new design
was devised using specially
drawn artworks at the top and
bottom. The centred layout of
type employed entirely centred
headings with justified text below
– all, of course set in Johnston
type.
Stocks of posters containing the
background were kept by printers
for later 2-colur overprints of type
when required.

backs was particularly unpleasant to
write on since it was soft and textured
to be absorbent to the poster paste).
This only applied to the red borders
and the window slips announcing
changes of timetable which contained
an illustration of a clock face. The
posters printed on coloured paper
had no border on them until the new
version with horizontal rules at the
top and bottom were introduced.

London, being a capital city, sees
a large number of visiting heads of
state from abroad, from monarchs
to presidents and prime ministers.
During my time at London Transport,
they generally arrived at Victoria
main line station, having travelled
by Pullman train from Gatwick
Airport, where they had landed by
plane. From Victoria station they
would travel by horse drawn coach
or motorcade along Victoria Street
to Parliament Square and then turn

left to head for Buckingham Palace
to pay their respects to the sovereign.
These journeys necessitated the
closure of streets to all traffic
including buses as well as providing
a spectacle for onlookers. Special
posters, announcing the event and
describing the route which also gave
times and details of the revised bus
services were produced in advance
of the occasion. (Before re-opening
and resumption of traffic a squad of
Westminster Council sweepers would
clear the road surface of evidence of
their former use by horses which, it
was rumoured, was delivered to the
Palace gardens for composting.)

Because of the traditional nature
of these state visits I evolved a layout
which could be recognised as being
less routine than the normal traffic
poster, but continued with the
established graphic style.

1946–71 **Pocket map covers**
Folded size: 150 × 75 mm
Printers: various

A selection of the range of pocket map covers produced following the end of World War II. By the end of the 1950s consistency in design was becoming blurred (the covers furthest to the right), with not only different layouts but also different type faces. The ranged left text on the Welcome and Sightseeing covers has difficulty balancing with the power of the symmetrical bullseye. The final design even dispenses with the use of a type style sharing any characteristics with the LT house typeface of Johnston.

1971 **Pocket map covers**
Folded size: 150 × 75 mm
Printers: Johnson Riddle & Co, St.Mary Cray, Kent (Underground); Waterlow & Sons, Watford, Herts (buses)

The ruling that no lettering should appear on the roundel bar triggered new designs for the Underground and bus map covers and gave the opportunity to devise a common style for all map covers

Pocket map covers

The various bullseyes that were now standardised into the re-proportioned roundel without lettering opened the door to my being able to look at every single printed item of design that was displaying a bullseye which would need to contain a replacement roundel. Many items that employed traditionally centred layouts were scrutinised when their bullseyes were replaced by roundels when reprints became due. A large number needed the addition of London Transport or Underground wording which would formerly have been combined with the bullseye bar.

This change – required at the highest level – gave me scope to re-design any item that needed to be updated, or that I wished to improve. My solution to timetable booklet covers is described in the timetable chapter. However, one of the earliest items that needed the new treatment was the range of map covers. From the 1920s, a distinctive style had been adopted, which was gradually updated while keeping the basic concept intact. But this process of development was interrupted in the late 1930s when a design was adopted for all map covers employing white lettering on different coloured panels and much smaller bullseyes (without lettering across the bar) but still employing a centred layout. The design was an attempt to reflect the *art deco* of the period, but lacked the classic distinction of the designs they had replaced. They were superseded themselves after World War II with a reversion to a development of the classic layout. The other hiccup occurred progressively from the late 1950s to the early 1970s, where an attempt was made to modernise the design by placing blocks containing the bullseye and lettering in different asymmetric positions.

These designs were still in print when I was looking at map cover replacement designs. It proved that when the symmetrical roundel is enlarged to more than half the width of the publication, a centred layout is the only way that a balanced design can be achieved – the roundel being such a dominantly powerful motif. So I reverted to the centred layout and at the same time standardised the size that maps would be folded to 150mm deep by 75mm wide – a size still used for the Underground pocket map today. Initially the Underground map employed a blue bar – devoid of lettering – to the roundel, such was the wrench from an application that had been in use for about 60 years. But the bar was later changed to the same red as the circle.

Once the design was established it was extended to the entire range of map covers. The bus and tube maps were the first to be introduced

and were the official flags of the London Transport system, both running to well over a million printed copies a year. London was added to Buses (replacing Bus Map formerly displayed) to bring the wording to the same size as that used on the Underground map. This was the first use of London Buses as a title and was to feature extensively as a replacement to London Transport on bus related matter and give it graphic equality to Underground as a title.

The design was applied next to the covers of tourist information maps, each being colour coded for language identification, mainly for staff. These particular cover designs had a short life caused by the adoption of what was called the 'Sunburst' roundel, designed by the advertising agency for promoting tourist travel. The design was later adapted within the same style to accommodate the Sunburst. Later I produced a Sunburst design for single colour printing, which was later used on a Conducted Coach Tours map cover. I had re-designed the Red Arrow map, giving it the diagrammatic treatment. So I used the opportunity to reduce the cover size from its former one third A4 to 150mm by 75mm. A black roundel was used to reflect the Red Arrow stop flags, which were already utilising a black bullseye as distinct from the red used on standard bus stops.

The London's Railways cover caused something of a problem in conforming to the established design, since British Rail's symbol was also to be used in conjunction with the roundel. However a compromise was made by using the same balancing of the two elements compared with the other covers.

Of passing interest is that the interior layouts of the tourist maps were also designed by myself – putting into practice my experience gained with foreign languages going all the way back to my days at Kynoch Press. This was, perhaps, the first occasion that the cover as well as the interior has been designed by a single person, certainly within the London Transport organisation. This wasn't to be the last time either, since I designed the Red Arrow and London's Railways diagrammatic maps, and their respective typographic texts, inside their respective covers. And much later, the Underground map, where I compiled and typeset the index as well as designing the map inside my own cover design.

Symbols

From time to time departments asked the Publicity Officer to produce symbols to identify themselves individually. In the past, a bullseye would be produced containing the department's name or function across the bar with, perhaps, a different colourway for the circle. Sometimes a simple solution was

1972   **Tourist Information pocket map covers**
Folded size: 150 × 75 mm
Printer: C. J. Petyt, London
1973–4   Pocket map covers
Folded size: 150 × 75 mm
Printers: C. J. Petyt, London
  Staples Printers
  and others

The design for this series of covers followed that developed for the bus and Underground pocket map covers.

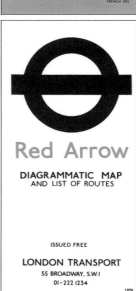

47

1976 London Transport International symbol

Initial design produced for the consultancy.

1980 London Transport International prospectus cover

Size: 297 × 210 mm
Printer: Staples Printers, St.Albans

The final form of the LT International symbol as used on a cover promoting LT's services and expertise available to other transport operators.

1976 London Transport Museum symbol

Symbol design submitted to the museum at Covent Garden in central London that opened in 1980 replacing the LT Collection at Syon Park. The museum rejected this design in favour of one they had commissioned themselves.

found, particularly since a number of bullseyes with lettering across the bar were requiring an alternative treatment without lettering across the bar as a matter of urgency when re-printing was required. Typical of this category were the Line identity bullseyes between car line diagrams – in this case the bullseye was changed to a roundel and the Line name placed underneath in the line colour.

More ambitious were a few special symbols, based on the roundel, which were designed especially for client departments. One of my more successful projects was the symbol designed for London Transport's consultancy arm, known as London Transport International. I approached the design with the attitude that if we were not allowed to add elements to the interior of the roundel then I must explore what could be added outside to explain the purpose of the design.

By adding a holder to the circle it became a globe. The original holder that I designed was altered at the request of the client to a less abstract shape by the addition of 'spikes to allow the globe to spin' – an alteration that I considered unnecessary and backward graphically.

Design manual

Nearly all of the design specifications that I was devising would be implemented by staff in other departments and workshops who needed guidance to produce their work consistently. Many design specifications were already recorded within booklets produced in house by the departments concerned.

Bryce asked me to produce an all-embracing manual to cover the aspects that we had already worked on. I followed the contents of the British Rail corporate identity manual. But they had a dedicated department looking at all aspects of corporate identity. London Transport had its monthly Design Committee meetings lasting one afternoon each, but no one to actually implement the design and keep control within the diverse departments unless they outsourced all of their requirements to Design Research Unit – a move that their budget could never afford. So I designed a cover and the first pages embracing the roundel and Johnston type. The artworks for each page were taken by Bryce to the Design Committee meeting for approval. The Design Committee originally intended that only Board Members, Chief Officers and Officers would receive a manual. I argued that while they should receive hard covered manuals containing all pages, so that they could hopefully see the overall picture emerging, their staff should receive paper covered versions containing the introduction and the pages relevant to the work they were handling. While this approach was accepted it left me with a headache as to how to implement the strategy – each time a set of pages was printed they would need to be despatched to a growing number of people throughout the organisation, as well as keeping in touch with changes of staff so that all could be kept updated. Bryce's secretary attempted to keep the list updated while Kathy's staff office was used to fill and address the envelopes.

I was successful in getting an additional person in my design section who would be entirely employed to produce the page artworks. I insisted on being part of the interview panel, which consisted of Bill Oswald and myself. We saw about ten very capable applicants, but it was Mike Welch who appeared to totally fit the job description, and I wasn't disappointed. With his talent to produce accurate artworks and discus aspects of design, Mike also understood corporate identity. His superbly detailed drawings of side views of buses and trains showing livery considerations, lettering and symbol positions, were all to the same scale (0 gauge – 1:43.5 or 7mm to the foot) so that they could be sold to modellers to cover their printing costs.

I also handled the printing of pages, which were divided according to their subject matter between the printers used by the Publicity Office. But Bryce was nearing his retirement and his successors lacked neither commitment nor the enthusiasm to continue with this project.

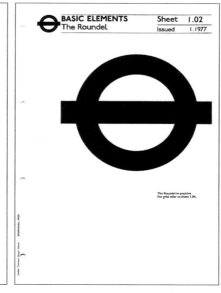

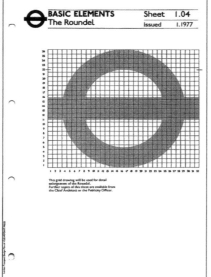

1977   **London Transport Design Manual**
Size: 297 × 210 mm
Printers: Bournehall Press;
           Clearpoint Press;
           Clifford-Thames Printing
           and others

Some of the initial pages, showing the grid all were designed to and with a page numbering system devised to make additional pages easy to insert.

1977 **London Transport Design Manual**
Size: 297 × 210 mm
Printers: Bournehall Press:
Clearpoint Press;
Clifford-Thames Printing
and others

More of the initial pages, showing
the grid all were designed to
and the page numbering system
devised to make additional pages
easy to insert.

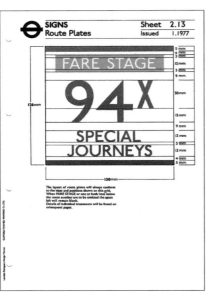

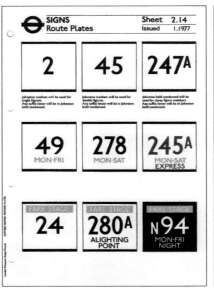

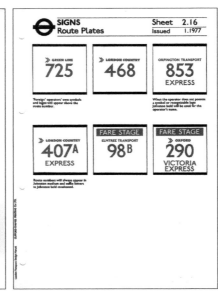

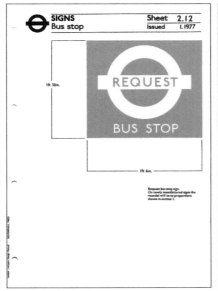

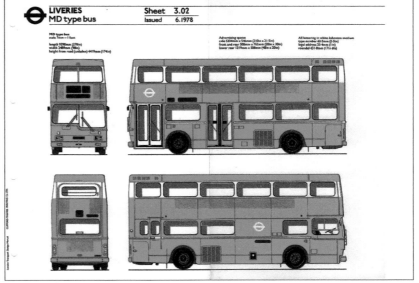

Train and bus livery interlude

During this busy period in the 1970s, I had Bryce Beaumont's encouragement to suggest design improvements and initiatives on any aspect of London Transport's corporate public image. He was happy to submit them to Design Committee meetings for discussion, with the support of his superior, Eric Wilkins, the Chief Public Relations Officer, who viewed these self motivated projects as his department acting pro-actively. At this time, Ken Livingstone was leader of the Greater London Council, LT's owner, and the government was Labour-run with Kenneth Robinson as Minister of Transport, both individuals being sympathetic to the use of good design as an important tool in the promotion of better public transport.

I viewed the continuance of my design projects as compensation for a job in the new Corporate Design Department that I had applied for and failed to get. The successful applicant was the always immaculately presented Roger Hughes, whom I was asked to initiate into corporate design and the workings of London Transport. So I took him to lunch at the *Olive Branch* in Homer Street and conversed on every subject I could think of, except design!

I pondered the current vehicle liveries, both bus and train, but from different standpoints. The aluminium coloured trains lacked the fast corporate look of the red trains that they were progressively replacing. As the aluminium aged, its surface became pitted, trapping minute particles of dust, giving the trains a worn and grubby look. Whilst accepting that painting would defeat the object of using a material for the bodywork that did not require it, I considered that a small quantity of paintwork could enhance these dull looking vehicles. Indeed, the roofs were already painted – the rolling stock superintendent told me that the roofs had a rubberised material sandwiched between the plates at the joins to keep water from seeping between them, which were then painted to stop the rubberised material from seeping out!

At the same time the buses were represented by a very monotonous all red fleet. There used to be country buses in a green livery, relieved by a little cream and the Green Line coaches, also in green and relieved by pale green, which could be seen in the centre of the capital mingling with the red buses. But when London Transport introduced their Red Arrow limited stopping single deck buses and advertised as something special which would make commuting from the main line stations to the City and West End quicker, they appeared in the same red livery relieved by lilac grey that most other red buses carried. The most noticeable difference from the norm was not to the buses, but to

their bus stops which displayed black flags. I used coloured pens on tracing paper overlaying photographs to see how the addition of some extra colour might help to make the Red Arrow buses more distinctive. Obviously red had to remain the predominant colour. I had been impressed with the Midland Red coaches passing Griffith House, where I was at that time working, on their way to and from Birmingham and other towns in the midlands. These coaches displayed black roofs as a secondary colour to their red livery. Connecting with their bus stops, the secondary colour for Red Arrows could be black.

I devised a scheme which could be applied to buses as well as trains which made a feature of roofs and the bottom area of the body appearing in a different colour. I accepted that the vast bus fleet would stay in red, secondary colours being applied only to vehicles performing special functions. Trains would all be liveried in grey, whether natural aluminium or painted on older stock, with red roofs and lower panels (called 'skirts' by transport people). The roofs of both buses and trains posed no problems since vehicle washers were equipped to clean them as part of the same action as cleaning bodies, unlike British Rail whose washers only cleaned the sides of carriages, but not the roofs or the ends. At a very early stage I decided not to pursue the representation of Line

1975   Red Arrow bus livery
The picture on the left shows a mock up of a photograph to give the effect of a possible livery. Inset is the Midland Red coach displaying a black roof as the secondary colour.

1975   Proposed train livery
Red painted areas superimposed on a black and white photograph of a Circle Line train. Other versions were produced with red across the lower portions of doors. On this proposal the doors were left bare of paint since they were prone to scrape the door recesses when opening and closing, rubbing away the paint from parts of the surface.

1978   Experimental bus livery

Application of experimental livery
scheme onto a bus converted to
a mobile shop and information
centre. The roof and lower panels
were painted in standard bus red
with white in between.

1979   Easter bus rally

The mobile shop and information
centre forms a background to
LT's publicity stall at the Easter
Parade of more than 40 buses,
commemorating 150 years of
London buses in Battersea Park.
Manning the stall either side of
myself are Frank Mussett and the
visually more charming Elaine
Cooper.

colours as part of the train livery. The Circle-Hammersmith & City-District (Wimbledon) trains would always have caused problems, even if the operators proceeded with my proposal of integrating the Wimbledon branch with the Hammersmith branch as the same Line. Jubilee Line trains would have carried the same grey for the secondary colour as their host colour. Northern Line trains would have appeared rather drab. The operators would also have argued that trains would need to be repainted if they were transferred from one Line to another, even though they accepted Line dedicated melamine maps inside.

I was asked to design a livery for a bus which was being converted to a mobile shop selling London Transport souvenir merchandise. So I used this opportunity to experiment with a full size test for my livery scheme. In this case I kept the roof and skirts in red and had the main bodywork painted white. This allowed for the maximum contrast of tones in black and white photographs and gave a chance for me to test the balance. The bus toured various transport open days and proved to be valuable to refer directors to a life size bus in the livery, rather than just a drawing. It went a long way in persuading the Chairman, Ralph Bennett and an ex-bus man known to have little time for aesthetics, that alternative liveries could usefully promote different products within the overall organisation.

I think it might have been largely as a result of this livery work that I was asked to devise a livery for the proposed Speedbus. The GLC was converting sections of the nearside of roads to accommodate bus lanes, with reserved space for buses and taxis only. In association with local borough councils, LT stipulated the roads which were prone to congestion and would benefit from an uncluttered nearside lane. The roads were generally those forming the spokes connecting the suburbs to the West End and the City. London Transport believed that these roads could be used to run fast commuter services, rather like short distance Green Lines. (They did not address the fact that bus lanes are rather like tramways, in that the speed of vehicles is only as fast as the slowest, since overtaking onto the rest of the road is often difficult.)

Originally I had been asked to design a symbol only. As an introduction to my proposals I emphasised the handicaps imposed over the years by restrictions, first to the style of lettering across the bar of the bullseye, then the prohibition of lettering altogether from the bar of the newly proportioned roundel. In my submission, I included some symbols but played them down; indeed, my livery proposals included no symbols at all, just the Speedbus title carefully positioned and sized in, of course, Johnston lettering. I also went into the reasons for choice of

Speedbus

colour and rejection of others, such as green as being likely to be confused with Green Line coaches. I felt that red should form a prominent part of the livery. This really only left yellow as a colour that would harmonise with red. Yellow was also the best colour that could be seen at a distance on murky days from a bus stop. Bus stops were also considered, but just by distinctive yellow route plates under the flags rather than the flags themselves. In addition to mocking up and colouring photographs to show the bus from different angles, I also devised different roundels and logos. However, what really endeared the project to the Chairman were

1977   Speedbus livery
Some of the illustrations that appeared in my submission for a livery treatment. In addition to the full livery, the style and position of the lettering and roundel on buses, the route plates on bus stops and symbol design suggestions can all be seen.

The many holidays spent with my granny in Bournemouth may have influenced my choice of colour. One of the Corporation's modern primrose liveried trolleybuses emerges from the turning circle at the start of its journey from Christchurch.

1980   Bus livery variations

Repainted photograph showing possible livery for tourist dedicated buses.

The Shoplinker bus livery was based on the livery suggestions for Speedbus.

the Dinky model buses that I had painted in the proposed livery. It was Eric Wilkins who felt that I should present the livery proposals to the Chairman myself – something that was most unusual in those days where a strict protocol and pecking order was normally observed. I left Ralph Bennett pushing a selection of models liveried in tradition red together with hand painted Speedbus red and yellow models across the top of his desk. The greatest test and accolade of all, was when he crouched down to get his eyes on the same level as the buses – back to boyhood, with no shame!

Alas, these proposals, having been accepted in principal and with the blessing of the Chairman, never went any further. The motorists' lobby delayed the imposition of bus lanes by arguing that their roads would effectively become narrower. The DMS buses that would have operated the network became too unreliable

to be entrusted with this key service and were also creating shortages of vehicles for the running of traditional routes. But this proposal was a useful exercise and formed the basis of livery proposals for other later schemes.

The Greater London Council had ambitions to take control of all main line railways beginning and ending their journeys within its area (this transfer would have embraced far fewer lines than when the government, in 1940, ruled that all trains that began and ended their journeys within the LPTB area would lose their first class accommodation). Services being viewed by the GLC for take over were: Ealing Broadway – Greenford; Liverpool Street – Enfield Town and Chingford; Tottenham Hale – North Woolwich; Charing Cross – Bromley North; Victoria – Beckenham Junction; Victoria – London Bridge via Denmark Hill and Norwood Junction; Wimbledon – West Croydon;

Wimbledon – Sutton and West Croydon; Waterloo – Hampton Court; Waterloo – Shepperton; Waterloo – Kingston – Putney – Waterloo. All of the services would have meant specially liveried trains which would no longer be interchangeable with those running services into the 'out counties' running over tracks which would continue to be owned by British Rail. However, there was one service, the North London Line, over which trains ran between Richmond and Broad Street via Willesden Junction, where the self contained line as well as the trains might be transferred to Underground ownership. It was on this basis that I had photographs of BR standard North London Line slam door stock, normally painted in plain BR 'Rail' blue, airbrushed in my red and grey Underground scheme to illustrate how the traditional rolling stock might be transformed.

However, the line was not as self

contained as its passenger service implied, since extensive use of sections of the track was made by freight trains, which the Underground would have wanted removed to stop any interference with their intensive passenger service. While BR was keen to have any loss making line transferred from their responsibility, they would have been required to pay for the alteration of the signalling system to conform with Underground standards. It seemed that the transfer of freight trains to other lines could have been resolved, but the proposal floundered over the cost of signal conversion, since BR had been kept as financially broke under the Labour Government in the 1970s as it was later to be under successive Tory Governments in the '80s and '90s.

Proposals for Underground rolling stock liveries were proceeded with in a small way. Service stock needed to be made more visible to people working on the line. My connections with the Underground's Permanent Way Safety Committee, in the work that I, and my colleague Kate Murphy, were doing for them designing posters, manuals and calendars, opened the door to my being chosen to submit designs. Because service vehicles did not officially form part of London Transport's perception to the public, approval was not needed at the highest level, therefore speeding the process of putting a scheme into practice.

When producing a corporate

change that may be sweeping away traditions, I like to speak to the people who are close to the existing scheme. They will often let me know why things have been done for as long as they have: for instance, why a particular shade of paint is used, or why the lettering is in the size and position that it is. Or even what they wish could be done but can't, themselves, think of a way to implement it. From these chats with the lads, most of whom worked at Neasden Depot, but also some that

I spoke to repairing tracks on site, I learned that most were keen to keep maroon as the colour for their rolling stock. This was, of course, the Metropolitan Railway's engine colour and became partially lost when the last steam locomotives were replaced by two green painted diesel locomotives. Lettering needed to be made very visible due to the often poor lighting. The depot staff and others' comments helped me take certain decisions and incorporate their wishes, especially when they

didn't conflict with the concept. This explains my inclusion of maroon as the secondary colour, although I had already decided that yellow should form the primary colour because of its qualities of visibility. Maroon also had an advantage of masking dirt, especially in oily and dusty conditions that these trains operated in. Because these trains did not operate in public I argued that roundels should not appear as part of the livery, since the definition of the roundel was 'the face of London Transport to the public'.

A few trains were actually painted in the liveries that I had proposed, but painting occurs much less frequently than for passenger stock. Following retirements, both within Publicity and in the Rail Operating department, I lost contact with the characters who relied on and appreciated my help. The new advertising orientated regime at Publicity had no interest in service vehicles – indeed, they had very little interest in any vehicle liveries, except crude non-corporate one-offs promoting particular individual

1978   North London Line

With the possible transfer of the North London Line to Underground ownership and operation its trains, running between Richmond, Willesden Junction, Hampstead and Broad Street might have looked like this. An additional darker grey was added around the window area, as was then commonly applied to French Railways' rolling stock, to unite the multiplicity of narrow openings and highlight the passenger area.

Yellow was applied due to its high visibility in dimly lit environments. However, it was limited to the areas least likely to attract the most dirt (engineering rolling stock was cleaned less often than service stock). In the case of the diesel locomotive above, the coupling rods connecting the driving wheels were also painted yellow due to their vertical and horizontal movement close to track level. Maroon was used as a secondary colour for traditional as well as practical reasons.

markets. On the rail service vehicles, while yellow was accepted as a safety visible colour, vehicles were re-painted entirely in that colour, removing any subtlety and attention to form that these, usually antique and fascinating pieces of equipment had enjoyed either from me or my predecessors in the workshops. What today's people don't appreciate is that

yellow, being very visible, is also very prone to showing dirt. This was an aspect that was recognised all those years ago by limiting yellow to the parts that would be least likely to attract oil and dirt.

However, in the 1990s I again had contact with Underground service vehicle liveries but this time on their road vehicles. As a development of

the 'red, white and blue' train liveries designed by Henrion Ludlow & Schmidt they then applied the blue at the base and white to road service vehicles. The Distribution Services vehicle department was expected to implement the new livery within their existing very limited budget when, to save costs, much of their stock had been left in the painted schemes

that they carried when bought. I was asked to visit the Distribution Services vehicle park in Bollo Lane, Acton, to apply lettering to some newly painted vehicles for the approval of HLS and I suspected that my appearance would not be welcomed by those in the park. Liaison between their manager, Peter Forsdick, and myself was done through my colleague Clare Charnley, one of the Advertising & Publicity client representatives. She was blond with model-like proportions with an upper class confidence and, on the very hot day of our visit, appeared wearing very tight shorts. This was not lost on Peter, who spent the afternoon fetching cold drinks and chatting to Clare (who was in a permanent state of giggles at the coincidental connection of name and location).

I followed the HLS specification by ranging the cap height of the first line of the title on the Underground roundel and positioned towards the front of the vehicle. They approved the nearside but on the offside had the roundel moved from the left to the right so that it was at the forward end of the vehicle. This produced the strange effect of wording ranged left counterbalanced by the roundel on the right, but also the roundel out of balance with the letter closest to it which was lower case. If HLS had done some rough designs in their studio I am sure they would not have come to this conclusion.

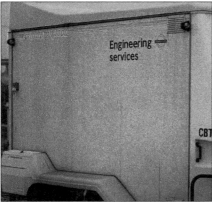

Back to the buses

Following the Thatcher Conservative government's privatisation of British Telecom and British Gas, on the promise of lower prices due to competition (which rings rather hollow in the first decade of the new century), they turned their attention to Britain's buses. First, the assets of the individual subsidiary companies forming the National Bus Company were offered for sale – most being bought initially by their employees (mainly managers). Under the Act privatising the bus companies, each individual route was required to make a profit, or be trimmed back until it did, or seek a subsidy from the local council whose area it operated through. This had a lesser effect on the NBC-owned companies, which had already been pruned to profitability over the previous fifteen years. But it dramatically effected the fortunes of the municipal fleets, which were obliged to be re-formed as subsidiaries of their parent metropolitan councils. Many of the larger councils had applied policies of cheap subsidised fares and integrated services to keep their passengers loyal to them. Much of the vast fleets became redundant and were therefore put up for sale.

As part of the 1984 act, every individual route operated by London Buses that couldn't cover its costs was to be put out to tender to any private operator as well as the London Buses

1990   Rail engineering road
        liveries

Nearside and offside of vehicles showing the unfortunate positioning of lettering in relation to the roundel on the offside. The Emergency Control Unit vehicle was lettered more recently and displays the tendency to centre the entire graphic

But the decision was made by the HLS representative – the studio were probably never asked.

Clare had joined the Advertising & Publicity office in the late 1980s. I had no more than a working relationship with her over the various jobbing projects that I designed and she progressed. But, in conversation with her on the train to Acton, I found that

some members of her family lived around Amersham which, of course, is where I had lived and commuted from since the early 1970s. So we had more common interests than we had originally thought. She later married Hugh Sumner who was a Chief Officer grade based at LT's headquarters at 55 Broadway. On leaving to have their baby, Clare was summoned to the

LT Passes & Permits office to hand in her staff pass giving her free travel on LT buses and trains and privilege rail pass allowing her to pay a quarter of the normal fare on British Rail journeys. On being issued with a tube ticket to get her home to Fulham, Clare gleefully reminded the clerk that her marital status now allowed her free travel on both systems!

subsidiary already operating it. Other London Buses' subsidiaries were not allowed to tender, which points to the direction that this political move was expected to take. To give the appearance of a level playing field, the winner was allowed to operate its buses in their existing livery, which obviated the expense of repainting its vehicles red (when KentishBus won a central London route it hired

traditional red RMs which it then repainted in its own maroon and cream colour scheme). The Tendered Bus Unit was run by Mike Weston who appeared to be as loyal an implementer of the dissection of the London Buses network as he was of the desecration of the corporate red livery. Tory MPs could look with pride at their handiwork as traditional red buses were replaced by a rainbow

assortment – one of the first routes to be privatised was the 24, whose green and grey buses ran around Parliament Square and would have beeen observed from the windows of government offices in Whitehall.

To identify the different coloured buses as those offering the same facilities as those of London Buses, such as the acceptance of Travelcards, I devised a symbol that could be either

applied to the livery or slid into a holder on the vehicle depending on whether the bus was dedicated to a London Buses route or operating one of its own company's services.

At about the same time the decision was made to specifically market the increasing fleet of minibuses. The future of many routes was being pinned on minibuses since they were cheaper to operate (the drivers did

not need full PSV licenses and could therefore be paid less) but had an image of tinniness and bumpiness. These minibuses were to be marketed as 'hoppers' to give the impression of nippiness and hopping on and off to do local shopping and make other short rides. I designed a standard logo based on the word 'hoppa' – which was the pronunciation used by many Londoners – incorporating a related roundel and area name. It had to be visible on any coloured livery but still retaining the roundel in red to comply with the current LT guidelines – there was a lot to take into account.

In London, buses remained the property of London Transport, for the time being. But the districts that the bus network had been divided in 1979 were turned into subsidiary companies in 1990, all with profit as their first motivation above all

other priorities. The companies were encouraged to devise their own names and symbols. Many of their names implied that they were central bus operators although, to be fair, all operated through central London to varying degrees. They came to Advertising & Publicity to have their symbols designed and the job was given to me. Any preferences that the new bus managements had were taken into account, in much the same way that individuals' likes and dislikes are considered when designing personal items such as business cards. Individual company names with their symbols were to be displayed on buses, as a secondary element to the London Buses identity.

Having mocked up the symbols, a standard form of lettering was devised as well as standard positions, taking into account the increased space

required on bus sides for commercial advertising. I designed symbols for all of the companies – except Metroline. I just could not come up with anything that would satisfy the Metroline directors (or myself) – my old friend and colleague, Mike Welch, saved the day with his design. London United, based at the old LUT tram depot at Fulwell, were offered a redraw of their original rather spidery coat of arms from tramway days. Eric Ravilious had drawn a griffin for use on LPTB directors' announcements and later used to publicise the LT canteen and 'Griffin' food products. He had also designed a sitting version of the griffin, and it was this that I adapted in left and right facing directions to face the shield on a redrawn London United coat of arms. Later, when the company had been sold to its directors, the coat of arms reverted to its original version – Ravilious and Frank Pick probably turned in their graves by this act of ignorance by the ultra conservative element of the bus fraternity. Other symbols have fared better since privatisation, notably London General and London Central which both retain the symbols that I designed. And, in 2007 Leaside and Selkent dusted off the motifs designed by me and re-applied them to their vehicles. A manual was produced for the different garages to apply their logos in standardised positions on each type of bus.

The next project was to deal with

a request from the London Buses management to brighten up what was left of their dwindling fleet and bring back some discipline that had been allowed to descend to a state of anarchy by the managements of these still wholly owned subsidiaries. Part of the brief was to find ways to hide the dirt that gathered on the lower parts of the bodywork, particularly during wet weather. I looked back at the livery schemes that I had worked on in the past and endeavoured to reduce the amount of unrelieved red that is seen.

London Buses subsidiary companies symbols, which replaced the district symbols and lasted until complete privatisation. Some – London General and South London – retained theirs after privatisation, while two, Leaside and Selkent have been reinstated by their new owners.

1988 London Buses livery

The first bus to be dealt with following approval of rough designs.

The grey 'skirt' would cover the lowest panel up to the division to the upper panel, which meant that grey areas would differ according to types of vehicle. The position of white mid-decks surround would also differ according to vehicle type – all positions having obstructions as demonstrated here.

1988 Production liveries 1

A newly painted Leyland Titan – complete with my own design of private blind – waits outside Albany House in Petty France to be shown off to members of the LT and LBL boards.

Fortunately, early in 1988, a snow storm helped, by concentrating far more dirt than was normal onto the sides of the buses. I went to Stockwell Garage with a Pantone colour swatch book where I matched the colour of the mud and dirt once it had dried – this became the grey 'skirt' as it became known. The relief of a white horizontal line to divide the upper and lower decks, as had persisted on RM buses needed to be reflected on the newer front exit and rear engined vehicles. There was no clear unobstructed area above the lower deck windows on the rear engined fleet compared to that forming part of the design on RMs. However, a compromise was possible using 40mm wide white vinyl tape that could be bought as a standard item in rolls.

The scheme that was finally approved didn't come about straight away. I gave illustrations of a number of representative bus types to a studio to draw up in the same scale and add overlays indicating the depths of grey and thicknesses and positions of the white lines to double deckers and single deckers. Tony Waldron, the reliable stalwart at the Redgrave Graphics studio in Denbigh Mews in Pimlico, prepared the displays. I had built a relationship over time with Redgrave which meant that I always had a quick turnaround from them. And I needed it – the entire scheme was achieved in about two weeks, from initial briefing to submissions of designs to the London Buses Chairman.

Next to receive attention were the Airbuses running between central London and Heathrow Airport and the Red Arrow express buses. The new red with grey 'skirts' colour scheme was applied, but the white lines were given variations. The brief for the

Airbus included retaining the extra bold lettering, which was in the style of Antique Olive as devised by the advertising agency for their launch campaign in 1980. So I had a variation of New Johnston lettering drawn as an extra bold italic that would be used on Airbus, Red Arrow any other service needing dedicated vehicles. On the Red Arrow the white horizontal line began with an arrow head at the front. In fact it was half an arrow head so that the Red Arrow lettering could more forcefully run along the upper side of the shaft. The shaft ended just short of the back of the bus by sweeping upwards and over the roof to join the upswept shaft on the other side, reflecting a fashion trend applied by some coach firms.

Other liveries were devised, mainly in the region of vinyl applications to highlight different services. I not only visited garages to supervise but also went to body manufacturers, on one occasion travelling overnight to Falkirk in Scotland, to advise on the positioning of a set of vinyls – and as it

1989   Production liveries 2
The majestic Alexandria bodied Scania wears the new livery together with its LBL subsidiary name and logo. The name and logo's position can also be seen on the RM in the background.

1989   Production liveries 3 & 4
Two buses of different types show the flexibility of the livery.

1988   Single deck livery

As with the double deckers, the grey 'skirt' covered the lowest panel up to the division to the upper panel, and the position of the white was above the windows on the lowest available portion of uncluttered roof.

turned out, apply – to one vehicle as a guide for application to the build.

By visiting garages, advising any painters having difficulty finding the most suitable positions to apply the additional colours and generally supervising, a tight control could be kept on a livery that had been

designed to suit a wide variation of vehicle shapes with a highly disciplined result. I also policed any versions seen that were definitely unsympathetic, for instance: black skirts, or white roofs on single deckers. It was estimated at the time that the additional cost of painting

and lining each bus, including addition labour time, amounted to £60 per bus – LBL still owned 5,000 buses, still the largest bus operator in the country.

This livery was not to last many years since the mid-1990s saw the entire fleet sold off on the cheap,

very often to garage managers who wanted to put their own livery stamp on history. However, some of the new owning companies were more sympathetic, notably London General.

These liveries were distinctive enough to be reproduced for posterity on models made by Corgi and EFE.

1988   Red Arrow livery

On Red Arrows the horizontal white line was raised to align with the bar of the roundel.
The extra bold lettering, based on New Johnston italic, was especially drawn for application to the Red Arrow and Airbus fleets.

1988   Airbus livery

The position of the roundel in relation to the Airbus lettering was specified by Airbus Industries when they allowed the use of their copyright name. The lettering used was the same adaptation of a New Johnston extra bold italic as had been applied to Red Arrows.

On the front, various panels dictated the off-centred position of the logo, which unintentionally gave it a more dynamic appearance (and related it to the off-centred air intake grill).

1988   Short run liveries

The operators of Gold Arrow pinched the Red Arrow graphics giving, in my view, the impression that Gold Arrows were a limited stopping high speed network, which it was not. Having lost the battle however, I devised and supervised a disciplined livery. London Buses' own hoppas needed no specialised identification since they were always painted in the standard LBL livery.

The pictures below show a section of the Croydon Food Production Centre and an item of packaging then in use enclosing their particularly meaty and reasonably priced sausages.
The picture on the right shows a wedding spread produced by the Centre of a real wedding. They prepared and delivered spreads such as this most weekends of the year at any venue within the London area. (Couples supplied their own clothing to their preferred designs!)
The pictures were commissioned by me as part of the production of the Centre's promotional booklet, some of the pages being shown opposite.

Catering

The fun and diversity of working at London Transport was that the organisation covered so much more than just running buses and trains. Those were the days when it was considered to be cheaper and more efficient to perform ancillary and support work in-house rather than buy it in from outside. To list just a few non-transport-operational subjects, I worked on the following:
London Transport Catering
St.John's Ambulance Brigade
London Transport Medical Section
Station Gardens Competition
Permanent Way Safety Committee
London Transport Players
St.Marylebone Parish Church.

London Transport had its own kitchens in Croydon – called the Croydon Food Production Centre – which supplied food to all London Transport premises: canteens at bus garages and rail depots as well as mobile canteens at rail heads and bus turning points, office canteens and restaurants Most also supplied staff with previously ordered items to take home. In the 'eighties, together with all other departments, it was forced to break even financially or be closed down. So they doubled their efforts to cater for special functions involving staff members, retirement parties, promotion parties, special openings and even weddings.

I did quite a lot of work for them, from the happier more secure days to

the end. I made use of Stradivarius, a script like typeface designed by Imre Reiner and cast by Bauersche Giesserei of Frankfurt-am-Main in 1945, for their messages, which seemed to contrast well with the formality of the griffin, originally designed by Eric Ravilious, and the Johnston lettering surrounding it which appeared on their crockery.

But these extra activities only added to London Transport Catering's financial woes: the very reason why they had been challenged to clear this hurdle, so their demise was of their own making rather than closure being imposed upon them, as had befallen other departments before and after them.

1976   London Transport Catering

The italic lettering used for leaflets of various types to publicise the LT Catering Service was Bauer Stradivarius while text was set in Antique Olive by Founderie Olive, Marseille.

1979   Griffin Home Care booklet

Once the London Transport Catering service became a profit centre they came to Publicity for help in the production of items to boost their sales. Shown here is the design stage of a spread and the cover of a booklet showing staff the range of food items available for them to order for delivery to their place of work to be taken home. The catering was privatised, the Croydon Food Production Centre was closed and prices inevitably rose before the booklet was printed.

1972   **Bus Stop timetable**
Size: 300 × 218 mm
Printer: Bournehall Press, Welwyn

The typographic standard of London Transport timetable set in 1972 and, with adaptations to typeface and heading, still in use today.

Strand *Aldwych*	1821	1829	1839	1902	1913	1925	1948	1959	2011	2034	2045	2057	2120	2131	2143	2206	2229	2252

Mortlake Garage	2236	2259	2322	0015	0036
Barnes *Red Lion*	2241	2304	2327	0020	0041
Hammersmith Broadway....	2247	2310	2334‡	0026	0047
Kensington Church	2257	2320	——	0036	0057
Hyde Park Corner	2304	2327	....	0043	0104
Charing Cross *Trafalgar Square*	2312	2335	....	0051	0112
Strand *Aldwych*	2315	2338	....	0100§	0121§

Additional buses, Saturdays: Mortlake Garage to Strand *Aldwych* at 1014, 1028, 1043, 1128, 1158, 1314, 1343, 1413, 1443, 1458, 1514, 1613 and 1643.

Sundays (also Easter, Spring and Summer Bank Holidays)

Mortlake Garage	0606	0626	0635	0702	0729	0753	0816	0839	0858	0916	0932	0947	1002	1017	1032	1047	1102	1109
Barnes *Red Lion*	0611	0631	0640	0707	0734	0758	0821	0844	0903	0921	0937	0952	1007	1022	1037	1052	1107	1114
Hammersmith Broadway....	0617‡	0637‡	0645	0712	0739	0803	0826	0849	0908	0926	0942	0957	1013	1028	1043	1058	1113	1120
Kensington Church	——	——	0652	0719	0746	0810	0833	0856	0915	0933	0949	1005	1023	1038	1053	1108	1123	1130
Hyde Park Corner	....	....	0659	0726	0753	0817	0840	0903	0922	0940	0956	1012	1030	1045	1100	1115	1130	1137
Charing Cross *Trafalgar Square*	....	....	0705	0732	0759	0823	0846	0909	0928	0946	1003	1020	1038	1053	1108	1123	1138	1148†
Mansion House Station	....	....	0713	0740	0807	0831	0854	0917	0936	0954	1012	1029	1047	1102	1117	1132	1147	....
Tower Hill Station	....	....	0716	0743	0810	0834	0857	0920	0939	0957	1016	1033	1051	1106	1121	1136	1151	....
Aldgate Station	....	....	0719	0746	0813	0837	0900	0923	0942	1000	1020	1037	1055	1110	1125	1140	1155	....

Mortlake Garage	1117	1130	1143	1155	1208	1221	1233	1246	1259	1311	1324	1337	1349	1402	1416	1429	1443	1457
Barnes *Red Lion*	1122	1135	1148	1200	1213	1226	1238	1251	1304	1316	1329	1342	1354	1407	1421	1434	1448	1502
Hammersmith Broadway....	1128	1141	1154	1206	1219	1232	1244	1257	1310	1322	1335	1348	1400	1413	1427	1440	1454	1508
Kensington Church	1138	1151	1204	1216	1229	1242	1254	1307	1320	1332	1345	1358	1410	1423	1437	1450	1504	1518
Hyde Park Corner	1145	1158	1211	1223	1236	1249	1301	1314	1327	1339	1352	1405	1417	1430	1444	1457	1511	1525
Charing Cross *Trafalgar Square*	1153	1206	1219	1231	1244	1257	1309	1322	1335	1347	1400	1413	1425	1438	1452	1505	1519	1533
Mansion House Station	1202	1215	1228	1240	1253	1306	1318	1331	1344	1356	1409	1422	1434	1447	1501	1514	1528	1542
Tower Hill Station	1206	1219	1232	1244	1257	1310	1322	1335	1348	1400	1413	1426	1438	1451	1505	1518	1532	1546
Aldgate Station	1210	1223	1236	1248	1301	1314D	1326	1339	1352D	1404D	1417	1430	1442	1455	1509	1522	1536	1550D

Mortlake Garage	1511	1521	1532	1539	1547	1559	1611	1623	1635	1647	....	1702	1717	1733	1740	1752	1804	1816
Barnes *Red Lion*	1516	1526	1537	1544	1552	1604	1616	1628	1640	1652	....	1707	1722	1738	1745	1757	1809	1821
Hammersmith Broadway....	1522	1532	1543	1550	1558	1610	1622	1634	1646	1658	1705	1713	1728	1744	1751	1803	1815	1827
Kensington Church	1532	1542	1553	1600	1608	1620	1632	1644	1656	1708	1716	1723	1738	1754	1801	1813	1825	1837
Hyde Park Corner	1539	1549	1600	1607	1615	1627	1639	1651	1703	1715	1723	1730	1745	1801	1808	1820	1832	1844
Charing Cross *Trafalgar Square*	1547	1557	1608	1618†	1623	1635	1647	1659	1711	1723	1734†	1738	1753	1809	1819†	1831†	1843†	1855†
Mansion House Station	1556	1606	1617	——	1632	1644	1656	1708	1720	1732	——	1747	1802	1818	....	....	....	....
Tower Hill Station	1600	1610	1621	....	1636	1648	1700	1712	1724	1736	....	1751	1806	1822	....	....	....	....
Aldgate Station	1604	1614	1625	....	1640	1652D	1704D	1716	1728D	1740	....	1755	1810	1826	....	....	....	....

Mortlake Garage	1829	1842	....	1855	1908	1921	1934	1947	1959	2012	2025	2038	2051	2104	2117	2129	2142	2155
Barnes *Red Lion*	1834	1847	....	1900	1913	1926	1939	1952	2004	2017	2030	2043	2056	2109	2122	2134	2147	2200
Hammersmith Broadway....	1840	1853	1859	1906	1919	1932	1945	1958	2010	2023	2036	2049	2102	2115	2128	2140	2153	2206
Kensington Church	1850	1903	1910	1916	1929	1942	1955	2008	2020	2033	2046	2059	2112	2125	2138	2150	2203	2216
Hyde Park Corner	1857	1910	1917	1923	1936	1949	2002	2015	2027	2040	2053	2106	2119	2132	2145	2157	2210	2223
Charing Cross *Trafalgar Square*	1908†	1918	1928†	1931	1947†	2000†	2013†	2023	2038†	2048	2104†	2117†	2130†	2143†	2156†	2208†	2221†	2234†
Mansion House Station	——	1927	——	1940	....	....	....	2032	....	2057	....	....	....	....	....	....	....	....
Tower Hill Station	....	1931	....	1944	....	....	....	2036	....	2101	....	....	....	....	....	....	....	....
Aldgate Station	....	1935	....	1948	....	....	....	2040D	....	2105D	....	....	....	....	....	....	....	....

Mortlake Garage	2208	2221	2234	2247	2259	2314	2329
Barnes *Red Lion*	2213	2226	2239	2252	2304	2319	2334
Hammersmith Broadway....	2219	2232	2245	2258	2310	2325	2340
Kensington Church	2229	2242	2255	2308	2320	2335	2350
Hyde Park Corner	2236	2249	2302	2315	2327	2342	2357
Charing Cross *Trafalgar Square*	2247†	2300†	2313†	2323	2338†	2350	0005
Mansion House Station	——	——	——	2332	....	2359	0014
Tower Hill Station	....	....	....	2336	....	0003	0018
Aldgate Station	....	....	....	2340D	....	0007D	0022D

†—Time at Strand *Aldwych*.   ‡—Time at Hammersmith *Brook Green*.   §—Time at Mansion House Station.
D—To Dalston Garage via Commercial Street and Kingsland Road.   G—To Dalston Garage via Kingsland Road.

Note—While every effort will be made to keep to the timetables, London Transport does not undertake that its buses will be operated in accordance with them, or at all. London Transport will not be responsible for any loss, damage or inconvenience caused by reason of any operating failures or in consequence of any inaccuracies, in the timetables. At Christmas, New Year, Easter and Spring and Summer holiday weekends, some services have special timetables and some

The progressive typographic design movements of the early twentieth century in Germany, Poland and the fledgling Soviet Union were joined in the '30s by a number of art and design groups which were gathering momentum in Britain and the USA. A collection of printers also became design led but, unlike their continental counterparts, tended toward the refinement of traditional design and production. Some printers commissioned type designs for their exclusive use from up and coming leading typographers and calligraphers. Other type faces were commissioned by type founders, in England notably the Monotype Corporation. A by no means exhaustive list of designers of type during the twentieth century would include, with their more well known type faces:

Morris Benton, 1872–1948 (USA), *Alternate Gothic, Bank Gothic, Broadway, Clearface, Cloister Old Style, Franklin Gothic, Goudy Catalogue, News Gothic, Stymie*;

Lucian Bernard 1883–1972 (Germany), *Bernard Roman, Lucian*;

Jakob Erbar 1878–1935 (Germany), *Candida, Erbar, Koloss*;

Eric Gill 1882–1940 (Great Britain), *Gill Sans, Golden Cockerel Type, Joanna, Perpetua, Pilgrim*;

F. W. Goudy 1865–1947 (USA), *Goudy, Italian Old Style, Kennerley, Venezia*;

Edward Johnston, *Underground Railway Type*;

David Kindersley 1915–95 (Great Britain), *Octavian*;

Rudolf Koch 1876–1934 (Germany), *Holla, Kabel, Locarno, Nueland, Wallau*;

Robert Hunter Middleton 1898–1985 (USA), *Flair, Karnak, Record Gothic, Tempo, Umbra*;

Stanley Morison 1889–1967 (Great Britain), *Times New Roman*;

Imre Reiner 1900–87 (Hungary), *Bazaar, Corvinus, London Script, Reiner Black/Script, Stradivarius*;

Paul Renner 1878–1956 (Germany), *Futura*;

Jan Tschichold 1902–1974 (Germany/Switzerland), *Sabon, Transit, Saskia, Zeus*;

Berthold Wolpe 1905–89 (Germany/Great Britain), *Albertus, Hyperion, Pegasus*;

Herman Zapf 1918– (Germany), *Aldus, Hunt Roman, Melior – the text face you are reading, Mergenthaler, Optima, Palatino, Sapphire, Venture*.

The new awareness spurned a flood of magazines devoted to discussions and displays showing the directions being pursued.

One of these design orientated publications was produced by the Shenval Press. In the Spring 1938 issue of TYPOGRAPHY was an article written by Christian Barman, who was at that time the Publicity Officer of London Transport. It was headed *Timetable Typography* and dealt with the development of typographic styles as used on timetables of the early railways up to rail, bus and air timetables currently then produced in this country and on the continent of Europe. The German and Swiss rail timetables were favoured by Barman, with a special description of the German REICHS KURSBUCH as being the most complete, the best edited and best printed timetable in the world. The publishers of these timetables had recently replaced the serifed type in which they were formerly set with some of the new grotesque sans serif faces then being designed and cast in type by continental type founders.

In Britain, Gill Sans had been available for use from the early 1930s having been commissioned by the London & North Eastern Railway for their signing, general publications and notably, timetables. Other railways (and bus companies) gradually changed from the traditional use of serifed type to the new sans serif style as budgets permitted. London Transport was already using Gill Sans for the figures in their pocket timetables, while the side headings were set in Monotype Grotesque No 1 (Mono series 215 and 216) which set narrower than Gill characters

Barman's article concludes with a description of the typographic revision to London Transport's timetables which was overseen by Francis Meynell making use of the typographic skills of Harry Carter, who had started his career at the Monotype Corporation and moved to the Kynoch Press in Birmingham in 1929 until 1936. Little did I know, during the first months of my career at Kynoch, of the hallowed atmosphere that was providing me with inspiration at Witton! Instead of developing a sans serif approach he had reverted to a serif type, utilising Times New Roman, which had been commissioned by the national newspaper and also made available for general use by Monotype. Carter then designed special serif figures for use with the Times New Roman side headings, but with the thickness transferred to the horizontal strokes to aid reading across lines. He also researched the width of setting, the leading and the use of rules.

By the 1960s London Transport's timetables were looking antiquated and were often badly set by a number of different printers of varying standards and without any concern for the reader.

Bus stop timetables formed the majority of settings. As services became less regular, so the number of times to be shown increased as every journey needed to be included in the production. Time columns were squeezed together and separated by brass vertical rules. Each rule had to be cut in a guillotine which, if blunt, tended to bend the ends as it cut them, before being inserted by hand.

Timetable frames on bus stops generally contained three panels

1972 **Route 267 bus stop panel timetable**

Size: A4 (297 × 210 mm)
Printer: Leonard Ripley, Vauxhall

The Bus 267 timetable is an example of the presentation which had been applied to this type of timetable information since the 1950s.

Bus 267 via Brentford, Twickenham and Fulwell
to HAMPTON COURT STN.

Mondays to Fridays
(Over the section marked ★ buses run every 7-10 minutes until 1830.)

Hammersmith Broadway
Turnham Green Church
Kew Bridge Star & Garter
Brentford Half Acre ★
Isleworth War Memorial ★
Twickenham King Street
Fulwell Jolly Blacksmith
Hampton Hill High St., Hampton Rd.
Hampton Court Station

Saturdays

Hammersmith Broadway
Turnham Green Church
Kew Bridge Star & Garter
Brentford Half Acre
Isleworth War Memorial
Twickenham King Street
Fulwell Jolly Blacksmith
Hampton Hill High St., Hampton Rd.
Hampton Court Station

Sundays

Hammersmith Met. Station
Turnham Green Church
Kew Bridge Star & Garter
Brentford Half Acre
Isleworth War Memorial
Twickenham King Street
Fulwell Jolly Blacksmith
Hampton Hill High St., Hampton Rd.
Hampton Court Station

†—Time at Fulwell Garage.

NOTE—No service operates on Christmas Day: a special timetable applies on Easter, Spring and Summer Bank Holidays and Boxing Day. While every effort will be made to keep to the timetables, London Transport does not undertake that its buses will be operated in accordance with them, or at all. London Transport will not be responsible for any loss, damage or inconvenience caused by reason of any operating failure or in consequence of any inaccuracies in the timetables.

LONDON TRANSPORT, 55 BROADWAY, S.W.I.   Telephone: 01-222 1234   3.1.71 (A)

371/1719K/500   L9529   Ripley

---

that small corrections could be made to the type by replacing characters using tweezers, where as film set (which was already on line in the 1970s) artwork entailed re-setting the entire production or pasting a patch onto the artwork.

In the early 1970s, following my own experience of trying to read and understand timetables (which were formed of closely set figures and a mass of vertical and horizontal rules) and struggling to fathom out the time of the next bus before boredom set in, I looked into ways of giving a timetable in a bus stop frame a clearer appearance, both initially and in practice. As with nearly all projects which I set out to do off my own bat, it could only be justified if the final result cost no more to produce than at present. There were a lot of people to persuade when seeking to make changes as fundamental as timetable designs. And it was best to be aware of as many hurdles as possible, and cross them, before approaching the key departmental officers for support to even embark on the exercise.

From my previous experience of working at printers, the greatest saving in production costs that could be made was to reduce the amount of hand operation and increase the amount of keyboard work. The vertical brass rules between the columns of times could contribute a large amount to cost saving if they were replaced by space between the columns, which could easily be accomplished by a keystroke. And the vertical space could be better emphasised if all columns appeared at regular intervals. However, the columns between vertical rules were set to irregular widths – those with footnote reference marks were set wider than those without. The setting of space between the columns therefore needed to be wide enough to allow for any footnote reference marks. The price of replacing vertical rules by space was that fewer columns within the width could be accommodated on a very full timetable.

Existing timetable settings employed varying sizes of type (ranging from 6pt to 12pt) depending on the amount of information on them and therefore the number of columns (and their depths) that were to appear. I proposed that 8pt Gill Sans was readable outside in not always the best lit conditions. Gill Sans was the closest style to London Transport's house type of Johnston, which was not available as a metal type below 36pt. Johnston figures were also of varying width, the face not having been designed for keyboard or tabular operation. The Gill fount, however possessed fairly narrow and very clear figures.

A conference in the early 1960s, of provincial and municipal bus operators, had settled on the use of Monotype Grotesque 215 and 216 for the setting of timetables which

and had been fixed at 36 inches deep by 12 inches wide in the 1920s. This meant that timetables were printed on paper very close to A4 size, and following the trend towards international paper sizes in the 1960s A4 width became standard together with its depth, which was multiplied twice or three time depending on the bulk of information. The other timetables were for the less frequent Underground services. All timetables were set in various styles of Gill Sans and were printed by letterpress. Letterpress with individually cast metal figures did have the advantage

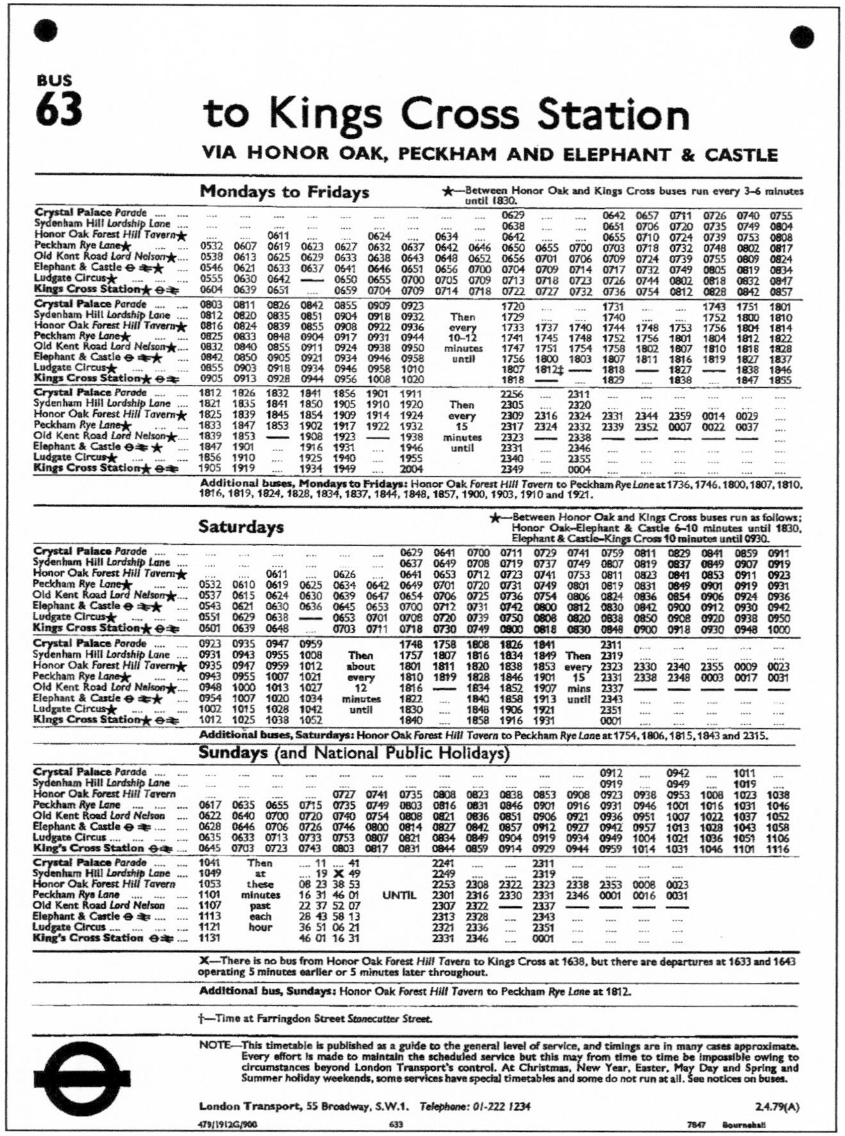

BUS 63 — to Kings Cross Station

VIA HONOR OAK, PECKHAM AND ELEPHANT & CASTLE

Mondays to Fridays ★—Between Honor Oak and Kings Cross buses run every 3–6 minutes until 1830.

Crystal Palace Parade	...	...	...	...	...	...	...	0629	...	...	0642	0657	0711	0726	0740	0755			
Sydenham Hill Lordship Lane	...	...	...	...	...	...	0638	...	...	0651	0706	0720	0735	0749	0804				
Honor Oak Forest Hill Tavern★	...	...	0611	...	...	0624	...	0642	...	0655	0710	0724	0739	0753	0808				
Peckham Rye Lane★	0532	0607	0619	0623	0627	0632	0637	0642	0646	0650	0655	0700	0703	0718	0732	0748	0802	0817
Old Kent Road Lord Nelson★	0538	0613	0625	0629	0633	0638	0643	0648	0652	0656	0701	0706	0709	0724	0739	0755	0809	0824
Elephant & Castle ⊖ ≷★	0546	0621	0633	0637	0641	0646	0651	0656	0700	0704	0709	0714	0717	0732	0749	0805	0819	0834
Ludgate Circus★	0555	0630	0642	...	0650	0655	0700	0705	0709	0713	0718	0723	0726	0744	0802	0818	0832	0847
Kings Cross Station★ ⊖≷	0604	0639	0651	...	0659	0704	0709	0714	0718	0722	0727	0732	0736	0754	0812	0828	0842	0857

(morning/daytime continuation)

Crystal Palace Parade	0803	0811	0826	0842	0855	0909	0923		1720		1731		1743	1751	1801
Sydenham Hill Lordship Lane	0812	0820	0835	0851	0904	0918	0932	Then	1729		1740		1752	1800	1810
Honor Oak Forest Hill Tavern★	0816	0824	0839	0855	0908	0922	0936	every	1733	1737	1740	1744	1748	1753	1756	1801	1804	1814
Peckham Rye Lane★	0825	0833	0848	0904	0917	0931	0944	10–12	1741	1745	1748	1752	1756	1801	1804	1812	1822
Old Kent Road Lord Nelson★	0832	0840	0855	0911	0924	0938	0950	minutes	1747	1751	1754	1758	1802	1807	1810	1818	1828
Elephant & Castle ⊖ ≷★	0842	0850	0905	0921	0934	0946	0958	until	1756	1800	1803	1807	1811	1816	1819	1827	1837
Ludgate Circus★	0855	0903	0918	0934	0946	0958	1010		1807	1812½		1818		1827		1838	1846
Kings Cross Station★ ⊖≷	0905	0913	0928	0944	0956	1008	1020		1818		1829		1838		1847	1855

(evening continuation)

Crystal Palace Parade	1812	1826	1832	1841	1855	1901	1911		2256	2311
Sydenham Hill Lordship Lane	1821	1835	1841	1850	1905	1910	1920	Then	2305	2320
Honor Oak Forest Hill Tavern★	1825	1839	1845	1854	1909	1914	1924	every	2309	2316	2324	2331	2344	2359	0014	0029
Peckham Rye Lane★	1833	1847	1853	1902	1917	1922	1932	15	2317	2324	2332	2339	2352	0007	0022	0037
Old Kent Road Lord Nelson★	1839	1853	...	1910	1927	...	1938	minutes	2324	2338						
Elephant & Castle ⊖ ≷★	1847	1901	...	1916	1931	...	1946	until	2331	2346						
Ludgate Circus★	1856	1910	...	1925	1940	...	1955		2340	2355						
Kings Cross Station★ ⊖≷	1905	1919	...	1934	1949	...	2004		2349	0004						

Additional buses, Mondays to Fridays: Honor Oak Forest Hill Tavern to Peckham Rye Lane at 1736, 1746, 1800, 1807, 1810, 1816, 1819, 1824, 1828, 1834, 1837, 1844, 1848, 1857, 1900, 1903, 1910 and 1921.

Saturdays
★—Between Honor Oak and Kings Cross buses run as follows: Honor Oak–Elephant & Castle 6–10 minutes until 1830, Elephant & Castle–Kings Cross 10 minutes until 0930.

Crystal Palace Parade	...	...	...	...	...	0629	0641	0700	0711	0729	0741	0759	0811	0829	0841	0859	0911
Sydenham Hill Lordship Lane	...	...	...	...	...	0637	0649	0708	0719	0737	0749	0807	0819	0837	0849	0907	0919
Honor Oak Forest Hill Tavern★	...	...	0611	...	0626	0641	0653	0712	0723	0741	0753	0811	0823	0841	0853	0911	0923
Peckham Rye Lane★	0532	0610	0619	0625	0634	0642	0653	0700	0720	0731	0749	0801	0819	0831	0849	0901	0919	0931
Old Kent Road Lord Nelson★	0537	0615	0624	0630	0647	0654	0706	0725	0736	0754	0806	0824	0836	0854	0906	0924	0936
Elephant & Castle ⊖ ≷★	0543	0621	0630	0636	0645	0653	0700	0712	0731	0742	0800	0812	0830	0842	0900	0912	0930	0942
Ludgate Circus★	0551	0629	0638	...	0653	0701	0708	0720	0739	0750	0808	0820	0838	0850	0908	0920	0938	0950
Kings Cross Station★ ⊖≷	0601	0639	0648	...	0703	0711	0718	0730	0749	0800	0818	0830	0848	0900	0918	0930	0948	1000

(Saturday continuation)

Crystal Palace Parade	0923	0935	0947	0959		1748	1758	1808	1826	1841	2311
Sydenham Hill Lordship Lane	0931	0943	0955	1008	Then	1757	1807	1816	1834	1849	Then	2319
Honor Oak Forest Hill Tavern★	0935	0947	0959	1012	about	1801	1811	1820	1838	1853	every	2323	2330	2340	2355	0009	0023
Peckham Rye Lane★	0943	0955	1007	1020	every	1810	1819	1828	1846	1901	15	2331	2338	2348	0003	0017	0031
Old Kent Road Lord Nelson★	0949	1000	1013	1027	12	1816	...	1834	1852	1907	mins	2337	2343				
Elephant & Castle ⊖ ≷★	0954	1007	1020	1034	minutes	1822	...	1840	1858	1913	until	2343					
Ludgate Circus★	1002	1015	1028	1042	until	1830	...	1848	1906	1921		2351					
Kings Cross Station★ ⊖≷	1012	1025	1038	1052		1840	...	1858	1916	1931		0001					

Additional buses, Saturdays: Honor Oak Forest Hill Tavern to Peckham Rye Lane at 1754, 1806, 1815, 1843 and 2315.

Sundays (and National Public Holidays)

Crystal Palace Parade	...	...	...	...	...	...	...	...	...	...	0912	...	...	0942	...	1011	...
Sydenham Hill Lordship Lane	...	...	...	...	...	...	...	...	...	0919	...	...	0949	...	1019	...
Honor Oak Forest Hill Tavern	...	...	...	...	0727	0741	0735	0808	0823	0846	0901	0916	0931	0938	0953	1008	1023	1038
Peckham Rye Lane	0617	0635	0655	0715	0735	0749	0803	0816	0831	0846	0901	0916	0931	0946	1001	1016	1031	1046
Old Kent Road Lord Nelson	0622	0640	0700	0720	0740	0754	0808	0821	0836	0851	0906	0921	0936	0951	1007	1022	1037	1052
Elephant & Castle ⊖ ≷	0628	0646	0706	0726	0746	0800	0814	0827	0842	0857	0912	0927	0942	0957	1004	1021	1036	1106
Ludgate Circus	0635	0653	0713	0733	0753	0807	0821	0834	0849	0904	0919	0934	0949	1004	1031	1046	1101	1106
King's Cross Station ⊖≷	0645	0703	0723	0743	0803	0817	0831	0844	0859	0914	0929	0944	0959	1014	1031	1046	1101	1116

(Sunday continuation)

Crystal Palace Parade	1041		11 ... 41		2241		2311	
Sydenham Hill Lordship Lane	1049	Then	19 X 49		2249		2319	
Honor Oak Forest Hill Tavern	1053	these	08 23 38 53		2253	2308	2323	2353	0008	0023
Peckham Rye Lane	1101	minutes	16 31 46 01	UNTIL	2301	2316	2330	2346	0001	0031
Old Kent Road Lord Nelson	1107	past	22 37 52 07		2307	2322				
Elephant & Castle ⊖ ≷	1113	each	28 43 58 13		2313	2328		2343		
Ludgate Circus	1121	hour	36 51 06 21		2321	2336		2351		
King's Cross Station ⊖≷	1131		46 01 16 31		2331	2346		0001		

X—There is no bus from Honor Oak Forest Hill Tavern to Kings Cross at 1638, but there are departures at 1633 and 1643 operating 5 minutes earlier or 5 minutes later throughout.

Additional bus, Sundays: Honor Oak Forest Hill Tavern to Peckham Rye Lane at 1812.

†—Time at Farringdon Street *Stonecutter Street.*

NOTE—This timetable is published as a guide to the general level of service, and timings are in many cases approximate. Every effort is made to maintain the scheduled service but this may from time to time be impossible owing to circumstances beyond London Transport's control. At Christmas, New Year, Easter, May Day and Spring and Summer holiday weekends, some services have special timetables and some do not run at all. See notices on buses.

London Transport, 55 Broadway, S.W.1. Telephone: 01-222 1234

479/1912G/900 633 7647 Bournehall 2.4.79(A)

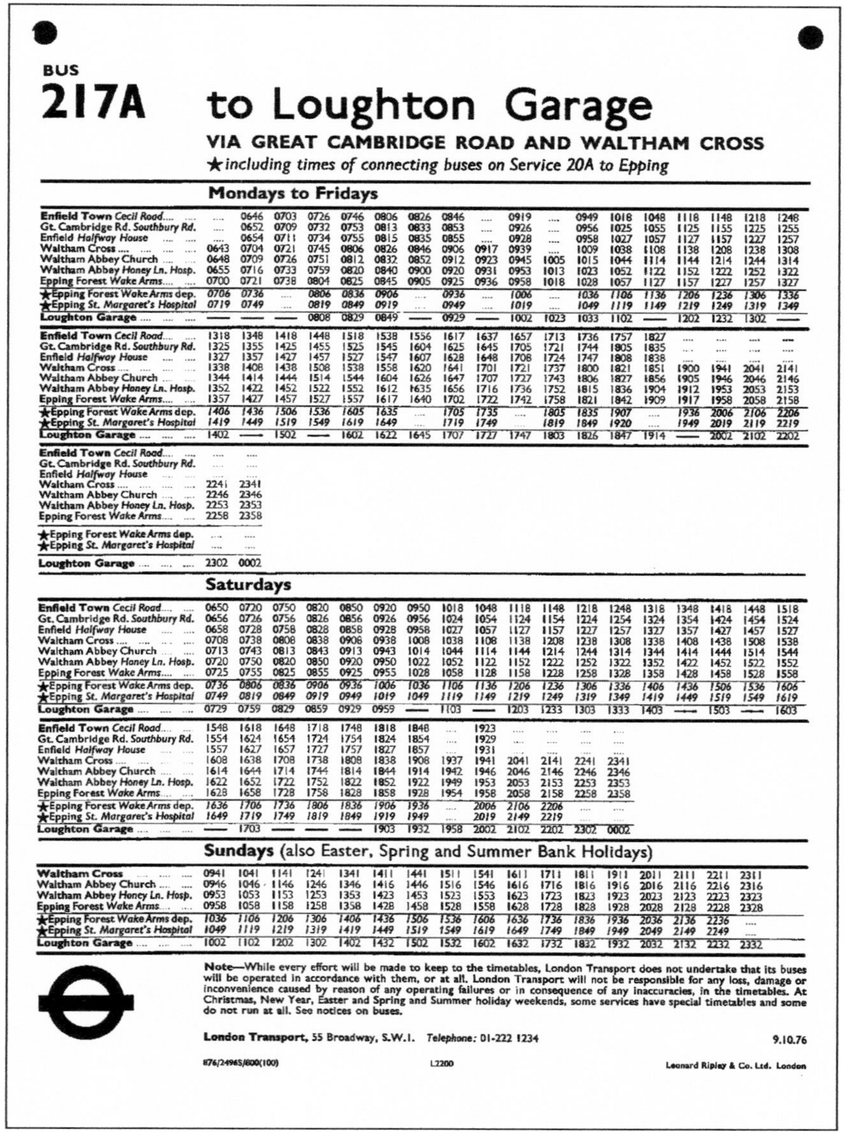

BUS 217A — to Loughton Garage

VIA GREAT CAMBRIDGE ROAD AND WALTHAM CROSS
★ *including times of connecting buses on Service 20A to Epping*

Mondays to Fridays

Enfield Town Cecil Road	...	0646	0703	0726	0746	0806	0826	0846	...	0919	...	0949	1018	1048	1118	1148	1218	1248
Gt. Cambridge Rd. Southbury Rd.	...	0652	0709	0732	0753	0813	0833	0853	...	0926	...	0956	1025	1055	1125	1155	1225	1255
Enfield Halfway House	...	0654	0711	0734	0755	0815	0835	0855	...	0928	...	0958	1027	1057	1127	1157	1227	1257
Waltham Cross	0643	0704	0721	0745	0806	0826	0846	0906	0917	0939	...	1009	1038	1108	1138	1208	1238	1308
Waltham Abbey Church	0648	0709	0726	0751	0812	0832	0852	0912	0923	0945	1005	1015	1044	1114	1144	1214	1244	1314
Waltham Abbey Honey Ln. Hosp.	0655	0716	0733	0759	0820	0840	0900	0920	0931	0953	1013	1023	1052	1122	1152	1222	1252	1322
Epping Forest Wake Arms...	0700	0721	0738	0804	0825	0845	0905	0925	0936	0958	1018	1028	1057	1127	1157	1227	1257	1327
★Epping Forest Wake Arms dep.	0706	0736		0806	0836	0906		0936		1006		1036	1106	1136	1206	1236	1306	1336
★Epping St. Margaret's Hospital	0719	0749		0819	0849	0919		0949		1019		1049	1119	1149	1219	1249	1319	1349
Loughton Garage	...	...		0808	0829	0849		0929	...	1002	1023	1033	1102	——	1202	1232	1302	

Enfield Town Cecil Road	1318	1348	1418	1448	1518	1538	1556	1617	1637	1657	1713	1736	1757	1827			
Gt. Cambridge Rd. Southbury Rd.	1325	1355	1425	1455	1525	1545	1604	1625	1645	1705	1721	1744	1805	1835			
Enfield Halfway House	1327	1357	1427	1457	1527	1547	1607	1628	1648	1708	1724	1747	1808	1838			
Waltham Cross	1338	1408	1438	1508	1538	1558	1620	1641	1701	1721	1737	1800	1821	1851	1900	1941	2041	2141
Waltham Abbey Church	1344	1414	1444	1514	1544	1604	1626	1647	1707	1727	1743	1806	1827	1856	1905	1946	2046	2146
Waltham Abbey Honey Ln. Hosp.	1352	1422	1452	1522	1552	1612	1635	1656	1716	1736	1752	1815	1836	1904	1912	1953	2053	2153
Epping Forest Wake Arms...	1357	1427	1457	1527	1557	1617	1640	1702	1722	1742	1758	1821	1842	1909	1917	1958	2058	2158
★Epping Forest Wake Arms dep.	1406	1436	1506	1536	1605	1635		1705	1735		1805	1835	1907		1936	2006	2106	2206
★Epping St. Margaret's Hospital	1419	1449	1519	1549	1619	1649		1719	1749		1819	1849	1920		1949	2019	2119	2219
Loughton Garage	1402	——	1502	——	1602	1622	1645	1707	1727	1747	1803	1826	1847	1914	——	2002	2102	2202

Enfield Town Cecil Road	...	...	...	...	...
Gt. Cambridge Rd. Southbury Rd.	...	...	...	...	...
Enfield Halfway House	...	...	...	...	...
Waltham Cross	2241	2341			
Waltham Abbey Church	2246	2346			
Waltham Abbey Honey Ln. Hosp.	2253	2353			
Epping Forest Wake Arms	2258	2358			
★Epping Forest Wake Arms dep.	...	...			
★Epping St. Margaret's Hospital	...	...			
Loughton Garage	2302	0002			

Saturdays

Enfield Town Cecil Road	0650	0720	0750	0820	0850	0920	0950	1018	1048	1118	1148	1218	1248	1318	1348	1418	1448	1518
Gt. Cambridge Rd. Southbury Rd.	0656	0726	0756	0826	0856	0926	0956	1027	1057	1124	1154	1224	1254	1324	1354	1427	1454	1524
Enfield Halfway House	0658	0728	0758	0828	0858	0928	0958	1027	1057	1127	1157	1227	1257	1327	1357	1427	1457	1527
Waltham Cross	0708	0738	0806	0838	0906	0938	1008	1038	1108	1138	1208	1238	1308	1338	1408	1438	1508	1538
Waltham Abbey Church	0713	0743	0813	0843	0913	0943	1014	1044	1114	1144	1214	1244	1314	1344	1414	1444	1514	1544
Waltham Abbey Honey Ln. Hosp.	0720	0750	0820	0850	0920	0950	1022	1052	1122	1152	1222	1252	1322	1352	1422	1452	1522	1552
Epping Forest Wake Arms	0725	0755	0825	0855	0925	0955	1027	1058	1128	1158	1228	1258	1328	1358	1428	1458	1528	1558
★Epping Forest Wake Arms dep.	0736	0806	0836	0906	0936	1006	1036	1106	1136	1206	1236	1306	1336	1406	1436	1506	1536	1606
★Epping St. Margaret's Hospital	0749	0819	0849	0919	0949	1019	1049	1119	1149	1219	1249	1319	1349	1419	1449	1519	1549	1619
Loughton Garage	0729	0759	0829	0859	0929	0959	...	1103	...	1203	1233	1303	1333	1403	——	1503	——	1603

Enfield Town Cecil Road	1548	1618	1648	1718	1748	1818	1848	...	1923	...								
Gt. Cambridge Rd. Southbury Rd.	1554	1624	1654	1727	1754	1824	1854	...	1929	...								
Enfield Halfway House	1557	1627	1657	1727	1757	1827	1857	...	1931	...								
Waltham Cross	1608	1638	1708	1738	1808	1838	1908	1937	1942	2041	2141	2241	2341					
Waltham Abbey Church	1614	1644	1714	1744	1814	1844	1914	1942	1946	2046	2146	2246	2346					
Waltham Abbey Honey Ln. Hosp.	1622	1652	1722	1752	1822	1852	1923	1953	2053	2153	2253	2353						
Epping Forest Wake Arms	1628	1658	1728	1758	1828	1858	1928	1954	1958	2058	2158	2258	2358					
★Epping Forest Wake Arms dep.	1636	1706	1736	1806	1836	1906	1936	...	2006	2106	2206							
★Epping St. Margaret's Hospital	1649	1719	1749	1819	1849	1919	1949	...	2019	2119	2219							
Loughton Garage	...	1703	...	1903	1932	1958	2002	2102	2202	2302	0002							

Sundays (also Easter, Spring and Summer Bank Holidays)

Waltham Cross	0941	1041	1141	1241	1341	1411	1441	1511	1541	1611	1711	1811	1911	2011	2111	2211	2311					
Waltham Abbey Church	0946	1046	1146	1246	1341	1416	1446	1516	1541	1616	1716	1816	1916	2016	2116	2216	2316					
Waltham Abbey Honey Ln. Hosp.	0953	1053	1153	1253	1353	1423	1453	1523	1553	1623	1723	1823	1923	2023	2123	2223	2323					
Epping Forest Wake Arms	0958	1058	1158	1258	1358	1428	1458	1528	1558	1628	1728	1828	1928	2028	2128	2228	2328					
★Epping Forest Wake Arms dep.	1036	1106	1206	1306	1406	1436	1506	1536	1606	1636	1736	1836	1906	1936	2036	2136	2236					
★Epping St. Margaret's Hospital	1049	1119	1219	1319	1419	1449	1519	1549	1619	1649	1749	1849	1949	2049	2049	2149	2249					
Loughton Garage	1002	1102	1202	1302	1402	1432	1502	1532	1602	1632	1732	1832	1932	2032	2132	2232	2332					

Note—While every effort will be made to keep to the timetables, London Transport does not undertake that its buses will be operated in accordance with them, or at all. London Transport will not be responsible for any loss, damage or inconvenience caused by reason of any operating failures or in consequence of any inaccuracies, in the timetables. At Christmas, New Year, Easter and Spring and Summer holiday weekends, some services have special timetables and some do not run at all. See notices on buses.

London Transport, 55 Broadway, S.W.1. Telephone: 01-222 1234 9.10.76

876/2496S/800(100) L2200 Leonard Ripley & Co. Ltd. London

1972 Route 63 bus stop panel timetable

Size: A4 (297 × 210 mm)
Printer: Bournehall Press

A prototype setting in which the vertical rules between the columns were replaced by extra space. A continental style figure 1 has been used to test the effect of reducing the space either side of it when compared with the standard figure for this font which resembles a capital I.

1976 Route 217A bus stop panel timetable

Size: A4 (297 × 210 mm)
Printer: Leonard Ripley, Vauxhall

A production timetable which also shows journeys by Bus 20A connecting at Epping Forest which are shown in italics to emphasise that they refer to a separate service. This timetable, as all others, was set following a detailed type specification supplied to all printers, but only specified Johnston setting for the heading by the printers that held the type.

---

was adopted by many of them. Their agreed timetables also employed space between columns instead of vertical rules used formerly. However, one problem was the presentation of four-figure numbers on the 24-hour timing system. Some times, for instance 2014, could easily be expressed as two thousand and fourteen, instead of a group of two double figures meaning, correctly, twenty-fourteen. Continental timetables had, for many years employed slightly smaller figures to express the minutes, aligned at the top with the hour figures, as did the timetables designed by Harry Carter. This style persisted to some degree into the Gill Sans era of London Transport timetables, but was not consistent between the various printers of the timetables because of no quality supervision by them or at the publicity timetable end of the operation. To use smaller minute figures would have meant using a smaller size than the optimum size of 8pt for use on bus stop panel timetables. Therefore, a change of weight was seen as an equally effective way to break up the four figures into two groups. Bold hour figures with medium minutes

1950   **Monotype Gill Sans**
Size: 8pt enlarged

Comparison of original Gill
Sans figures (left) and those
re-drawn (right) by the Monotype
Corporation to look similar to
figures commonly seen on the
European continent. In the 1950s,
'60s and '70s Monotype supplied
a considerable amount of
typesetting equipment to central
and eastern Europe, particularly
for the setting of bus and rail
timetables in those countries.

1234567890   1234567890

1975   **Metropolitan Line
timetables**
Size: 40 × 25 in
Printer: Waterlow & Sons

Early examples of the
typographic presentation
following the typographic style of
bus stop panel timetables.

were tried, as well as medium hour figures with light minute figures. The latter group was selected as having a subtlety between the two weights that did not draw attention to the difference. Printers were encouraged to make use of the Gill Sans alternative figures produced by Monotype for the European market. Their style similar to Futura and possessed the advantage of a figure 1 with a serif (or nose) at the top which reduced the space between them compared with the standard Gill 1 similar to a capital I. The alternative numbers also specified were: 4 (which was open) and 8 (whith its different size circles).

Finally, the setting for the headings meant that Johnston could be used, in 36pt which was the smallest size that the face was available as metal type. This application was reverting to a style used for London General Omnibus timetables up to the 1930s, although route numbers were set in the same size as the Johnston headings, but in Gill Sans bold – Johnston bold was not available in this size. A standard type size was used on all timetables, so that none was seen to compete with the next.

The Publicity Officer, Bryce Beaumont, was very supportive and took the initial timetable settings to his regular weekly timetable meeting with the bus operating directorate. The operators, having been left to fend for themselves for so long since

everyone had more important and interesting things to do than deal with timetable designs, were not receptive to the new designs, possibly because they had not thought of doing it themselves. So they sited the quantity of bus stop timetable panels (which only measured in single figures) that could no longer be accommodated by using the new layout, to which I listed the larger number of timetables of the existing layout that were only accommodated by replacing some of the short journeys with footnotes – and often the footnotes were anywhere but at the foot of the timetables.

However, Bryce won reluctant approval when he threatened the involvement of the Design Committee.

The new timetable designs were introduced only as re-timing of bus routes made re-setting necessary. When the bus operating department saw the ease of calculating the depth of any timetable, they became very eager to have grids drawn up for drafting new timetables now that a known number of columns could he allowed for.

A similar style was adopted for double royal size poster timetables displayed on Underground station

platforms and inside ticket offices. Besides the Metropolitan Line timetables, of which many also included timings of the parallel running British Rail Marylebone – Aylesbury services, full timetables were also displayed for outer parts of the District and Central lines.

Departure lists were also dealt with, using a range of type sizes and styles standardised for all posters, replacing the former practice of setting each poster with type of varying sizes to fill the area.

The heads and feet of the timetable posters were not changed since

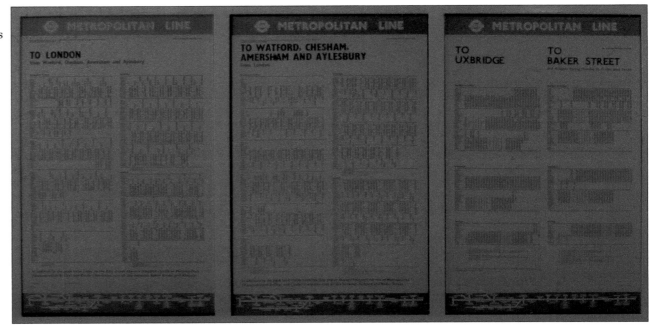

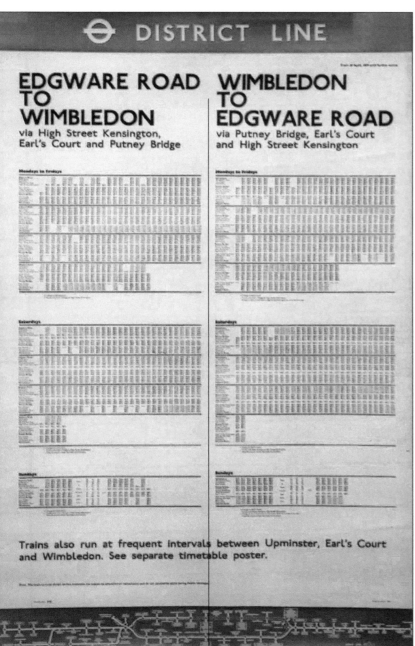

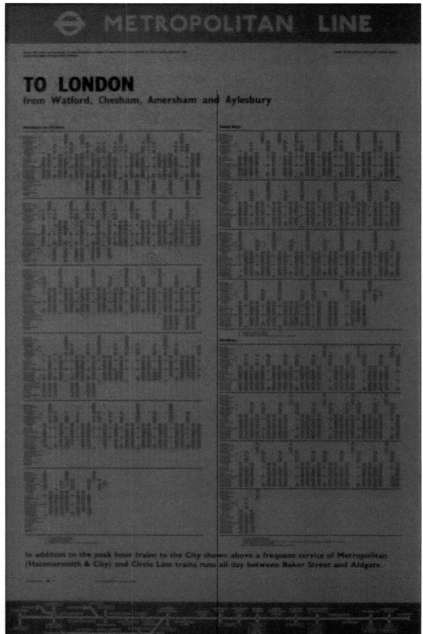

1975 **District Line and Metropolitan Line timetables**

Size: 40 × 25 in
Printer: Waterlow & Sons

While the tops and bottoms remained the same – to use up pre-printed backs – the timetable presentation following the typographic style of bus stop panel timetables.

1975   **Central Line timetables**
Size: 40 × 25 in
Printer: Waterlow & Sons

For portions of lines with frequent services departure lists were cleaned up typographically, while sections with less frequent services displayed traditional timetables set to the updated standard.

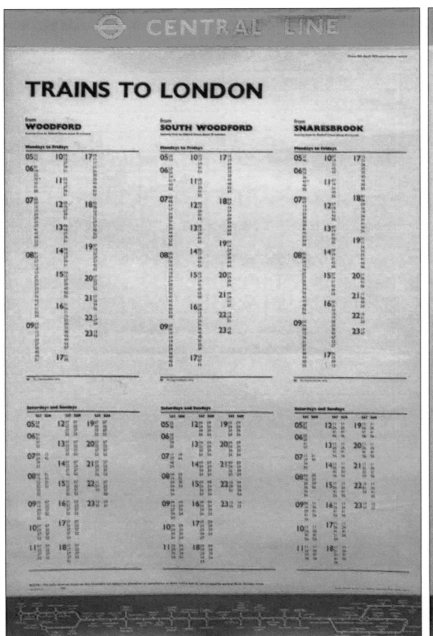

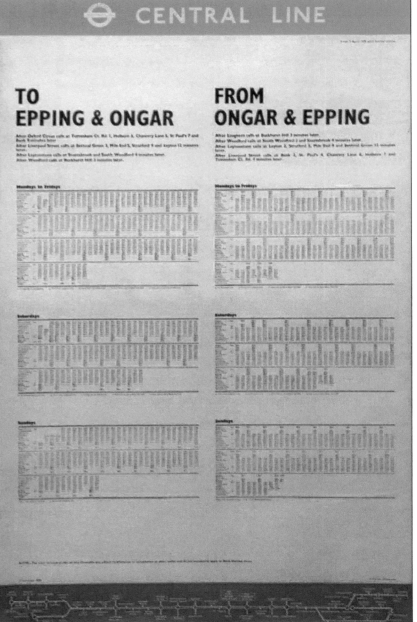

LONDON TRANSPORT
UNDERGROUND
GUIDE

13 November, 1972 until further notice

CONTENTS

ENQUIRIES

For any information about travel in London please Transport Travel Enquiry Office. These are at Euston, Victoria, Oxford Circus, King's Cross an Underground stations. You can also write to t Officer, London Transport, 55 Broadway, SW1H 01-222 1234 at any time, day or night.

A

INFORMATION

Car Parks
There is accommodation for cars at many Underground stations, especially outside London. This enables you to leave your car at or near the station and complete your journey to work or shop in the comfort of the Underground. The cost is low. Please see pages (ii) & (iii) or the Underground map at the end of the book for a list of stations where there are car parks.

Children
Children under 3 years old travel free when accompanied by a fare paying adult or child passenger. Children of 3 and under 14 years old travel at half the adult fare, fractions of 1p charged as 1p.

Dogs and other Animals
You must buy a ticket for your dog. Other small and inoffensive animals may be taken free of charge. All animals must be on a lead or carried, and must in all circumstances be carried on escalators. It is a punishable offence not to do this.

---

provided the opportunity to bring the typographic style into line with the work being done on the bus stop and rail poster timetables. As with all the other timetable typographic

I judged them to be satisfactory, although the artwork for the line diagrams were re-drawn to conform with the designs being revised for the car interior diagrams.

Early in 1973 the Underground Guide booklet was due to be completely reset amendments as had formerly been sufficient. This was because of the prevailing economic conditions making considerable changes (reductions) necessary to timetables on all lines. This

---

London Transport

Underground
Guide

00 May, 1973 until further notice

Contents

Enquiries

For any information about travel in London please call at any London Transport Travel Enquiry Office. These are at Piccadilly Circus, Euston, Victoria, Oxford Circus, King's Cross and St. James's Park Underground stations. You can also write to the Public Relations Officer, London Transport, 55 Broadway, SW1H 0BD, or telephone 01-222 1234 at any time, day or night.

Information

Car Parks
There is accommodation for cars at many Underground stations, especially outside London. This enables you to leave your car at or near the station and complete your journey to work or shop in the comfort of the Underground. The cost is low. Please see pages (ii) & (iii) or the Underground map at the end of the book for a list of stations where there are car parks.

Children
Children under 3 years old travel free when accompanied by a fare paying adult or child passenger. Children of 3 and under 14 years old travel at half the adult fare, fractions of 1p charged as 1p.

Dogs and other Animals
You must buy a ticket for your dog. Other small and inoffensive animals may be taken free of charge. All animals must be on a lead or carried, and must in all circumstances be carried on escalators. It is a punishable offence not to do this.

Escalators
Do not allow clothing or anything you may be carrying to touch any part of the escalator. Disregard of this warning may cause damage for which London Transport can accept no responsibility. Stand on the right so that others in a hurry may be able to pass. If you have a dog with you, it MUST be carried.

Fog
In foggy weather it may be necessary to vary the times of trains, or even to cancel them. On these occasions London Transport tries to save passengers discomfort and inconvenience, but cannot be responsible for delays which may unavoidably occur.

Hand Luggage
Hand luggage only may be taken on the Underground. Please make sure it does not obstruct other passengers and do not allow it to block the train doors.

Holidays
The timetables shown in this book do not necessarily apply on public holidays. On Easter, Spring and Late Summer holiday Mondays, first trains run at Sunday times, last trains run at normal Monday to Saturday times and at Christmas special services operate. Some stations are open only on certain days. For information please see blackboard notices displayed at stations, and page 149 of this Guide.

Interchange Stations
Five minutes must be allowed for changing trains at interchange stations, with the exception of Bank-Monument where 10 minutes should be allowed.

Left Luggage
Left Luggage facilities are normally open during Underground traffic hours. For a list of stations see index pages (ii) & (iii).

Lost Property
If you find lost property on a London Transport train or station you should hand it at once to the nearest London Transport official. This is a Department of Environment regulation. If you leave something behind, you can apply for it at the Lost Property Office at 200 Baker Street, NW1 5RZ, close to Baker Street Station, which is open Mondays to Fridays from 10 00 to 18 00. It is closed on Saturdays, Sundays and public holidays. You can write if it is more convenient than calling.

Parties
There are special Day Return rates for parties of 20 or more. The Party age-limit for Children's half fares is raised to 18. These special rates must be arranged in advance. Please write for details to the Fares and Charges Office, London Transport, 55 Broadway, London, SW1H 0BD.

Prams and Bicycles
Folding prams, provided they are closely folded, may be taken at any time on London Transport trains, free of charge

v

1972 **Timetable booklet of Underground services**
Size: 171 × 109 mm
Printer: Waterlow & Sons

Style of the introductory pages that had been in use since the 1950s, shown here as a comparison to the revised style of 1973.

1973 **Timetable booklet of Underground services**
Size: 171 × 109 mm
Printer: Waterlow & Sons

Typographic revisions show the development achieved using exactly the same text typefaces but a revised layout. The upper and lower case heading on the lower spread is set in Johnston in its smallest size as metal type.

1972 **Timetable booklet of Underground services**
Size: 171 × 109 mm
Printer: Waterlow & Sons

The style that had been introduced in the 1940s and still persisted on Underground timetables, was the reduction of hour figures to the heads of columns and changes of hour. The effect can be seen here, with the appearance of a conflict within the column of centred leader dots and vertical time joiners fighting the right ranging minute figures.

1973 **Timetable booklet of Underground services**
Size: 171 × 109 mm
Printer: Waterlow & Sons

The reset timetable gives a more uniform appearance, using space in place of vertical rules.

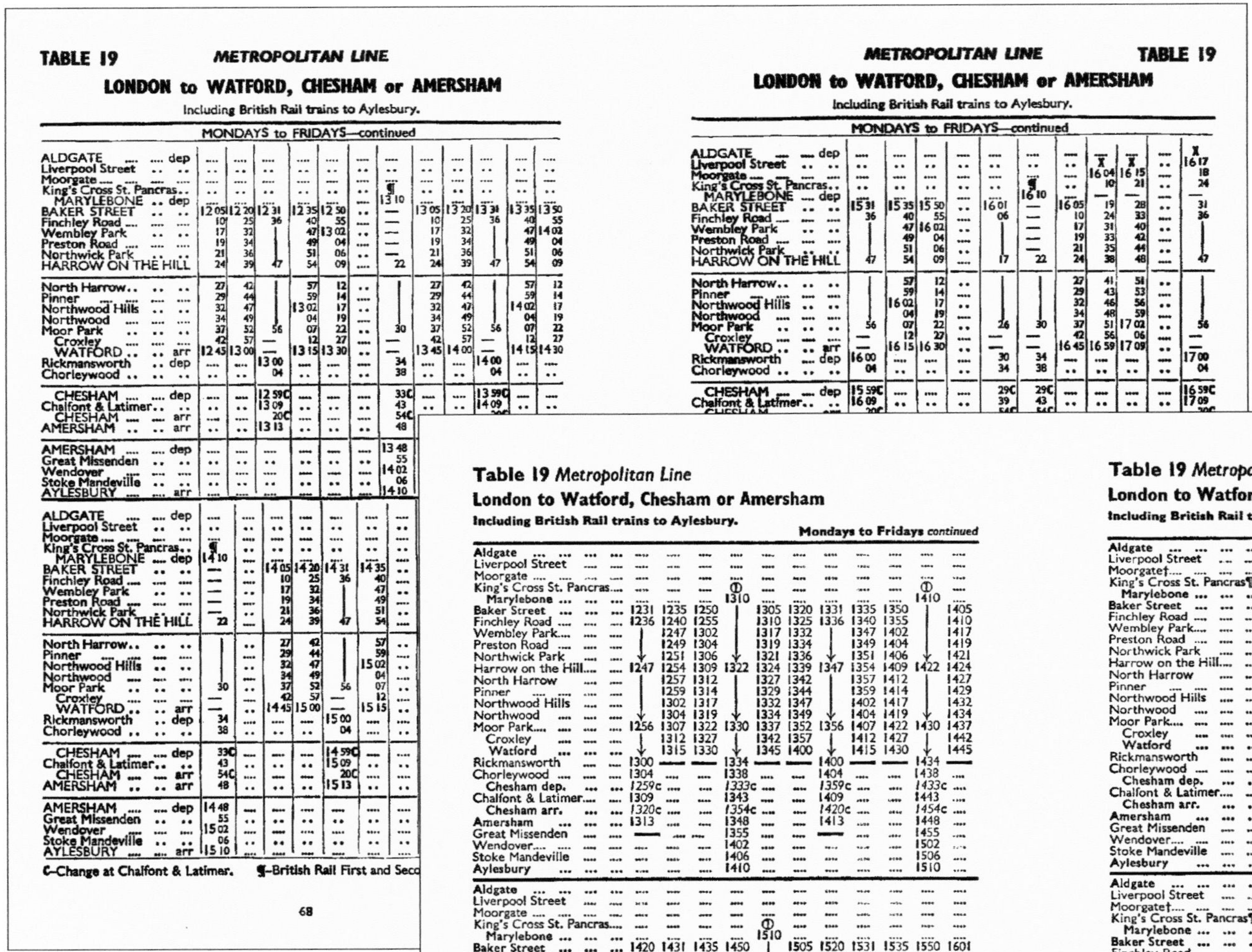

useful arrangement, although using the slightly bolder weight Gill Sans medium (Monotype (262) with the light (362). Full typographic layouts were prepared for all pages so that

revisions, the new style had to take no more space than the one that it was replacing (in fact the total number of pages remained the same, while some individual timetables spread over more and others fewer). The timetables in the existing booklet were set in Gill Sans light (Monotype 362), in a special casting of a 6pt body on 5½pt which meant that all lower case descenders descended no lower than the base of the x-height. The new setting continued with this

---

TABLE 19 METROPOLITAN LINE

LONDON to WATFORD, CHESHAM or AMERSHAM

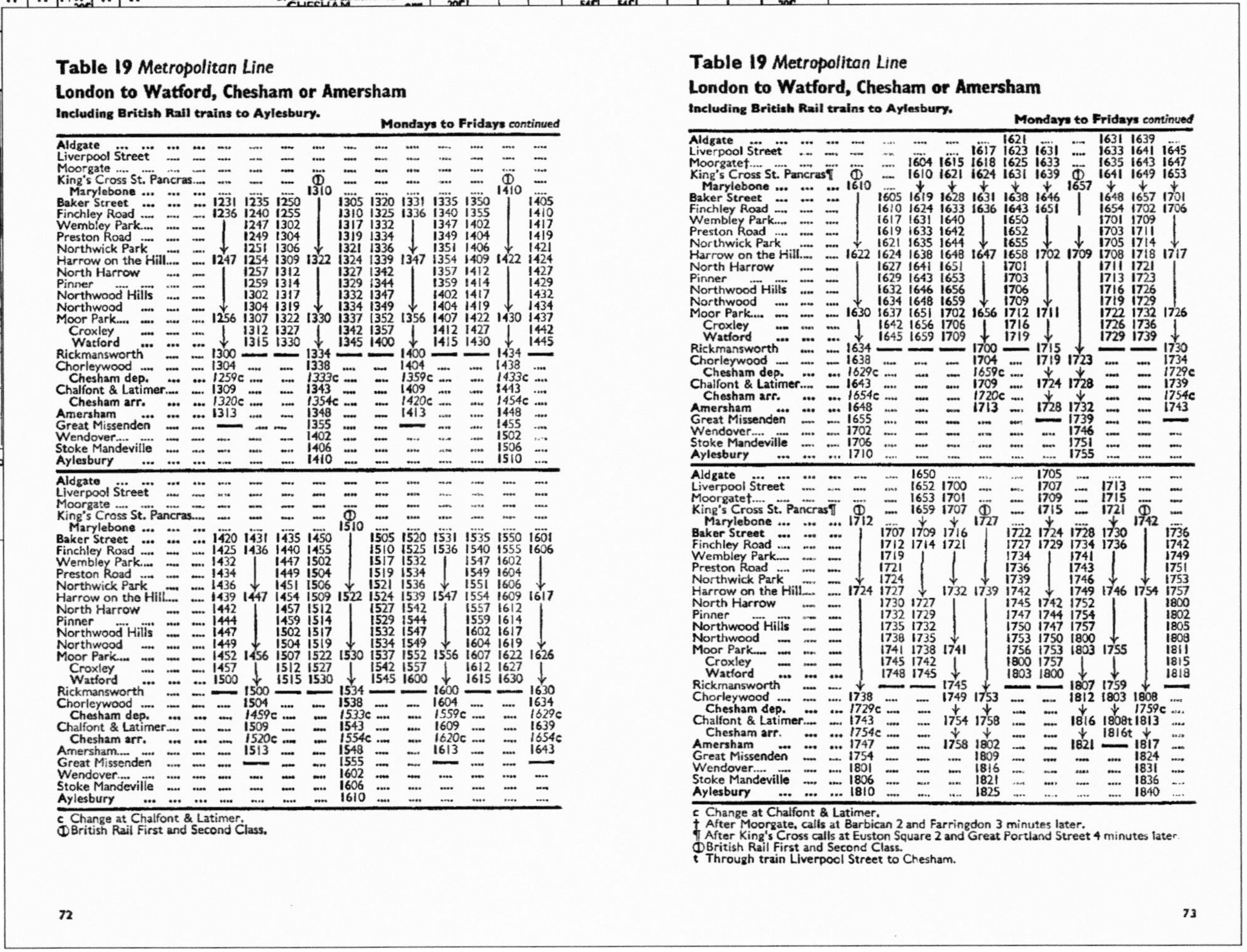

Including British Rail trains to Aylesbury.

MONDAYS to FRIDAYS—continued

(Stations in order: Aldgate, Liverpool Street, Moorgate, King's Cross St. Pancras, Marylebone, Baker Street, Finchley Road, Wembley Park, Preston Road, Northwick Park, Harrow on the Hill, North Harrow, Pinner, Northwood Hills, Northwood, Moor Park, Croxley, Watford, Rickmansworth, Chorleywood, Chesham, Chalfont & Latimer, Amersham, Great Missenden, Wendover, Stoke Mandeville, Aylesbury)

c–Change at Chalfont & Latimer.
¶–British Rail First and Second Class.

Table 19 *Metropolitan Line*

London to Watford, Chesham or Amersham

Including British Rail trains to Aylesbury.

Mondays to Fridays *continued*

(Stations in order: Aldgate, Liverpool Street, Moorgate, King's Cross St. Pancras, Marylebone, Baker Street, Finchley Road, Wembley Park, Preston Road, Northwick Park, Harrow on the Hill, North Harrow, Pinner, Northwood Hills, Northwood, Moor Park, Croxley, Watford, Rickmansworth, Chorleywood, Chesham dep., Chalfont & Latimer, Chesham arr., Amersham, Great Missenden, Wendover, Stoke Mandeville, Aylesbury)

c Change at Chalfont & Latimer.
① British Rail First and Second Class.

Table 19 *Metropolitan Line*

London to Watford, Chesham or Amersham

Including British Rail trains to Aylesbury.

Mondays to Fridays *continued*

(Stations in order: Aldgate, Liverpool Street, Moorgate, King's Cross St. Pancras, Marylebone, Baker Street, Finchley Road, Wembley Park, Preston Road, Northwick Park, Harrow on the Hill, North Harrow, Pinner, Northwood Hills, Northwood, Moor Park, Croxley, Watford, Rickmansworth, Chorleywood, Chesham dep., Chalfont & Latimer, Chesham arr., Amersham, Great Missenden, Wendover, Stoke Mandeville, Aylesbury)

c Change at Chalfont & Latimer.
† After Moorgate, calls at Barbican 2 and Farringdon 3 minutes later.
¶ After King's Cross calls at Euston Square 2 and Great Portland Street 4 minutes later.
① British Rail First and Second Class.
t Through train Liverpool Street to Chesham.

editorial could be achieved before any setting, saving the expense of moving blocks of type around and creating further proofs. This also allowed the selection and positioning of the special filler advertisements that had been designed to harmonise with the timetable settings.

However, the Underground Guide got only as far as proofing stage, when the economic straight jacket engulfing London Transport (the original reason for the re-print) necessitated altering the timetables again and again at such a rate that even the poster timetables could hardly keep up with the changes. These conditions were caused by the government imposing a national wage freeze in an attempt to reduce inflation. Track maintenance staff, as well as others, left their employment with London Transport to seek higher paid jobs elsewhere, leading to speed restrictions on the portions of track which required attention through lack of maintenance. Fewer drivers and guards also led to train cancellations and gaps in service making published timetables irrelevant to the dwindling service. As conditions improved, production of the all Underground pocket timetable was switched to individual line guides, although only the Metropolitan, followed by the Central line booklets, were completed.

Thoughts were then given to a re-introduction of local bus and rail timetables. Since the transfer in

January 1970 of green buses and Green Line coaches to the new Reigate-based London Country Bus services, together with their timetable booklets, London Transport had lost control of pocket timetables for its own services. A person had already been employed in the Publicity Office to edit the Underground line timetables, whose duties were expanded to nurture these local timetable booklets which would include all modes of public transport within each re-defined area.

Table 20 *Metropolitan Line*

Uxbridge to Baker Street

Sundays

Uxbridge							0653	0710	0726	0744	0759	0814 0829
Hillingdon							0656	0713	0729	0747	0802	0817 0832
Ickenham							0658	0715	0731	0749	0804	0819 0834
Ruislip			Dep.	Dep.			0700	0717	0733	0751	0806	0821 0836
Ruislip Manor			Neas-	Neas-			0702	0719	0735	0753	0808	0823 0838
Eastcote			den	den			0704	0721	0737	0755	0810	0825 0840
Rayners Lane			at	at			0707	0724	0740	0758	0813	0828 0843
West Harrow			0703a	0707a			0709	0726	0742	0800	0815	0830 0845
Harrow on the Hill							0713	0729	0745	0803	0818	0833 0848
Northwick Park							0715	0731	0747	0805	0820	0835 0850
Preston Road							0717	0733	0749	0807	0822	0837 0852
Wembley Park		0656d			0708d	0721d	0736	0752	0810	0825	0840	0855
Finchley Road		0708	0712	0716	0720	0733	0743	0800	0817	0832	0847	0902
Baker Street		0714	0718	0722	0726	0739	0748	0805	0822	0837	0852	0907

Uxbridge		0844	0859	0914	0929	0944	....	59 14	29 44
Hillingdon		0847	0902	0917	0932	0947	....	02 17	32 47
Ickenham		0849	0904	0919	0934	0949	....	04 19	34 49
Ruislip		0851	0906	0921	0936	0951	....	06 21	36 51
Ruislip Manor		0853	0908	0923	0938	0953	Then at	08 23	38 53
Eastcote		0855	0910	0925	0940	0955	these	10 25	40 55
Rayners Lane		0858	0913	0928	0943	0958	minutes	13 28	43 58
West Harrow		0900	0915	0930	0945	1000	past each	15 30	45 00
Harrow on the Hill		0903	0918	0933	0948	1003	hour	18 33	48 03
Northwick Park		0905	0920	0935	0950	1005	....	20 35	50 05
Preston Road		0907	0922	0937	0952	1007	....	22 37	52 07
Wembley Park		0910	0925	0940	0955	1010	....	25 40	55 10
Finchley Road		0917	0932	9947	1002	1017	....	32 47	02 17
Baker Street		0922	0937	0952	1007	1022	....	37 52	07 22

Uxbridge		2214	2229	2244	2257	2317	2332	2351
Hillingdon		2217	2232	2247	2300	2319	2334	2354
Ickenham		2219	2234	2249	2302	2321	2336	2356
Ruislip		2221	2236	2251	2304	2324	2339	2358
Ruislip Manor		2323	2238	2253	2306	2325	2340	2400
Eastcote	until	2225	2240	2255	2308	2327	2342	0002
Rayners Lane		2228	2243	2258	2311	2330	2345	0006
West Harrow		2230	2245	2300	2313	2332	2347	0008
Harrow on the Hill		2233	2248	2303	2317	2335	2352	0011
Northwick Park		2235	2250	2305	2319	2337	2354	0013
Preston Road		2237	2252	2307	2321	2340	2356	0015
Wembley Park		2240	2255	2310	2324d	2342d	2359d	0018
Finchley Road		2247	2302	2317	2336	2359‡	0011	——
Baker Street		2252	2307	2342	2342	0004‡	0017	

a After Neasden calls at Dollis Hill 1, Willesden Green 4, Kilburn 6 and West Hampstead 8 mins. later.
d After Wembley Park, calls at Neasden 3, Dollis Hill 4, Willesden Green 7, Kilburn 9 and West Hampstead 11 mins. later.
‡ Change at Wembley Park.

Travel Enquiries?

Ring 01-222 1234 at any time, day or night

115

A HISTORY OF LONDON TRANSPORT

Passenger Travel and the Development of the Metropolis, by Dr. T. C. Barker and Michael Robbins. Volume 1—The Nineteenth Century. *Published by George Allen and Unwin. From all booksellers, Price £4.* Vol 2 The Twentieth Century—in preparation, publication Autumn 1973.

Country Walks

These books are guides to footpaths and country ways easily reached by Underground or Bus. There are photographs to whet your appetite beforehand, Ordnance Survey Maps with your route clearly marked, and notes on local curiosities and places of interest. Complete with details of how to get there and back.

1973 (Book II) now on sale. Price 40p each from all London Transport Travel Enquiry Offices and most Underground Station Ticket Offices.

London Transport Posters

Full size reproductions of many recent London Transport posters are available at 77p *including VAT* plus 11p postage and packing. A new range of postcard size reproductions of posters dating back to 1913 is also available at 4½p each.

Write for an illustrated folder of the reproductions currently available to the Publicity Poster Shop, London Transport, Griffith House, 280 Old Marylebone Road, London NW1 5RJ.

The Metropolitan Line
The Bakerloo Line
The Piccadilly Line

by Charles E. Lee, F.C.I.T.

Special brief histories illustrated with photographs and maps. From any London Transport Travel Enquiry Office. Or by post from the Publicity Officer, London Transport, 280 Old Marylebone Road, London, NW1 5RJ.

1973 **Timetable booklet of Underground services**

Size: 171 × 109 mm
Printer: Waterlow & Sons

Many timetables are shorter than the page depth. I therefore designed a selection of filler advertisements to make up the depth of those pages, as well as providing some relief from solid timetable matter. For the typographer these would be both fun and a challenge, finding suitable typefaces and ornaments from the depths of forgotten type cabinets in the printer's composing room. Notice the way the advertisements are laid out on the same grid as the timetables, with the indent of text matching that of the times columns area, thereby linking the two unrelated elements.

1975 Prototype local area timetable booklets

Page size: A6 (105 × 148 mm)
Typesetter: Wace & Co

The first specimen pages envisaged a possible A6-size booklet which would have been convenient for pockets and handbags (these illustrations are 75 per cent full size).

Anticipating future production, which would have utilised computer typesetting, Gill Sans side-headings were combined with Univers condensed times figures. Compared to the 6pt side-heads the figures are set in 6.5pt on a 6pt body since no descenders were used with them (only footnote reference letters without descenders were used). On the bus route diagrams at the heads of timetables, it was envisaged that computers would be used in production to update the connecting bus numbers of connecting routes.

The roundel and silhouette double-decker bus forming the heading, as well as the British Rail double-arrow symbol, and the roundel in the Table 14 heading were all criticised by the bus schedules department representatives as likely to be not understood by the public!

---

166 ⊖ 🚌 **Beckenham Junction – Croydon – Chipstead Valley**
Mondays to Saturdays (Saturdays between Shirley and Chipstead Valley only)

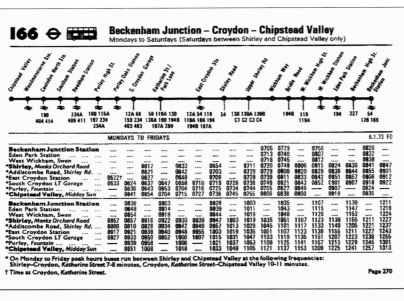

MONDAYS TO FRIDAYS   6.1.73 FO

Beckenham Junction Station	….	….	….	….	….	….	….	0705	0729	….	0756	….	….	0820	….
Eden Park Station								0713	0740		0807			0832	
West Wickham, Swan								0718	0745		0812			0838	
*Shirley, Monks Orchard Road			0612		0633		0654	0711	0720	0748	0806	0815	0824	0830	0841	0847
*Addiscombe Road, Shirley Rd. ..			0621		0642		0703	0720	0728	0739	0811	0833	0842	0852	0857	0908	0912
*East Croydon Station	0522†		0627		0648		0709	0725	0734	0744	0755	0827	0849		0907		0924	
*South Croydon LT Garage	0533	0624	0637	0647	0658	0710	0719	0726	0738	0749	0821	0843	0852	C901	0907	0918	0922
*Purley, Fountain		0630	0643	0653	0704	0716	0725	0734	0744	0755	0827	0849	—	0907	—	0924	—
*Chipstead Valley, Midday Sun		0641	0654	0704	0715	0727	0736	0745	0755	0806	0838	0900	—	0918	—	0935	—
Beckenham Junction Station	0836			0903			0929			1003			1035			1107			1139			1211
Eden Park Station	0848			0914			0939			1011			1043			1115			1147			1219
West Wickham, Swan	0854			0919			0944			1016			1048			1120			1152			1224
*Shirley, Monks Orchard Road	0852	0857	0916	0922	0930	0939	0947	1003	1019	1035	1051	1107	1123	1138	1155	1211	1227
*Addiscombe Road, Shirley Rd. ..	0806	0910	0928	0934	0942	0949	0957	1013	1029	1045	1101	1117	1133	1149	1205	1221	1237
*East Croydon Station	0917	0921	0940	0946	0955	1003	1019	1035	1047	1103	1119	1135	1151	1207	1223	1239	1255
*South Croydon LT Garage	0827	0933	0950	0952	1000	1007	1015	1031	1047	1103	1119	1125	1141	1157	1213	1229	1245	1301
*Purley, Fountain		0939	0958		1006			1021	1037	1053	1109	1125	1141	1157	1213	1229	1245	1301
*Chipstead Valley, Midday Sun		0951	1008		1018			1033	1049	1105	1121	1137	1153	1209	1225	1241	1257	1313

* On Monday to Friday peak hours buses run between Shirley and Chipstead Valley at the following frequencies: Shirley–Croydon, Katharine Street 7-8 minutes, Croydon, Katharine Street–Chipstead Valley 10-11 minutes.
† Time at Croydon, Katharine Street.

Page 270

Bus 166   MONDAYS to FRIDAYS continued   8.1.73 FO

Beckenham Junction Station		1243		1315		1347		1419		1451			1522		1552	1614
Eden Park Station		1251		1323		1355		1427		1459			1530		1600	1622
West Wickham, Swan		1256		1328		1400		1432		1504			1535		1605	1627
*Shirley, Monks Orchard Road	1243	1259	1315	1331	1347	1403	1419	1435	1451	1507		1523	1539	1555	1609	1630
*Addiscombe Road, Shirley Rd. ..	1253	1309	1325	1341	1357	1359	1428	1447	1503	1519		1533	1548		1605	1618	1640
*East Croydon Station	1259	1315	1331	1347	1403	1419	1435	1451	1507	1523		1539	1554		1611	1624	1646
*South Croydon LT Garage	1311	1327	1343	1359	1415	1431	1447	1503	1519	1535		1541	1606	1615	1623	1636	1659
*Purley, Fountain	1317	1333	1349	1405	1421	1437	1453	1509	1525	1541		1549	1557	1612	1621	1629	1644	1707
*Chipstead Valley, Midday Sun	1329	1345	1401	1417	1433	1449	1505	1521	1537	1553		1601	1609	1624	1633	1641	1656	1717
Beckenham Junction Station	1634	1656	1721	1740			1802			1824		1846			1916	
Eden Park Station	1644	1706	1731	1750			1812			1834		1854			1924	
West Wickham, Swan	1650	1712	1737	1756			1818			1839		1859			1929	
*Shirley, Monks Orchard Road	1652	1714	1739	1758	1759	1816	1820	1826	1832	1842	1846	1901	1904	1916	1931
*Addiscombe Road, Shirley Rd. ..	1701	1723	1748	1807	1808	1825	1829	1835	1841	1851	1855	1910	1913	1925	1940
*East Croydon Station	1710†	1732†	1757†	1813		1814	1831	1835	1841	1847	1857	1901	1916	1919	1931	1946
*South Croydon LT Garage	—	—	—	1826		1827	1843	1847	1851	1857	1907	1911	1926	1929	1941	1956
*Purley, Fountain					1835	1849			1903			1917	1932		1947	2002
*Chipstead Valley, Midday Sun					1846	1900			1914			1928	1943		1958	2013
Beckenham Junction Station		46		16			2216			2244					THEN AT THE FOLLOWING MINUTES PAST EACH HOUR
Eden Park Station		54		24			2229			2252					
West Wickham, Swan		59		29			2229			2257					
*Shirley, Monks Orchard Road	46	01	16	31		2231	2246	2254	2259	2309	2324	2341			
*Addiscombe Road, Shirley Rd. ..	55	10	25	40	UNTIL	2240	2255	2303	2308	2318	2333	2350			
*East Croydon Station	01	16	31	46		2246	2301	2309	2314	2339	2339	2356			
*South Croydon LT Garage	11	26	41	56		2256	2311	2319	2324	2334	2349	0006			
*Purley, Fountain	17	32	47	02		2302	2317			2330					
*Chipstead Valley, Midday Sun	28	42	58	13		2313	2328			2341					

SATURDAYS

Shirley, Monks Orchard Road	….	….	0624	0654	0715	0735	0755	….	0815	0835	0850	0805	0920	0935	0950	1008	1022
Addiscombe Road, Shirley Rd. ..	….	….	0634	0704	0725	0745	0805	….	0825	0845	0900	0815	0930	0945	1000	1016	1032
East Croydon Station	….	….	0641	0711	0732	0752	0812	….	0832	0852	0907	0922	0937	0952	1009	1025	1041
South Croydon LT Garage	0821	0841	0651	0721	0742	0802	0822	0837	0842	0902	0917	0832	0947	1003	1020	1036	1052
Purley, Fountain	0629	0848	0658	0728	0749	0809	0829	0844	0849	0909	0924	1010	1027	1043	1058	
Chipstead Valley, Midday Sun	0639	0859	0709	0739	0800	0820	0840	0855	0900	0920	0935	0950	1005	1022†	1039	1055	1111

* On Monday to Friday peak hours buses run between Shirley and Chipstead Valley at the following frequencies: Shirley–Croydon, Katharine Street 7-8 minutes, Croydon, Katharine Street–Chipstead Valley 10-11 minutes.
† Time at Croydon, Katharine Street.

Bus 166 Page 271

Table 14 ⇄⊖ **London – Watford, Chesham, Amersham or Aylesbury**
Complete service

MONDAYS TO FRIDAYS

Aldgate						1612		1627	1637					1654				1702
Liverpool Street						1614	1624	1629	1639					1655				1704
Moorgate						1615	1625	1630	1640					1657				1705
Barbican						1617	1627	1632	1642					1658				1707
Farringdon						1618	1628	1633	1643					1658				1708
King's Cross						1621	1631	1636	1646					1701				1711
Euston Square						1623	1633	1638	1649					1703				1713
Great Portland Street						1626	1636	1640	1650					1705				1715
Marylebone					1610							1712			1727		
Baker Street	1510	1530	1533	1550		1610	1613	1628	1640	1643	1657	1702		1710	1712		1719
Finchley Road	1515	1535	1538	1550		1615	1618	1633	1645	1648		1705	1706		1715	1717		1724
Wembley Park	1522	1542		1602		1604		1622	1642		1655	1708					1726
Preston Road	1524	1544		1604		1624		1642		1657	1709		1716				1729
Northwick Park	1526	1546		1606		1626		1645		1700	1710				1729
Harrow-on-the-Hill	1530	1550	1549	1610	1622	1630	1629	1647	1656	1702	1713	1708	1722	1724		1732	1738	1735
North Harrow	1533	1553		1613		1633		1652		1705	1716				1735		1737
Pinner	1535	1555		1615		1635		1652		1707	1718			1727			1740
Northwood Hills	1538	1558		1619		1638		1655		1710	1721			1730			1743
Northwood	1541	1601		1621		1641		1658		1713	1724			1733			1746
Moor Park	1544	1604	1558	1624	1630	1644	1638	1701	1705	1716		1736		1735	1747	1749
Croxley	1548	1608		1628		1648		1705		1721	1722	1743				1753
Watford	1551	1611		1631		1651		1708		1724	1743					1757
Rickmansworth			1602		1634		1642		1709			1739	1752	
Chorleywood			1606		1638		1648		1713			1723		1743	1756	1752
Chalfont & Latimer			1611		1643		1651		1718		1728		1748	1801	1757
Chesham				1622	1654	1702		1723			1758	1758	1817
Amersham			1615		1648	1655		1722		1732		1747	1752	1805	1801
Great Missenden						1656					1739					1809
Wendover						1702					1746		1801			1816
Stoke Mandeville						1708					1751		1806			1821
Aylesbury						1710					1755		1810			1825

Roman figures denote through trains
Italic figures denote connecting services
First class included on this train

Table 14   Page 373

Table 26 ⇄ **Shoeburyness – Southend – Tilbury – Rainham – Fenchurch Street**
All trains First and Second Class

MONDAYS TO FRIDAYS

Shoeburyness	…	…	0510	0535	0600	0622		0652	0707		0727		0734		0754		0804		0841	0910	0940
Thorpe Bay	…	…	0514	0539	0604	0631		0655	0711		0730	0737		0803		0814		0844	0914	0944
Southend East	…	…	0517	0542	0607	0634		0658	0714		0733	0740		0806		0820		0847	0917	0947
Southend Central	…	…	0520	0545	0610	0637		0709	0717		0736	0743		0808		0822		0852	0922	0952
Westcliff	…	…	0522	0547	0612	0639		0711	0719		0738	0745		0810		0824		0854	0924	0954
Chalkwell	…	…	0525	0550	0614	0641		0714	0721		0740	0747		0813		0827		0857	0927	0957
Leigh-on-Sea	…	…	0527	0552	0617	0644		0716	0724		0743	0749		0818		0829		0902	0932	1002
Benfleet for Canvey I.	…	…	0532	0557	0622	0649		0721	0729		0748	0754		0818		0838		0910	0940	1010
Pitsea	…	…	0537	0605	0635	0655		0730	0734		0752	0804		0822		0845		0917	0947	1017
Stanford-le-Hope	…	…	0544	0611	0642	0702		0737	0741		0758	0811		0829		0845		0917	0947	1017
East Tilbury	…	…	0548	0616	0646	0706		0741	0745		0803			0834		0849		0921	0951	1021
Tilbury Riverside	0532	0602	0627	0657	0717	0732	0757		0751	0759	0809	0814	0821	0829	0843	0901	0914	0934	1004	1034
Tilbury Town	0538	0608	0633	0709	0723	0738		0754	0803	0813	0818	0825	0831	0843	0848	0905	0918	0938	1008	1038
Grays	0543	0613	0638	0708	0728	0743		0800	0808		0823	0830	0838		0853	0909	0923	0944	1014	1044
Purfleet	0548	0618	0643	0713	0733	0748		0805	0813	0843	0852		0858		0910	0915	0928	0949	1019	1049
Rainham	0552	0622	0647	0717	0737	0752		0808	0817		0832	0839	0847		0902	0919	0932	0952	1022	1052
Dagenham Dock	0557	0627	0652	0722	0742	0758		0822		0837		0845		0907		0940	0957	1027	1057
Barking	0606	0635	0700	0730	0750	0806		0831		0846		0901		0918		0949	1006	1036	1106
Stepney East			0803																
Fenchurch Street	0610	0640	0705	0735	0755	0810		0825	0836	0840	0850	0856	0906	0910	0929	0935	0953	1010	1040	1110

Page 370

76

A prototype design with a book size of A6 (105 by 148 mm), as being pocket or handbag size, had already been developed in conjunction with Peter Sims who, at that time, very capably ran the Publicity Office timetable section. We had regular meetings in our respective rôles as editor and designer and did a lot of bouncing of ideas between each other. I had complete faith in him doing his part of the job extremely efficiently and I think he felt equally regarding my sympathy to the job. Most importantly, both of us were confident that this project was entirely within our grasp.

The page size provided space for enough times columns to be able to be read across easily, but not too many for the eye to stray onto the wrong line. Univers condensed was used for the times columns, which allowed for one more column than the conventional Gill Sans. This was combined with Gill Sans for the side headings – all in 6pt, the normal readable size for timetable booklets. In those days, when hot metal was still the normal method of mechanically setting type – and the best for producing specimen pages by allowing small changes between each proof, there were not enough options on the keyboard to combine both type faces. If this setting was to become the production standard, special mats would have been made up holding both typefaces for use at the chosen printers. However, I had in mind future

1975   Prototype local area timetable
Page size: 108 by 210 mm
Typesetter: Ramsay Typesetting
Printer: Index Printers

A page from the ill-fated and bulky trial local timetable booklet. There would have been 11 booklets covering areas around central London. They could have gone into publication, but by the time the editor was ready – after many pointless delays mainly due to apprehension – his budget was withdrawn in the next round of economic cuts.

149 ⊖ Ponders End – Tottenham – Liverpool St – Waterloo – Victoria

Daily service between Lower Edmonton and Liverpool Street: Mondays to Fridays only, Liverpool Street-Victoria

Railway stations served or near: Southbury ≷, Lower Edmonton ≷, Bruce Grove ≷, Seven Sisters ⊖ ≷, South Tottenham ≷, Stoke Newington ≷, Rectory Road ≷, Dalston Junction ≷, Liverpool Street ⊖ ≷, Bank ⊖, Mansion House ⊖, Cannon Street ⊖ ≷, Monument ⊖, Waterloo ⊖ ≷, Victoria ⊖ ≷.

MONDAYS TO FRIDAYS   11.2.74

The service works in two sections: Ponders End or Lower Edmonton—Liverpool Street / Stamford Hill or Stoke Newington—Victoria

First buses

Ponders End *Enfield Garage* ◆	E E: ... ... 0526 0538 ... 0649
Lower Edmonton *Tramway Avenue*	0420 0450 0531 0543 ... 0654
Edmonton *Fore Street*|*Angel Road*	0427 0457 0538 0550 ... 0701
Tottenham *Swan*	0434 0504 0545 0557 ... 0708
Stamford Hill *Broadway*	0438† 0510 0551 0603 0645 0714
Dalston Junction *Church*	0520 0601 0613 0655 0724
Shoreditch *Church*	0527 0608 0620 0702 0732
Liverpool Street Station	0531 0612 0624 0706 0738
Bank	0709
Waterloo Station	0720
Millbank *Thames House*	0726
Victoria Station	0732

Victoria Station	... ... 0734 1641
Millbank *Thames House*	0739 1647
Waterloo Station	0747 1655
Bank	0800 1707
Liverpool Street Station	0538 0554 0805 1712
Shoreditch *Church*	0542 0558 0809 1717
Dalston Junction	E E 0549 0605 0817 1725
Stamford Hill *Broadway*	0453† 0505† 0523† 0559 0615 0825‡ 1735
Tottenham *Swan*	0458 0510 0528 0605 0621
Edmonton *Fore Street*|*Angel Road*	0506 0518 0536 0613 0629
Lower Edmonton *Tramway Avenue*	0514 0526 0544 0621 0637
Ponders End *Enfield Garage* ◆	0519 0531 0642

Last buses

Ponders End *Enfield Garage* ◆	... 1822 1848 ...
Lower Edmonton *Tramway Avenue*	1828 1853 2254 2354
Edmonton *Fore Street*|*Angel Road*	1836 — 2301 0001
Tottenham *Swan*	1843 — 2308 0008
Stamford Hill *Broadway*	0815 1811‡ 1849 2314 0013†
Dalston Junction	0826 1821 1859 2324 —
Shoreditch *Church*	0834 1829 1906 2331
Liverpool Street Station	0840 1835 1910 2335
Bank	0845 1838
Waterloo Station	0858 1849
Millbank *Thames House*	0903 1855
Victoria Station	0910 1901
Victoria Station	... 1903 ...
Millbank *Thames House*	1908
Waterloo Station	1913
Bank	1924
Liverpool Street Station	1743 1927 2342
Shoreditch *Church*	1748 1931 2346
Dalston Junction	1756 1938 2353
Stamford Hill *Broadway*	1806 1948 0003
Tottenham *Swan*	1815 — 0009
Edmonton *Fore Street*|*Angel Road*	1825 — 0017
Lower Edmonton *Tramway Avenue*	1834 — 0025
Ponders End *Enfield Garage* ◆	1840 0025

Service intervals

Ponders End—Lower Edmonton peak hours, 7–8 minutes
Lower Edmonton—Stoke Newington 15 minutes (peak hours 7–8 minutes, evenings 20 minutes)
Stoke Newington—Liverpool Street 7–8 minutes (peak hours 3–4 minutes, evenings 20 minutes)
Liverpool Street—Victoria 15 minutes (peak hours 7–8 minutes)
The intervals between buses may be longer in the early morning and late evening.

◆—The service is extended from Ponders End to Lower Edmonton during the following periods only: at 0526, 0538, from 0649 to 0934, at 1206, 1236, from 1507 to 1848.

◆—The service is extended from Lower Edmonton to Ponders End during the following periods only: at 0514, 0526, from 0637 to 0922, at 1155, 1221, and from 1453 to 1834.

E—Individual early journey.
†—Time at Stamford Hill *Egerton Road*.
‡—Time at Stoke Newington *Common*.

10

166 ⊖ Beckenham Junction – Croydon – Chipstead Valley

Mondays to Saturdays (Saturdays between Shirley and Chipstead Valley only)

PAY AS YOU ENTER exact fares please

Railway stations served or near: Beckenham Junction ≷, Eden Park ≷, West Wickham ≷, East Croydon ≷, Purley Oaks ≷, Purley ≷, Reedham ≷, Smitham ≷, Coulsdon North ≷, Woodmansterne ≷.

MONDAYS TO FRIDAYS   6.1.73 FO

Beckenham Junction Station	... ... 0705 0729 ... 0756 ... 0820 ... 0836 ... 0903 ... 0928 ... 1003
Eden Park Station	0713 0740 0807 0832 0848 0914 0939 1011
West Wickham *Swan*	0718 0745 0812 0838 0854 0919 0944 1016
★ Shirley *Monks Orchard Road*	0612 0633 0654 0711 0720 0748 0806 0815 0824 0830 0841 0847 0852 0857 0903 0918 0930 0939 0947 1003 1019 1035
★ Addiscombe Road *Shirley Road*	0621 0642 0703 0720 0729 0800 0820 0829 0838 0844 0855 0901 0906 0910 0928 0934 0942 0949 0957 1013 1029 1045
★ East Croydon Station	0522† 0627 0648 0709 0728 0739 0811 0833 0842 0851 0857 0908 0912 0917 0921 0939 0945 0948 0955 1003 1019 1035 1051
★ South Croydon *LT Garage*	0533 0624 0637 0647 0658 0710 0719 0728 0738 0749 0821 0843 0852 0901 0907 0918 0922 0927 0933 0950 0952 1000 1007 1015 1031 1047 1103
★ Purley *Fountain*	0630 0643 0653 0704 0716 0725 0734 0744 0755 0827 0849 0907 0924 0939 0956 1006 1021 1037 1053 1109
★ Chipstead Valley *Midday Sun*	0641 0654 0704 0715 0727 0736 0745 0755 0806 0838 0900 — 0918 0935 0951 1008 1018 1033 1049 1105 1121
Beckenham Junction Station	1035 ... 1107 ... 1139 ... 1211 ... 1243 ... 1315 ... 1347 ... 1419 ... 1451 ... 1522 ... 1552 1614 1634 1655 1721
Eden Park Station	1043 1115 1147 1219 1251 1323 1355 1427 1459 1530 1600 1622 1644 1705 1731
West Wickham *Swan*	1048 1120 1152 1224 1256 1328 1400 1432 1504 1535 1605 1627 1650 1712 1737
★ Shirley *Monks Orchard Road*	1051 1107 1123 1139 1155 1211 1227 1243 1259 1315 1331 1347 1403 1419 1435 1451 1507 1523 1538 1555 1608 1630 1652 1714 1739
★ Addiscombe Road *Shirley Road*	1101 1117 1133 1149 1205 1221 1237 1253 1309 1325 1341 1357 1413 1429 1445 1501 1517 1533 1548 1605 1618 1640 1701 1723 1748
★ East Croydon Station	1107 1123 1139 1155 1211 1227 1243 1259 1315 1331 1347 1403 1419 1435 1451 1507 1523 1539 1554 1611 1624 1646 1710* 1732* 1757†
★ South Croydon *LT Garage*	1119 1135 1151 1207 1223 1239 1255 1311 1327 1343 1359 1415 1431 1447 1503 1519 1535 1543 1551 1606 1615 1623 1638 1659
★ Purley *Fountain*	1125 1141 1157 1213 1229 1245 1301 1317 1333 1349 1405 1421 1437 1453 1509 1525 1541 1543 1559 1629 1644 1707
★ Chipstead Valley *Midday Sun*	1137 1153 1209 1225 1241 1257 1313 1329 1345 1401 1417 1433 1449 1505 1521 1537 1553 1601 1609 1624 1633 1641 1656 1717
Beckenham Junction Station	1740 ... 1802 ... 1824 ... 1846 ... 1916 ... 46 ... 16 ... 2216 ... 2244
Eden Park Station	1750 1812 1834 1854 1924 54 ... 24 2224 2252
West Wickham *Swan*	1756 1818 1840 1859 1929 59 ... 29 2229 2257
★ Shirley *Monks Orchard Road*	1758 1759 1816 1820 1828 1832 1842 1846 1901 1904 1916 1931 THEN 46 01 16 31 PAST 2231 2246 2254 2259 2309 2324 2341
★ Addiscombe Road *Shirley Road*	1807 1808 1825 1829 1835 1840 1851 1855 1910 1913 1925 1940 AT 55 10 25 40 EACH 2240 2255 2303 2308 2318 2333 2350
★ East Croydon Station	1813 1814 1831 1835 1841 1847 1857 1901 1916 1919 1931 1946 01 16 31 46 HOUR 2246 2301 2309 2314 2324 2339 2356
★ South Croydon *LT Garage*	1826 1827 1843 1847 1851 1857 1907 1911 1926 1929 1941 1956 11 26 41 56 UNTIL 2256 2311 2319 2324 2334 2349 0006
★ Purley *Fountain*	— 1835 1849 — 1903 — 1917 1932 — 1947 2002 17 32 47 02 2302 2317 2330
★ Chipstead Valley *Midday Sun*	— 1846 1900 — 1914 — 1928 1943 — 1958 2013 28 43 58 13 2313 2328 2341

★ On Monday to Friday peak hours buses run between Shirley and Chipstead Valley at the following frequencies: Shirley—Croydon *Katharine Street* 7–8 minutes, Croydon *Katharine Street*—Chipstead Valley 10–11 minutes.

† Time at Croydon *Katharine Street*

12

1976 **Line timetable guides**
Page size: A5 (148 × 210 mm)
Printer: Tapp & Toothill,
Leeds and London

The style of this timetable is a development of the specimen pages of the former ill-fated timetable editions. The cover utilises an illustration of a section of one of the trains operating the Metropolitan Line and scanned using a line screen, both for effect and the fact that a course screen was required by the method of printing. This style of illustration was used throughout the series, despite the train enthusiast element of the production staff being adamant that the entire elevation of a train should be used.

computer setting for the type, as I also had for the production of the diagram maps above, where route corrections could be made automatically on all maps whenever their details changed.

Unfortunately, Peter transferred to another section within the office at this critical time, leaving his successor David Pickles, who possessed his own entrenched views on design and production, to progress through these publications (as well as processing the range of panel timetables and notices that formed the work of the timetable section), but lacking the confidence to actually process the work to completion. So endless proofs and re-proofs were produced by Index Printers to an enlarged page size (108 by 210 mm) which was deemed to be a more economic than the original and handy smaller size. It was film set by the last of a number of typesetters that had entered into this challenging new project (all other typesetters having one-by-one pulled out as more and more proofs were requested with no sign at all of any payment for them or future production contacts). So this local timetable booklet project was overtaken by another series of budget cuts from a constantly beleaguered Central Finance Department and died, perhaps helping to bring down Index Publishers (who, as ABC Travel Guides, would have edited the production while Index Printers would have printed them).

With the cancellation of the all-Underground timetable booklet, individual line timetables were seen as cheaper alternatives. This was to be the first Pickles project that had a deadline on production. Whilst I had hoped to use the experience gained on the A6 size local guides layouts, I was forced into A5 size pages on savings of cost, which was considerably less (a hatched vertical line was printed down the middle of the cover so that the reader could fold the publication down to A6 size. However, my recommendation was excepted on the paper that was used – produced by Spicers, it was very opaque and at the same time very thin and light weight, but not very cheap. I was able to utilise the recommendations of Francis Maynell 50 years before, by inserting horizontal leads (extra space) at intervals down the timetable to aid reading across – instead of every five or six lines – at points where the timetable information changed.

The Metropolitan Line timetable guide was followed by that for the Central Line and later the Bakerloo and Jubilee lines to cover the opening of the latter.

When I re-designed timetables (or anything else), I attempted to rectify the shortcomings that I had experienced with the existing designs. My advantage over the people who worked with the scheduling of services was that I wasn't very good at working out departure and arrival

ISSUED FREE BY
LONDON TRANSPORT
55 BROADWAY
LONDON SW1H 0BD
TRAVEL ENQUIRIES 01-222 1234

Metropolitan Line
and British Rail

timetables

Services between
Aylesbury, Amersham,
Chesham, Watford,
Uxbridge, Harrow-on-
the-Hill and London

FROM
12 DECEMBER
1977

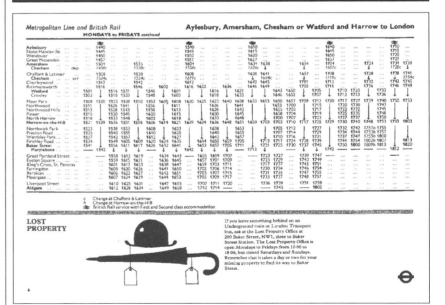

Central Line

timetables

Services between
West Ruislip,
Ealing Broadway,
London, Hainault,
Epping and Ongar

departures	Notting Hill Gate to Gants Hill and Hainault
trains leave	Queensway 1 minute later
	Lancaster Gate 3 minutes later
	Marble Arch 5 minutes later
	Bond Street 7 minutes later
Journey time	Notting Hill Gate to Hainault about 50 minutes

	MONDAYS to FRIDAYS	SATURDAYS	SUNDAYS

n to Newbury Park only

departures	Oxford Circus to Gants Hill and Hainault
trains leave	Tottenham Court Road 1 minute later
	Holborn 3 minutes later
	Chancery Lane (closed on Sundays) 5 minutes later
	St. Paul's 7 minutes later
	Bank 9 minutes later
Journey time	Oxford Circus to Hainault about 42 minutes

	MONDAYS to FRIDAYS	SATURDAYS	SUNDAYS

n to Newbury Park only

25

Epping or Hainault, Oxford Circus, Ealing Broadway or West Ruislip   *Central Line*

MONDAYS to FRIDAYS   —   First trains   —   Last trains

◊Epping 20
◊Theydon Bois 20
◊Debden 20
◊Loughton 20
◊Buckhurst Hill 20
◊Woodford 21
◊South Woodford 21
◊Snaresbrook 21

◊Hainault 24
◊Fairlop 24
◊Barkingside 24
◊Newbury Park 24
◊Gants Hill 24
◊Redbridge 24
◊Wanstead 24

Leytonstone
Leyton
Stratford
Mile End
Bethnal Green
Liverpool Street 13 17

Bank 13 17
St. Paul's 13 17
Chancery Lane 13 17
Holborn 13 17
Tottenham Crt Rd 13 17
Oxford Circus 13 18

Bond Street 13 18
Marble Arch 13 18
Lancaster Gate 13 18
Queensway 13 18
Notting Hill Gate 14 18
Holland Park 14 18

Shepherd's Bush 14 18
White City 14 18
East Acton 14 18
North Acton 14 19
◊West Acton 19
◊Ealing Broadway 19

◊Hanger Lane 14
◊Perivale 14
◊Greenford 14
◊Northolt 15
◊South Ruislip 15
◊Ruislip Gardens 15
◊West Ruislip

◊ For further details of times from or to these stations see page references

9

times. The timetable 'hairies' usually had a rough idea of the pattern of most services even before they saw an individual timetable and they definitely knew which routes went where, so they only needed to refer to timetables for the finer details of precise times, making me similar to the average passenger.

Once the advertising people moved in to run the Publicity Office, they employed 'focus groups' to ask passengers pertinent questions (but often not the vital ones) about their travel habits and needs. This was because the new intake of Publicity executives, in common with their counterparts in the advertising agencies, would never attempt to use the bus services that they were expecting their own passengers to negotiate, except for commuting from home at the start of each day (but not returning home at night, which was usually accomplished by taxi after yet another evening brain storming with advertising colleagues or attending one more advertising award ceremony). Coincidentally the focus group results were usually identical to the conclusions that I had formulated myself after actually experiencing the services, although not at the enormous cost that advertising agencies and market research agencies charge.

The typographic re-design of timetables coincided with the necessity to adapt the covers of timetable booklets to the inclusion

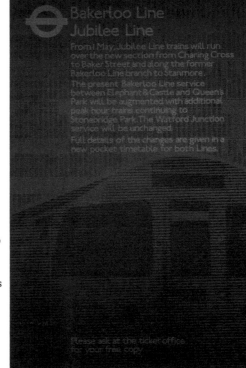

1981   Line timetable guides
Page size: A5 (148 × 210 mm)
Printer: —

Following a similar style to the Metropolitan Line timetable book, pages contained departure lists from particular individual points along the Central Line, as well as full timetables showing the first few trains and last few trains of the day when services were less frequent. Similar layouts were more familiar as double royal posters at central London stations.

1979   Line timetable poster
Page size: Double Royal (25 × 40 in)
Printer: Walter Brian

To match the timetable booklets and to inform of their availability, I designed a series of posters utilising a similar graphic treatment to the front of the train. The background was made up of columns of figures to represent timetable columns.

This poster announces the booklet covering the opening of the Jubilee Line on 1 May 1979.

1972   Timetable booklets:

Night Buses
Page size: 148 × 210 mm
Printer: Kelly & Kelly, London

Underground Guide
Page size: 172 × 108 mm
Printer: Waterlow & Sons

Central Bus Timetables
Page size: 172 × 108 mm
Printer: S. H. Peters & Sons Ltd

Covers of timetable booklets were
re-designed following the 1971
revisions to the London Transport
corporate identity and before
their contents were updated
typographically.

1974   How to get there booklet
Size: 169 × 98 mm
Printer: Staples Printers, Rochester

The cover of the staff edition,
followed the style the staff edition
for bus timetables. The inside was
the same as the public version.

1972   Times and Fares leaflets
Page size: 180 × 108 mm

Victoria Line
Printer: Frederick Printing Co.

Northern Line
Printer: Baynard Press

The picture at the base of the
leaflets was of the driving car of a
Victoria Line train which formed
the most modern tube stock
at that time – the policy was to
show the most modern stock in
publicity, even if it wasn't running
on the particular line being
highlighted. The photograph was
taken by Colin Tait, one of a small
band of freelance photographers
selling their services to LT, who
had a studio within walking
distance of the Publicity Office
at Old Marylebone Road. He
achieved the effect of movement
by dragging the photographic
paper across while being
exposed though the negative.

of the newly proportioned roundel
with no lettering across the bar. The
opportunity was therefore taken to
harmonise the design of all timetable
covers, which were at that time the
Underground Guide and the Night
Bus timetable, although certain
informational booklets were added
to the concept, notably the How to
Get There booklet, which contained
directions by bus and tube to well
known places in the London area.
There had been a uniform style of
cover design in the 1950s and '60s
consisting of Gill Sans type in white
out of a green background for the

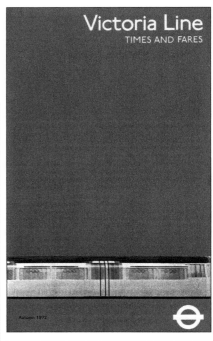

Green Line and Country bus books, out of a red background for Central bus and out of a maroon background for Underground timetables books. By the 1970s the Green Line and Country bus books had been devolved to the National Bus Company owned London Country Bus Services, and the Central Bus timetable was no longer issued to the public, but still updated and published for the use of bus inspectors as a guide to timings. Because it had become an internal document only, the Central Bus cover had reverted to a centred layout set in Times New Roman bold within heavy box rules and printed in black on a red card. As part of the re-design it seemed reasonable to retain the colour breakdown of black and red. It also meant that the bus schedules department couldn't accuse me of increasing the production cost (an accusation often levelled at the Publicity Office when publicity was seen to be a requirement that hadn't seemed necessary before, or if the people handling it at local level had thought that their efforts were sufficient). But the higher powers within the schedules office still accused me of interfering with their internal work, to which I replied that the staff deserved their information to be as well presented as that provided for the public.

Another timetable publication (or more strictly, abridged timetables containing first and last times) was

the leaflet that started with that produced for the opening of the Victoria Line in 1968 with a cover by Abram Games. I had re-designed the cover only, in preparation for the opening of the extension to Brixton on 23 July 1971. When a later reprint was required to give revised details consequent of the opening of Pimlico Station on 14 September 1972, a typographic re-design of the inside became desirable. With the likelihood that the leaflet might be joined by similar publications for all other lines I designed a common cover style to help their recognition. The design was much simpler to the one being replaced because some would be wanted at comparatively short notice. I attempted to reflect the contents by the use of a moving train. The effect of the moving tube car was achieved by simply sliding the bromide paper from left to right as the photographic negative was projected onto it. As with many projects that I viewed globally, this particular scheme got no farther than the Victoria and Northern lines before another was devised in the constant panic to retain passengers in an atmosphere of rising fares and progressively reduced services.

The Night Bus network had been allowed to gradually run down, as more and more night workers used their own cars, or taxis, to get to and from their places of work. Mike Parker was the Bus Marketing Manager who decided, through the use of publicity,

1995 **Steam on the Met leaflet**
Size: A5 210 × 148 mm
Printer: Cullum Litho, London

The poster and leaflet illustrated for this ever popular annual event was designed ostensibly in the same New Johnston typographic style as other Underground work at this period. However, a lettering style similar to that used by the Metropolitan Railway is used, as is the timetable set in a style similar to that used in the 1930s and '40s.

The timetable makes use of the Times typeface. The only deviation is the use of standard Times New Roman figures instead of those designed by Harry Carter with thickened horizontal strokes. I doubt if the designers adapting the 'font' for computer use were aware that special figures had ever existed!

P.M. times are in heavy figures	Metropolitan Line and British Railways	Watford - Rickmansworth - Amersham														1	

This table shews complete service of steam trains between Watford and Amersham.
For complete steam train service between Harrow on the Hill and Amersham see Table 2.

SATURDAY, and SUNDAY, 20 & 21 May—morning and afternoon

Baker Street ¶																		
Harrow on the Hill .... dep.	8 56	8 56	....	....	....	....	....	....	....	....	....	....	....	....	....	....	....	....
WATFORD .... dep.	......	9 18	9 49	1049	1119	1219	1249	1349	1419	1519	1549	1649	1719	1819				
RICKMANSWORTH	9 12	..	9 57	1057	1127	1227	1257	1357	1427	1527	1557	1657	1727	1827				
Chorley Wood & Chenies ...																		
Chalfont & Latimer																		
AMERSHAM .... arr.	9 29	..	1014	1114	1144	1244	1314	1414	1444	1544	1614	1714	1744	1844				
AMERSHAM .... dep.	1003	..	1033	1130	1203	1303	1333	1433	1503	1603	1633	1733	1803	1903				
Chalfont & Latimer																		
Chorley Wood & Chenies ...																		
RICKMANSWORTH	1018	..	1048	1145	1218	1318	1348	1448	1518	1618	1648	1748	1818	1918				
WATFORD .... arr.	1027	..	1058	1157	1227	1327	1357	1457	1527	1627	1657	1757	1827	M				
Harrow on the Hill															1936			
Baker Street ¶															W			

¶—Frequent electric trains to and from Baker Street connect with steam trains.
M—calls at Moor Park at 1924.   W—terminates at Wembley Park at 1944.

P.M. times are in heavy figures	Metropolitan Line and British Railways	Harrow on the Hill — Amersham										2

This table shews complete service of steam trains between Harrow on the Hill and Amersham.
For complete steam train service between Watford and Amersham see Table 1.

SATURDAY, SUNDAY and MONDAY, 27, 28 & 29 May—morning and afternoon

Baker Street ¶										
Wembley Park .... dep.	9 10									
HARROW on the Hill ......dep.	9 25	1025	1125	1225	1325	1425	1525	1625	1725	
Moor Park & Sandy Lodge ...	U									
RICKMANSWORTH										
Chorley Wood & Chenies ...										
Chalfont & Latimer										
AMERSHAM .... arr.		1100	1200	1300	1400	1500	1600	1700	1800	
AMERSHAM .... dep.		1130	1230	1330	1430	1530	1630	1730	1830	
Chalfont & Latimer										
Chorley Wood & Chenies ...										
RICKMANSWORTH										
Moor Park & Sandy Lodge ...	X									
HARROW on the Hill ....arr.	1024	1205	1305	1405	1505	1605	1705	1808	1906	
Wembley Park .... arr.	1032									
Baker Street ¶										

¶—Frequent electric trains to and from Baker Street connect with steam trains.
U—Steam train continues non stop to Uxbridge arriving 0947.   X—Steam train non stop from Uxbridge departing 1000.

A welcome sight on a dark night

LONDON NIGHT BUSES

⊖ **Going places**

1981   Night Bus timetable booklet

Page size: 99 × 210 mm
Printer: Staples Printers, St.Albans

At the time that these timetables were set in type, Gill Sans was not available as a photosetting type face. However, the result, which was set in Univers with its wide figures, worked well since no routes ran often enough to require more than one page for each direction. This was the first time that route maps headed production LT timetables.

Night Bus N97

Liverpool Street Station · Bank · Ludgate Circus · Strand *Aldwych* · Charing Cross *Trafalgar Square* · Hyde Park Corner · South Kensington Station · Earls Court Station · Fulham Broadway Station · Hammersmith Broadway · Turnham Green Church · Kew Bridge *Star & Garter* · Brentford · Hounslow · Hounslow West Station · Harlington Corner · Heathrow Airport North · Heathrow Airport Central

Sunday night/Monday morning to Thursday night/Friday morning

Liverpool Street Station				0004	0024	0044	0104
Bank				0007	0027	0047	0107
Ludgate Circus			2348†	0009	0029	0049	0109
Aldwych			2353	0013	0033	0053	0113
Charing Cross *Trafalgar Square*			2355	0015	0035	0055	0115
Piccadilly Circus			2400	0020	0040	0100	0120
Hyde Park Corner			0011	0031	0051	0111	0131
South Kensington Station			0017	0037	0057	0117	0137
Earl's Court Station			0025	0045	0105	0125	0145
Fulham Broadway Station			0030	0050	0110	0130	0150
Lillie Road *Fulham Palace Rd*			0034	0054	0114	0134	0154
Hammersmith Bdy. *King Street*			0037	0057	0119§	0137	0157
Stamford Brook Garage	2338	0008	0028	0042	0102	0142	0202
Turnham Green Church	2341	0011	0031	0045	0105	0145	0205
Kew Bridge *'Plough'*	2345	0015	0035	0049	0109	0149	0209
Brentford *Half Acre*	2348	0018‡	0038	0052	0112‡	0152	0212
Hounslow *Bus Stn (London Rd)*	2355	——	0045	0059		0159	0219
Hounslow West Station	0001		0051	0105		0205	0225
Harlington Corner	0008		0058	0112		0212	0232
Heathrow Airport North	0011		0101	0115		0215	0235
Heathrow Airport Central	0014		0104	0118T		0218T	0238T

Liverpool Street Station	0124			0225	0253	0320	0350	0411
Bank	0127			0228	0256	0323	0353	0414
Ludgate Circus	0129	0148†	0209†	0230	0258	0325	0355	0416
Aldwych	0133	0153	0214	0234	0302	0329	0359	0420
Charing Cross *Trafalgar Square*	0135	0155	0216	0236	0304	0331	0401	0422
Piccadilly Circus	0140	0200	0221	0241	0309	0336	0406	0427
Hyde Park Corner	0151	0211	0232	0252	0317	0344	0414	0435
South Kensington Station	0157	0217	0238	0258	0322	0349	0419	0440
Earl's Court Station	0205	0225	0246	0306	0330	0357	0427	0448
Fulham Broadway Station	0210	0230	0251	0311	0335	0402	0432	0453
Lillie Road *Fulham Palace Rd*	0214	0234	0255	0315	0339	0406	0436	0457
Hammersmith Bdy. *King Street*	0219§	0237	0258	0320§	0342	0409	0439	0500
Stamford Brook Garage	——	0242	0303	——	0347	0414	0444	0505
Turnham Green Church		0245	0306		0350	0417	0447	0508
Kew Bridge *'Plough'*		0249	0310		0354	0421	0451	0512
Brentford *Half Acre*		0252	0313		0357	0424	0454	0515
Hounslow *Bus Stn (London Rd)*		0259	0320		0404	0431	0501	0522
Hounslow West Station		0305	0326		0410	0437	0507	0528
Harlington Corner		0312	0333		0417	0444	0514	0535
Heathrow Airport North		0315	0336		0420	0447	0517	0538
Heathrow Airport Central		0318T	0339T		0423T	0450	0520	0541

Liverpool Street Station	0430	0450	0514		0554	
Bank	0433	0453	0517		0557	
Ludgate Circus	0435	0455	0519		0559	
Aldwych	0439	0459	0523		0603	
Charing Cross *Trafalgar Square*	0441	0501	0525	0555	0605	0629
Piccadilly Circus	0446	0506	0530	0600	0610	0634
Hyde Park Corner	0454	0514	0538	0608	0618	0642
South Kensington Station	0459	0519	0543	0613	0623	0647
Earl's Court Station	0507	0527	0551	0621	0631	0655
Fulham Broadway Station	0512	0532	0556	0626	0636	0700
Lillie Road *Fulham Palace Rd*	0516	0536	0600	0630	0640	0704
Hammersmith Bdy. *King Street*	0519	0539	0603	0633	0643	0707
Stamford Brook Garage	0524	0544	0608	0638	0648	0712
Turnham Green Church	0527	0547				
Kew Bridge *'Plough'*	0531	0551				
Brentford *Half Acre*	0534	0554				
Hounslow *Bus Stn (London Rd)*	0541	0601				
Hounslow West Station	0547	0607				
Harlington Corner	0554	0614				
Heathrow Airport North	0557	0617				
Heathrow Airport Central	0600	0620				

† – Time at Farringdon Street *Stonecutter Street*.
‡ – Time at Brentford *County Court*.
§ – Time at Hammersmith Broadway *Butterwick*.
T – Time at Heathrow Airport *Terminal 2*.

28

to re-build the network by aiming at night time leisure goers instead.

I had devised a campaign, incorporating a symbol of the moon surrounded by the outer London terminal points, a poster showing a couple on a damp night with a warmly lit bus in the distance, a diagrammatic map of routes and a revamp of the timetable. The size of the booklet was convenient for leaflet racks, but not very economic for setting of timetables, especially since they were to be filmset in the Univers typeface with its very wide figures. Each spread accommodated one route's timetable, however long or short its contents were.

The route diagrams I designed to go above the timetables were the first in regular production use as headings. In the early 1980s, when it was decided that route diagrams would replace headings at the tops of bus stop timetables the actual design work was done elsewhere, but reference for details was made to those on the Night Bus timetables.

Page grids for the night bus booklets were devided into sections that could accommodate standard depth advertisement fillers where there were short timetables. I had put forward the proposition that these booklets could be displayed in leaflet racks at the coat pick-up points at theatres, cinemas and especially night clubs that closed their doors after normal daytime services had finished.

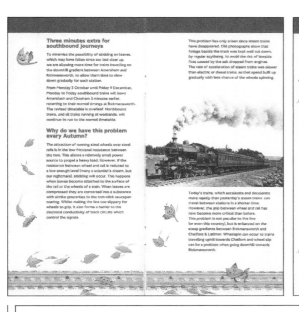
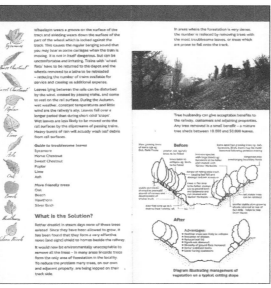

Autumn Leaves

Three minutes extra for southbound journeys

To minimise the possibility of skidding on leaves, which may have fallen since our last clear up, we are allowing more time for trains travelling on the downhill gradient between Amersham and Rickmansworth, to allow them time to slow down gradually for each station.

From Monday 3 October until Friday 9 December Monday to Friday southbound trains will leave Amersham and Chesham 3 minutes earlier, reverting to their normal timings at Rickmansworth. The revised timetable is overleaf. Northbound trains, and all trains running at weekends, will continue to run to the normal timetable.

Why do we have this problem every Autumn?

The attraction of running steel wheels over steel rails is in the low frictional resistance between the two. This allows a relatively small power source to propel a heavy load. However, if the resistance between wheel and rail is reduced to a low enough level

(many a scientist's dream, but our nightmare), skidding will occur. This happens when leaves become attached to the surface of the rail or the wheels of a train. When leaves are compressed they are converted into a substance with similar properties to the non-stick saucepan coating. Whilst making the line too slippery for wheels to grip, it also forms a barrier to the electrical conductivity of track circuits which control the signals.

This problem has only arisen since steam trains have disappeared. Old photographs show that foliage beside the track was kept well cut down, by regular scything, to avoid the risk of lineside fires caused by the ash dropped from engines. The rate of acceleration of steam trains was slower than electric or diesel trains. So that speed built up gradually with less chance of the wheels spinning.

Today's trains, which accelerate and decelerate more rapidly than yesterday's steam trains, can travel between stations in a shorter time. However, the grip between wheel and rail has now become more critical

than before. This problem is not peculiar to this line (or even this country), but is enhanced on the steep gradients between Rickmansworth and Chalfont & Latimer. Wheelspin can occur to trains travelling uphill towards Chalfont and wheel slip can be a problem when going downhill towards Rickmansworth.

Wheelspin wears a groove on the surface of the track and skidding wears down the surface of the part of the wheel which is locked against the track. This causes the regular banging sound that you may hear in some carriages when the train is moving. It is not in itself dangerous, but can be uncomfortable and irritating. Trains with 'wheel flats' have to be returned to the depot and the wheels removed to a lathe to be retreaded – reducing the number of trains available for service and causing us additional expense.

Leaves lying between the rails can be disturbed by the wind created by passing trains, and come to rest on the rail surface. During the Autumn, wet weather, constant temperatures and little wind are the railway's ally. Leaves fall over a longer period

than during short cold 'snaps'. Wet leaves are less likely to be moved onto the rail surfaces by the slipstreams of passing trains. Heavy bursts of rain will actually wash leaf debris from rail surfaces.

Guide to troublesome leaves: Sycamore, Horse Chestnut, Sweet Chestnut, Poplar, Lime, Ash.

More, friendly trees: Oak, Beech, Hawthorn, Silver Birch.

What is the Solution?

Rather drastic! In steam days none of these trees existed. Since they have been allowed to grow, it has been found that they form a very effective noise (and sight) shield to homes beside the railway.

It would now be environmentally unacceptable to remove all the trees – in many areas lineside trees form the only area of forestation in the locality. To reduce the problem many trees, on our own and adjacent property, are being lopped on their track side.

In areas where the forestation is very dense, the number is reduced by removing trees with the most troublesome leaves, or trees which are prone to fall onto the track.

Tree husbandry can give acceptable benefits to the railway, customers and adjoining properties. Any tree removed is a small benefit – a mature tree sheds between 10,000 and 50,000 leaves.

When it is necessary to remove a large number of trees, bushes are planted in their place. These are able to trap leaves blowing from the remaining trees, or those on adjoining land.

During the periods when leaves are blanketing the track, they are removed at night when trains are not running. Once this has been done, a solution called Sandite is spread along the track surfaces by a specially adapted train. Sandite is a mixture of sand (for grip), iron filings (to improve electrical conduction of track circuits) and gel (to hold the first two in suspension onto the track surface). This is normally laid shortly before first trains are due to run, but can also be used during the day between service trains. These special trains (and trains running on the Chesham branch) are also equipped with rail scrubbers, which remove Leaves that have become stubbornly crushed

onto the track, restoring the clean surface.

Each Autumn we have managed to reduce the delays to your trains, as our understanding of the problem has increased and machinery has been developed to cope. Hopefully this progressive sequence will continue into this Autumn.

1994   **Autumn Leaves leaflet**
Size: 210 × 99 mm
Designers:
cover   Set Square Design, Cheltenham
inside   Tim Demuth
Printer: Waterside Press, St.Albans

The revised service operated during the autumn months when leaves were expected to be falling.

The text, which was researched and written by myself, is reproduced here . The production was found to be so useful by schools in the Amersham area that it was used by them to form displays at local stations.

The printing is unusual that, while employing the 4-colour process, uses instead: blue (for the type), maroon (Metropolitan Line), red (roundel circle) and yellow, allowing self colour printing in a great many cases and a combination of colours to achieve the required effect. An innovation such as this can only come from an experience in the printing process with the designer working in harmony.

The following year budget cuts dictated a shorter version, containing a short introduction, a similar timetable and a new cover designed by me.

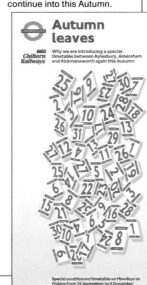

1974   **Individual station dedicated pocket timetables**

Size: 105 × 75 mm (folded)

Many attempts have been made to produce line dedicated timetables – some have succeeded for a while and then floundered because of budget cuts, others have never even been launched. Aided by computers the job is now far simpler – all that is needed is a very flexible specification from the designer and the rest can be done by the schedules people – in theory!

It will come as no surprise that the chosen cover designs were from the bottom row – very clear, austere and to the point – but where is the interest, the excitement? Yes, even a timetable cover can be exciting.

The same can be said of the timetables inside, where a series of layouts depending on the type and horizontal rules were overlooked in favour of the boxed treatment traditional to LT in the 1930s.

This 'in-house' campaign marked the resurrection of the Night Bus network which has expanded year by year to cover every corner of the greater London area. In many cases, buses now run every half an hour all through every night of the week.

The Night Bus campaign is one of a number of examples in this part of the chapter of using an inviting cover to give a less daunting impression of the timetables within. However, it is still possible to give a timetable an attractive appearance, just as can be done typographically with text, by the judicious use of face, size, letter and word spacing, leading and measure. This is something that experience and confidence was a large part of the learning process in the days of hot metal setting when communication with those setting and assembling the type was vital (another part is listening to others). Now, the initial design work can be done with the aid of computers, but only as far as interpreting the enthusiasm of the typographer. A timetable can even be used to set a periodic style or mood, such as is regularly done with the selection of different type faces for headings. There can be a particularly successful outcome if the designer keeps in constant touch with all aspects of jobs. Styles can be gradually and unknowingly altered by making a small exception to suit one instance which then becomes the norm.

I had to constantly look around

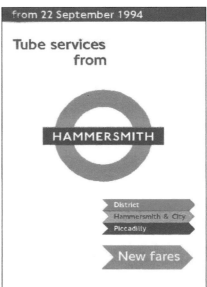

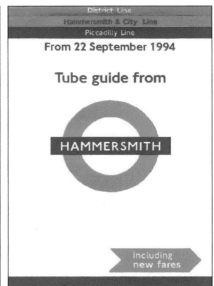

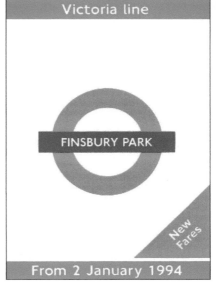

Departures to Richmond

Mondays to Fridays	
First train 0552	
Hours	**Minutes**
05	52
06	07, 16, 26, 36, 46, 56
07	05, 13, 24, 30, 37, 45, 52
08	00, 09, 17, 23, 32, 38, 46, 54
09	05, 16, 24, 32, 41, 50, 59
10	09, 20, 30, 39, 50
11	
12	01, 09, 20, 30, 39, 50
13	
14	
15	01, 09, 20, 30, 39, 48
16	00, 09, 17, 27, 38, 48, 55
17	03, 11, 19, 27, 35, 43, 51, 59
18	07, 15, 24, 34, 42, 51, 59
19	07, 17, 29, 38, 53
20	08, 22, 39, 52
21	04, 18, 32, 49
22	09, 29, 49
23	11, 33, 44
00	03, 26
Last train 0026	

Departures to Richmond

Saturdays	
First train 0552	
Hours	**Minutes**
05	52
06	07, 36, 56
07	16, 31, 51
08	11, 31, 51
09	11, 31, 44, 51
10	
11	
12	
13	
14	11, 24, 39, 54
15	
16	
17	
18	
19	
20	11, 31, 51
21	
22	
23	11, 33, 44
00	03, 26
Last train 0026	

Departures to Richmond

Sundays	
First train 0751	
Hours	**Minutes**
05	
06	
07	51
08	11, 31, 51
09	11, 31, 51, 59
10	13, 20, 30, 40, 50
11	
12	
13	
14	
15	00, 10, 20, 30, 40, 50
16	
17	
18	
19	
20	
21	11, 31, 51
22	
23	11, 33
00	
Last train 2333	

Departures to Ealing Broadway

Mondays to Fridays	
First train 0528 (Piccadilly line train. Change at Acton Town and Ealing Common)	
Hours	**Minutes**
05	28 (Piccadilly line train. Change at Acton Town and Ealing Common)
06	23, 41, 51
07	09, 18, 34, 48, 57
08	04, 14, 21, 30, 36, 48, 52
09	02, 07, 10, 18, 21, 27, 29, 36, 38, 43, 48, 54, 57
10	02, 12, 16, 26, 42, 56
11	
12	
13	12, 26, 42, 56
14	
15	
16	03, 14, 22, 33, 43, 52, 59
17	07, 16, 23, 31, 38, 47, 55
18	03, 11, 19, 29, 39, 45, 47, 53, 56
19	01, 04, 11, 14, 23, 25, 31, 34, 43, 48, 55, 58
20	01, 11, 15, 26, 31, 41, 44, 58
21	12, 23, 27, 42, 56
22	01, 21, 41
23	01, 22, 37, 54, 59
00	17, 28, 33, 37, 49
Last train 0049	

Departures to Ealing Broadway

Saturdays	
First train 0528 (Piccadilly line train. Change at Acton Town and Ealing Common)	
Hours	**Minutes**
05	28 (Piccadilly line train. Change at Acton Town and Ealing Common)
06	26, 46
07	06, 21, 41
08	01, 21, 41
09	
10	01, 19, 34, 49
11	
12	
13	
14	04, 19, 34, 49
15	
16	
17	
18	
19	04, 19, 24, 27, 36, 41
20	
21	01, 21, 41
22	
23	01, 22, 37, 59
00	17, 28, 33, 37, 49
Last train 0049	

Departures to Ealing Broadway

Sundays	
First train 0720	
Hours	**Minutes**
05	
06	
07	20, 34
08	01, 21, 41
09	
10	03, 24, 45
11	
12	
13	
14	05, 25, 45
15	
16	
17	
18	
19	
20	00, 05, 21, 25, 41
21	01, 21, 41
22	
23	01, 16, 24, 43, 53
00	04, 08, 14
Last train 0014	

to discover design work was not being done at all on jobs that I would normally have expected to be associated with or the subsequent design work was done by others with no sympathy with the original thinking. And these other people would often make crucial design decisions on a whim, often a personal one, instead of using design logic to lead the consideration.

A case in point was on panel timetables, where the weight of the hour figures was altered to bold and the minute figures to medium, with the effect that the hours swamped the relatively more important minute figures, the difference in weight of the two being too great – something that I had considered already myself and rejected.

Later, when digital computer setting became the norm and New Johnston, of which I had supervised the production of with its figures on the same width body, was in use London Transport's typesetters wrote programmes for the setting of timetables in Gill Sans, continuing the hot metal look. It was not until a generation later, on the recommendation of an outside design consultancy, that the present New Johnston setting of bus stop timetables came into use, thereby concluding the development process that I had initiated in the 1970s.

0756	0816	0836	0856
0802	0822	0842	0902
0810	0830	0850	0910
0818	0838	0858	0918
0828	0848	0908	0928
0838	0858	0918	0938
0849	0909	0929	0949
1620	1649	1709	1729
1626	1655	1715	1735
1632	1701	1721	1741
1639	1708	1728	1748

1140	**1156**	**1212**	**1228**
1149	**1205**	**1221**	**1237**
1155	**1211**	**1227**	**1243**
1201	**1217**	**1233**	**1249**
1205	**1221**	**1237**	**1253**
1628	**1644**	**1700**	**1716**
1637	**1653**	**1709**	**1725**
1643	**1659**	**1715**	**1731**
1649	**1705**	**1721**	**1737**
1653	**1709**	**1725**	**1741**

Details from two different bus stop panel timetables, both printed in 1981. The top detail shows the figures as they were set following my specification of ten years earlier. The detail below shows the figures set in a bolder weight than specified. If the two timetables had been displayed in the same frame the visual result would have appeared to be sloppy.

1978   **New Johnston typeface**
Designer: Banks & Miles

The three weights of the re-designed Johnston which was to become known as New Johnston. These three weights later became available as a digital keyboard face. The size shown here is about 36pt, which was the smallest size that the original Johnston was available as cast metal characters.

ABCDEFGHIJKLMNOPQRSTUVWXYZ
abcdefghijklmnopqrstuvwxyz
1234567890 .,:;''() £&!?

ABCDEFGHIJKLMNOPQRSTUVWXYZ
abcdefghijklmnopqrstuvwxyz
1234567890 .,:;''() £&!?

ABCDEFGHIJKLMNOPQRSTUVWXYZ
abcdefghijklmnopqrstuvwxyz
1234567890 .,:;''() £&!?

ABCDEFGHIJKLMNO PQRSTUVWXYZ&

abcdefghijklmnopqrs tuvwxyz
1234567890£?!/()-;:, ""
aegly14

1972 **Johnston type face**

The lettering designed for the Underground group in 1916 survived intact until 1972, when members of the LT Design Committee concluded that the house typeface might be updated. They commissioned the type designer, Walter Tracey, who suggested re-drawing certain letters to improve the spacing between them and the readability of the font as a whole. These are on the bottom row.

Johnston type

The history of the letter form designed by Edward Johnston in 1916 for use on signs and official printed posters of the London Underground, London General buses and the company owned tramways in the north-west and south-west of London is already well documented. Its use on pictorial posters was never compulsory until the 1980s, although it was often desired by designers or by the printers who adding typography to artists' paintings. It was the standard of design that made many of the posters recognisable as coming from the companies that were to become part of London Transport in 1933 and later London Transport itself, whatever the type faces used on them. Advertising agencies generally opted for the use of other type faces to cover their campaigns, although LT's use of agencies was never great.

From time to time, especially when London Transport was experiencing bad times, such as lower use of buses and trains in the evenings due to increased television ownership, or because of car ownership, or as a reaction to the general grubbiness of the buses, trains and stations, the board of LT would turn its attention to the typeface and throw down the challenge to the Publicity Officer that a change would cure the organisation's ills. The late 1960s was one such time, when car ownership was increasing and the replacement of the solidly built RF, RT and RM types

was by a new breed of plain looking rectangular box-like buses which were mechanically unreliable and rattled even when brand new. It was time for another look at a successor to the Johnston typeface!

In the early 1970s London Transport commissioned the eminent type designer, Walter Tracey, to conduct a research into the suitability of continuing to use Johnston or its replacement with a more modern letter form. This thinking was obviously influenced by British Rail's highly successful, and much copied,

corporate identity employing the Rail alphabet related to the Helvetica typeface, and backed by LT's retained design consultancy, Design Research Unit, who had already re-designed LT's head office letterheads using Helvetica. Tracey returned with a compromise, probably having already been briefed by LT's accountants that there was no money in the kitty to re-sign the entire Underground system in another style. His compromise was to retain the use of Johnston but replace some of its more awkward letters, which he deemed to be the: a,

e, g, l, y characters in the lower case and the figures 1 and 4. In the bold face nothing was to be altered. The letters were duly ordered as wooden display and metal text type from the type founders Stephenson Blake and Stevens Shanks and printers were instructed to change all the relevant letters in their standing forms. The letter cards used by the photo setting firms for setting type on film were never altered, nor were the sheets of rub down transfer lettering, both of which were used increasingly in the production of artworks and one off

ABCDEFGHIJKLMNOPQRSTUVWXYZ
abcdefghijklmnopqrstuvwxyz
1234567890 . , : ; ' ' ( ) £&!?

ABCDEFGHIJKLMNOPQRSTUVWXYZ
abcdefghijklmnopqrstuvwxyz
1234567890 . , : ; ' ' ( ) £&!?

The type faces as proposed by London Transport's advertising agency, Foote, Colne & Belding. The upper alphabet is Franklin Gothic condensed and would have been used for headlines. Below is the proposed text typeface, called Bookman. Both would have been set as horizontally centred lines in Upper and lower case.

displays. This limited action was to only stem the tide for a clamour for change which would lead to a later attack by LT's retained advertising agency, FCB.

In the late 1970s LT had changed their advertising agency to Foote Colne & Belding (FCB) following a long lasting relationship with Ogelvy Benson & Mather (OBM) and its predecessor S. H. Benson.

FCB had won the hearts of the LT management with their production of the memorable *Fly the Tube* poster. That this poster was clever in terms of the idea that it conveyed there can be no doubt. But because the theme expressed was so compelling, the lack of graphic subtlety or sophistication of the overall layout and typography was overlooked. Riding on this success, the agency were naturally keen to increase their sphere of influence by actually producing full sized mock ups of some carefully selected poster subjects in their prevailing type style, which was Franklin

Gothic condensed for the headlines, contrasting with a serifed face, which was Bookman, for text which was set smaller than the Johnston text that it was replacing. But they had not done their homework into the vast range of different types of informational posters and notices handled as a matter of routine by the Publicity Office layout staff and the printers to LT. The agency argued that they saw the main stumbling block in the way of modern looking typography to be the use of the Johnston typeface, which they regarded as old fashioned and limiting to the typographer. In its place they opted for a much bolder and larger face than Johnston for headings. Layouts would be centred and printed in black, instead of the very dark bronze blue ink which had been used since World War II.

Their analysis was wrong, in that they were blaming the Johnston typeface for a range of posters which often employed very bad typography. The agency were also not concerned

with associated sign designs, bus and train destination blind designs or any other aspect of corporate design, because their vision of corporate design only extended as far as one advertising campaign, which had a life ending with the start of the next campaign – they were not aware of anything bigger and many still aren't.

At the same time as FCB was pushing for change, Bryce Beaumont, who had resisted their overtures with his usual quiet diplomacy, had retired to be superseded by his deputy, Michael Levey. Levey had already displayed his vulnerability to persuasion by the agency, by instructing his Publicity Office printing section staff to adopt centred layouts for all informational posters. The range of letterpress posters, using Johnston bold caps for titles with medium upper and lower case for the text below, was altered to entirely centred layouts, printed in black instead of the very dark bronze blue. The red rules at the head and foot

of posters were removed and a large red roundel was placed in the centre at the base. The appearance of these poster layouts coincided with the arrival of a new regime of Thatcher-orientated higher managers at LT, who believed that the economic problems of the organisation would be solved by a more commercial approach in keeping with their mentor's market guided philosophy. The director whose portfolio covered publicity was driven to remark upon the harshness of the appearance of these new posters compared with the ones they had replaced, which was caused of course by the use of black ink instead of bronze blue for the type.

As these posters began to be seen more regularly on displays along the platforms and at station entrances, their stark appearance became more apparent even to the new intake of market orientated managers at LT who had originally approved them. Levey had already reported to me, on returning from a meeting of the International Union of Public Transport (U.I.T.P.) in Budapest, that they had discussed the standardisation of the use of the 'M' to denote urban rail systems. 'M', or 'Metro' was already used by Tyne & Wear, Paris, Madrid, Rome (Metropolitana), Moscow and other cities in the USSR (Metpo), as well as systems in the United States, Canada and South America, Australia and New Zealand and systems in Asia. I was fearful that the Underground's name and unique roundel might be in line for 'revision'. As for the lettering, the LT Design Committee instructed Levey not to cave in any further to the advertising agency and commission Banks & Miles to find ways to adapt Johnston to compete visually with the brash Franklin Gothic. Banks & Miles responded by re-designing the lower case with a larger x-height and adding a matching lower case fount to the bold. An entirely new light fount was designed. To counter the Franklin Gothic condensed a Johnston condensed was devised matching the other founts for x-height and weight. This was not as condensed as that used on bus blinds, but roughly equalled Monotype Gill Sans bold condensed or Stephenson Blake's Granby Bold condensed. It was at the point of the Banks & Miles rough designs that I was invited to view them and give my comments. The future production of posters was to lead to their printing by lithography

or silk screen from artwork using film set letters. The original Johnston face had been transferred to film letter cards which butted up on the left and contained a series of marks on the right in different positions according to which letter that was to follow. This system allowed for a degree of standardisation of letter spacing, similar to that used when wooden display letters are set next to other. It was this system using about 6cm high letters on letter cards that was proposed to be used for headlines. A similar system with letters on a 35mm film strip would be used to set text type. I already had in mind that a keyboard system would eventually need to be used to bring the cost of artworks and printing down to a similar level to that of letterpress printing. This would also allow for the setting of Johnston in much smaller sizes than had hitherto been possible. To that end I recommended that the figures were designed to be all the same width, which was normally half the set width of the typeface. This would allow tables to be set, which was not possible with the traditional Johnston, which didn't matter too much when limited to large display sizes and was often replaced with the more versatile Gill Sans in the smaller sizes. It was for this reason that I requested that the figure 1 should be given a 'nose', similar to most other sans faces, to reduce the space between it and other figures that it was

set next to. I would have preferred that its 'nose' sloped a little more.

Once approved by the LT Board and the Design Committee the final decision before the new type face was brought into production was a name for it. In view of the fact that it was only approved for printing, the implication was that Johnston's 1916 sans serif face would continue in use on signing. Various names, such as that of the Japanese designer, Eiichi Kono, employed by Banks & Miles, or of Banks & Miles themselves were suggested and rejected and it was my suggestion that we retain Johnston's name by adding *New* to the front to suggest the refinement such as has been applied to other type faces, that was accepted. And so the typeface was from then known as *New Johnston* light, medium and bold with their respective italic fonts, together with medium and bold condensed for use as headlines. A handful of film setters were briefed and given reels of each font on 35mm films which suited a system of photo setting display type used fairly commonly. The reels were produced by Star Illustration Works Ltd, typesetters and blockmakers, of 76 Wardour Street, London W1. Star Illustration were a family firm that had switched from copper and zinc letterpress blockmaking to photo-lithography. The family also owned Sheekey's Fish Restaurant in St.Martin's Court, Charing Cross Road, just around the corner from

1978   **London Transport informational posters**

An unfortunate introduction to this new poster layout embraced a design connected subject matter to the text. This graphically exemplifies the starkness and harshness of the black and red layout and shows how easily a policy that has taken years to establish and develop can be quickly destroyed.

Trafalgar Square Underground station – this fact emerged after I had established a working relationship with the firm and not before – I must insist! Star Illustration produced duplicate 35mm reels which were sent to Alphabet, Graphic Systems and others, but remained the property of London Transport to reduce the likelihood of the type face being used for other clients' work. It was stressed to type setters that if they were found to be using New Johnston on work other than for London Transport the New Johnston films would be returned and business with them would be terminated. The advertising agency, FCB, were also instructed to use New Johnston bold condensed in place of the Franklin Gothic that had caused the redrawing of Johnston. They used Conways as one of their typesetters, but Conways – arrogant to the end – decided to redraw certain characters

ABCDEFGHIJKLMNOPQRSTUVW
XYZ&.,:;!?''()/--* abcdefghijklmn
opqrstuvwxyz£1234567890

ABCDEFGHIJKLMNOPQRSTUVW
XYZ&.,:;!?''()/--*abcdefghijklmnop
qrstuvwxyz£1234567890

ABCDEFGHIJKLMNOPQRSTUVWX
YZ&.,:;!?''()/--* abcdefghijklmnopqrst
uvwxyz£1234567890

ABCDEFGHIJKLMNOPQRSTUVWXY
Z&.,:;!?''()/--* abcdefghijklmnopqr
stuvwxyz£1234567890

ABCDEFGHIJKLMNOPQRSTUVWXYZ&
.,:;!?''()/--*abcdefghijklmnopqrstuvw
xyz£1234567890

ABCDEFGHIJKLMNOPQRSTUVWX
YZ&.,:;!?''()-* abcdefghijklmnopqrs
tuvwxyz£1234567890

ABCDEFGHIJKLMNOPQRSTUVWXY
Z&.,:;!?''()-* abcdefghijklmnopqrstu
vwxyz£1234567890

ABCDEFGHIJKLMNOPQRSTUVWXYZ
&.,:;!?''()-* abcdefghijklmnopqrstuvwx
yz£1234567890

1978   New Johnston type
Design: Banks & Miles, Blackheath

The reason for the Banks & Miles re-design of Johnston was to counter the advertising agency's recommendation that Franklin Gothic be used for headlines. The particular Johnston font is the bold condensed which is forth from the top.

Both headings and text were set by headline photoset, with letter and word spacing judged by the eye of the operator. Both were pasted down as strips, similar to a telegram, in a centred position and re-photographed to a suitable size to then be pasted on the half-size to double royal size artwork mounting board that poster artworks were made to. Any alterations at artwork stage meant re-setting the relevant piece and pasting down onto the strips stage of the artwork before re-photographing for the final artwork.

This replaced the former letterpress method which consisted of setting the wooden type by hand, with generally standard spaces between the words, screwing it into a form, rolling the surface of the type with ink and running a few copies off on a proofing press. Corrections were made by removing the offending type characters and simply substituting others.

and their modified alphabet was used, not only for advertisements, but also for signing on the Underground, some of which can still be seen on the strips beneath the platform digital train describer signs. It proved predictably difficult to persuade the management of LT's Publicity Office that the advertising agency were using a bastardised version of this brand new typeface – they just could not believe that such a thing was possible.

The first posters to be set in New Johnston appeared with the very undistinguished form of centred layout. As their blandness became apparent to the point that comment was being made in the higher circles of LT, I thought it was about the right time to embark on a new identity that would cover posters as well as leaflets and booklet covers. Following Design Research Unit's recommendation that a plain roundel would cover all of LT's operations, needs had made themselves apparent that on occasions, the different modules did require identification. I used the bases of posters and other printed matter to also reflect the module that was speaking. A white roundel on a red background would therefore sign off bus related messages. A red roundel on a black background would denote the Underground, since that representation was already used on back illuminated signs directing to stations. London Transport messages would be signed off with a red roundel

on a white background. On all posters the roundel would be ranged left with the lettering above. Also on type only information posters, headings would be separated from text by a horizontal rule, always in a consistent position. This was done to reduce the contrast between posters with wordy headings and those with very short headings when seen adjacent to each other.

As I developed this project the directorship in charge of the Publicity Office was filled by Basil Hooper. He liked an audience and could slaughter feeble or unprepared opposition in front of that audience. The early mock ups of the new generation of information posters needed to be approved by him. My office was still at Griffith House Marylebone, while he required meetings in his office at 55 Broadway, usually in the early evening – he treated my poster meetings as a relaxation to wind down after a heavy day. I had to carry these large posters attached to rigid mounting boards half way around the Circle Line during the evening peak time. But my trouble was rewarded. I think, in hindsight, that Basil recognised my professionalism. He asked me to make minor alterations for further meetings, but generally accepted all my design proposals. We got on well, meetings were very good humoured and relaxed (on his part). These meetings followed the retirement of Michael Levey, who had been manoeuvred, manipulated and generally not supported by a succession of new, and often short lived, appointees to directorships responsible for the Publicity Office, resulting in a rudderless Publicity Office until the arrival of Basil who was originally perceived to follow the same mould. The future would show that Basil was a valuable ally.

With the setting of posters being done by hand to a predetermined size, the procedure was very similar to letterpress setting with wood and metal type – but much slower. The initial setting of the type was followed by the intermediate stages of producing photographic prints, then cutting the strips of typesetting and pasting the lines together before being photographed to enlarge it to the required size which was then pasted onto a piece of mounting board for the artwork which, if the final printing size was double royal, was half size. Trim marks were added on the corners by hand with a ruling pen. Once approved, the artwork was then photographed to provide film which was then retouched before being contacted to make a positive suitable for exposing onto a lithographic plate.

1978   London Transport informational posters

These centred layouts superseded those that were formerly ranged left and were the first in an offensive by the advertising agency to impose their own layouts and type faces onto the design of informational publicity.

The differing sized roundels in different positions gave the impression of a ping-pong ball bouncing when a bank of posters were seen along a tube station platform wall or bus shelter.

Altogether, a sad swan song for Edward Johnston's fragile masterpiece.

1978   Information poster mock-ups

A new generation of poster layouts was considered to coincide with the production of posters by new technology. Whilst the text was set in the original style of Johnston, the headings were set in Granby bold in anticipation of the arrival of the similar looking New Johnston bold. New technology also gave the opportunity to convert some of the lettering into outline or add shadow effects.

1981   **Informational posters**
Size: Double Royal

These posters are set in the first generation of new technology, entirely using headline type. The nearest poster has its heading set in New Johnston condensed with text set in Johnston. However, because each was set by different compositors using their own preferred letterspacing judgement the spacing is inconsistent, a problem that would become less likely once keyboard setting was available. The posters on the left and far right display the flexibility of using an illustration which would have entailed a large line block if the poster had been reproduced by letterpress. Also, as shown on the far right poster, of fitting type into other type with ease.

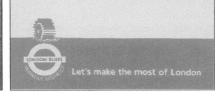

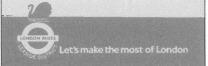

The process was slow and expensive compared to printing letterpress straight from raised type. This surprised some of the LT directors who had pushed for this new system but hadn't listened (or understood) when it had been explained to them beforehand that LT was a special case when it came to short runs of posters.

Keyboard type

I had always viewed the above procedure as an intermediate stage to production completely on the keyboard. Typesetters were queuing at the door to offer their services to satisfy LT's setting needs. But they were only interested in the leaflet work employing type sizes below 36 point. In those days film setting consisted of (usually) a spinning disc containing all the letters of the fount around the edge in negative form. As the text was tapped out on

the keyboard, a light would flash through the relevant letter – hence the name *film*setting, since the spinning disc formed a negative. The negative characters were about 6 to 8 point in size (about the size of this text), which was sufficient for text setting and headings up to about 48 point. But LT's artworks often utilised sizes larger than this, even on half full size artworks to double royal poster size. So even if the type could withstand the enlargement to half size, when the printer doubled the size, corners of type became very rounded and even straight lines were rather ragged.

I became aware of a system being developed where the type was built up with pixels, so that the size that a character appeared was the size that it originated, meaning that the larger the type the more pixels built it up. This was the system in use by the type foundry H. Bertold AG, Berlin, who had supplied the

computer setting equipment to the Setting Room at Tonbridge Wells. For the two directors, Maurice Turner and Brian Andre it was a labour of confidence since they were prepared to stand the development cost and experimentation work before the type was ready for production. They also brought in Tim Woods, who was marketing and development manager at the Monotype Corporation with particular responsibility servicing typesetters in eastern Europe, and who gave a very unbiassed and technical judgement. I had no money in my budget and none was forthcoming since Nick Lewis, who was by now the Publicity Officer following the retirement of Michael Levey, was not able to comprehend the necessity of opting for a new system of setting type when poster artworks were already being produced quite satisfactorily as far as he was concerned. The Chief Marketing

Manager, Basil Hooper, who had appointed Lewis and whom Lewis reported to, was more understanding. We very often shared the same train when commuting to and from work. On the Underground train or as we stood on the platform at Marylebone terminus waiting for the train to the Chilterns (but not on board since Basil made use of his First Class free pass) I explained to him the typographic problems of poster production. He had enough trust in me when I said that once the computer set artwork replaced the more expensive hand set artwork it would re-coup the development costs of the system in about a year (in fact we achieved it in six months). One of the stumbling blocks was that the New Johnston keyboard type was to be confined to London Transport work, whereas the huge development costs of a commercial type would normally be offset over a period by selling it to

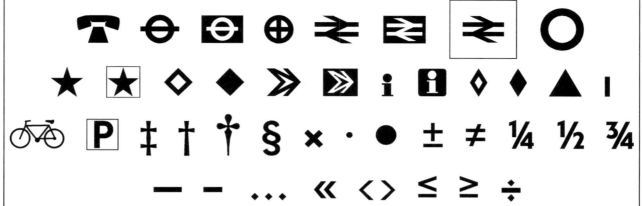

1981   **New Johnston special keyboard characters**

Banks & Miles were asked to design special characters to go with the digitised New Johnston for keyboard setting with timetables and the Underground diagram map. Of interest is the proportions of the roundel, which was drawn in this spindly way to avoid the centre filling in when set in small sizes which was a treatment also applied to small sizes of type. But once the fount came into the hands of the uninitiated, this roundel proportioned for sizes under 12pt appeared as large as 80mm across, apparently unnoticed by some of the very people who were judging my designs. The other interesting character is the traditionally shaped dagger. This was specifically asked for in place of the New Johnston dagger which looked like a crucifix when seen as small as is used on the tube pocket map.

approved typesetters. I therefore had to be completely sure that this system was going to be the most suitable for LT's work before we embarked upon it, and then agree to reimburse the Setting Room for the development costs that would normally be bourn by the type founder by guaranteeing them a large volume of work and a monopoly status for typesetting production for an initial period.

There were two basic stages in production. First was the unitisation, which was the production of letter cards with nicks on the bottom which would position each letter of the alphabet next to any other letter with the correct amount of space between. This was similar to the information on the original hand set lettercards, except that a computer keyboard only had 18 alternative letter widths per fount. Some characters had to be fractionally redrawn to fit into one of the 18 width categories. This process was performed by Robert Norton in his workshop in Princess Risborough. The process of unitisation also took account of the second stage which was the digitisation, by making sure that none of the curved edges of letters ended on a line of pixels thereby making them straight. Digitisation was performed on the letter cards by the type founder and it was that stage when each character was turned into a pixelated letter that the photographic process was left behind. Normally a typeface would be produced in three

digitised versions: i. from 5pt to 14pt; ii. from 15pt to 24/36pt; iii. above 36pt. Unlike all other users of type, LT's prime need was for sizes above 24pt, so the digitisation was stretched to the use of just one version, based on the larger sizes, with the option that one or both smaller versions would be added if necessary at an additional cost. The one version was found to be sufficient, which was to have a profound effect on the way type founders digitised their commercial type in future.

The procedure for producing type only information posters was to set the heading by hand in display film set type, usually in New Johnston bold condensed. Beneath that was the text set in New Johnston light by keyboard. Both would be run out on bromide paper which were pasted down on card in position half size to the finished double royal poster. The printer would enlarge and photograph the artwork which would be printed litho or silk screen. As confidence grew, the heading were also set on the keyboard, but in New Johnston bold since bold condensed was never digitised and remained only available as a hand set fount. While typesetters

were happy to electronically condense Bold to make it look like Bold condensed, the letters looked like bold seen at an angle. Typesetters were implored not to interfere with the type face by condensing or expanding it.

But Edward Johnston's lettering was still not safe. While it was excepted on purely typographic information posters for headings, the advertising agency pressed that a serif face (perhaps Bookman) be used for text. The agency needed to gather support for their use of a serif type face on their pictorial posters and they had an ally in Nick Lewis, the new Publicity Office leader, who was an ex-agency man. Many experiments were produced, all in the entirely centred layout that the agency, Nick Lewis and his recently recruited deputy, Thelma Wright, deemed to be the 'most friendly' – even if it was difficult to read and decidedly old fashioned by prevailing graphic standards. I employed a studio to produce full size double royal mock-ups. Their brief was to choose suitable sizes in a variety of typefaces, to a variety of measures – the permutations were endless – but they had every reason to make the brief succeed in the hope

that they would get more work in the future on the strength of its success. What is more, I chose one of the few studios from the many that I had built up a relationship with to provide the different types of work that a vast organisation requires, that had not received a ban from Mrs Wright for her own purely ideological reasons. This studio was Gwylim (Bill) Thomas, who had probably more typographic experience than any other of the studios that I used. What is more, he was adept at moving invoices around to match the final appearances of work, rather than how much actual time each had taken. Mrs Wright, despite her outward appearance of knowing the business viewed most work sympathetically if done by her friends and less so if they were not, however professionally each party produced the work.

The first mock-ups produced by Bill Thomas were rejected, as being difficult to read. So were the revised versions and the following revised versions, to the point that Nick Lewis accused me of sabotaging the exercise. What neither he nor Thelma Wright could grasp, was that a line of type centred under

London Transport Informational Posters

One argument for continuing with the style of basically centred poster layouts is that they are 'modern' and 'friendly'. Whilst experiments can be continued with centred, left ranging with first line indents and other varieties of typography and layout, there are many examples of each variation already existing.

Poster layouts generally

Centred layouts are an adaptation of the printed book title page which originate from about the seventeenth century. Nearly all posters produced from Victorian times until at least the second world war employed centred layouts. Some exceptions were the Underground posters commissioned by Frank Pick employing designers as innovative as E. McKnight Kauffer. These posters were distinctive in that the typography was worked into the layout, rather than (in the case of many) being treated as a large caption centred beneath a squared up illustration.

Underground informational posters generally employed a centred layout, but the clarity of the Johnston poster type compared very favourably with the heavy block type used by many of the main line railways. A clearer type, but with the traditional title page layout therefore, in the 'twenties, formed a distinct typographical advance.

The basis of all graphic design is to attain balance. A symmetrical (or centred) layout, by its nature, is already balanced. An asymmetrical layout must be consciously balanced by the designer. An asymmetrical layout requires the beholder's eye to ingest all of the qualities of the layout. The first impression may be one of imbalance, which is disturbing and unexpected. This is what makes the asymmetrical design all the more interesting to perceive. A balance is subconsciously looked for. More importantly, an asymmetrical design gives movement. The eye is directed by the design from one item to the next in importance, and so on.

London Transport poster layouts

London Transport's symbol, the roundel, whilst being a very strong and clear shape, is totally symmetrical and non-moving. It is such a powerful shape that even when it is placed symmetrically while other matter is not, the image is still totally static. When it is used asymmetrically the entire layout gains movement. (This can be seen to effect on the sides of buses. The centrally positioned roundel on an RM-type is merely the owner's symbol – it only moves when the bus moves. The forward placed roundel on a front entrance double-decker gives the bus movement, direction and urgency. It actually appears to be propelling the bus. This is correct, since the bus is operated by London Transport as symbolised by the roundel, rather than vice-versa.)

Left ranging headings and text are generally easier to read. They also have a neatness and clarity of purpose which reflects the organisation that they are speaking for.

A large amount of tabular matter must, by its nature, be ranged left to be read with the greatest ease. However, a left ranging layout often requires considerably more skill by the designer to achieve balance. This though, is no argument against having a more effective layout.

There is no reason to believe that a left ranging orderly layout is any less 'friendly' than a centred layout, or partially centred with enormous indents to the first lines of paragraphs. The 'friendliness' must come partially from copywriting.

One can envisage, in the near future, all poster copy being potentially 'good news'. Posters announcing the most disastrous news can usually conclude with a customer benefit. For example, a fares increase notice often contains a discount item to soften the blow. At present it is not fully exploited.

Other announcements could be injected with a hint of humour. Occasional posters can be less rigid typographically (but still adhere to the basic layout specifications) to emphasise a particular function.

The ultimate aim is to attract the public to read London Transport's posters; firstly, by a very distinctive layout and, secondly, by the copy nearly always announcing a benefit – however small.

Type

While there are distinct readability advantages between one typeface and another, often the typography is blamed when, in fact, the total layout is at fault. There are recognised acceptances of the most readable types and styles when applied to book typography. Whereas a novel set in sans serif typeface would make a reader aware of the type rather than the words, no such difficulty is apparent when posters are set in sans serif types. In fact, the reverse applies since the reader must first be attracted by the initial clarity of a poster – with a book the reader is first attracted by its cover.

The accepted typographic presentation rules of book by indenting first lines of paragraphs (but not the first one since that leads the reader in), punctuation and the use of italics and capital letters do not apply so rigidly on a poster, which is read in totally different environmental conditions. When poster readability can be enhanced by breaking the rules held dear to book typographers, then it must be done.

Lets make the most of London

This must appear in close relationship to the roundel – it is an informal invitation. It may come at the foot of some fairly complex traffic instructions. It must therefore be seen to form an informal relief. Since it is an invitation to make the most of London by all London Transport's services, rather than just those shown above on the particular poster, it must form part of the roundel. It must not be seen to be an appendage to the poster text.

In italic type it achieves these aims. In roman type it is merely a statement – perhaps an abrupt one.

Conclusion

London Transport posters, while harmonising with each other, must compete with all other commercial posters. London Transport's poster sites possess the unique advantage that a group of diverse posters can be seen together as a unit, competing for attention against the individual publicity items of other advertisers. (When London Transport's advertising posters are seen in a commercial advertising environment they, at present, appear to merge with their competitors with remarkable success.)

London Transport must have a distinctly pronounced poster style. The two ingredients that all the other advertisers grouped together do not share, are consistent layout and type, and consistent clarity.

London Transport must foster this unique advantage.

T. Demuth
Design section – Publicity Office
8 December 1979

an advertising illustration acts as a caption which has probably gone a long way to explaining the theme of the subject. Whereas the topic of a message contained on text only information posters is usually very dry and uninteresting, but it is also very important that it does get read – possibly meaning the difference between catching or missing a bus or train. More importantly, many of these posters carried safety messages (very few advertising agency posters do). Readability therefore was paramount, which goes back more than half a century to Frank Pick's brief to Edward Johnston in 1914.

There then followed an uneasy compromise – informational posters tended to be ranged left with a roundel in the middle at the base, while advertising posters centred their illustrations and each line of type. It was a tiring and uphill job keeping an eye on an imperfect system to try to stop it getting any worse, especially since diplomatic relations had virtually frozen between myself and the Lewis/Wright duo. However, whenever the occasional compliments came in from the outside world of graphics, they were usually unintentionally directed at work that I had handled. But there it ended – any compliments for anyone else's work resulted in the department being invited into Nick Lewis's office to enjoy a glass of wine (and cheeky giggly risqué asides with Thelma).

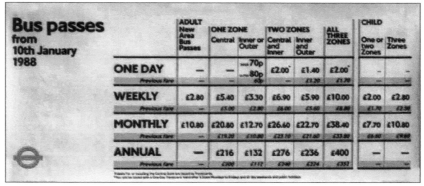

One form of typography which the advertising agency attempted a number of times but never completed, were the layouts for fares revision (increase) posters. I continued to handle them year after year – I wasn't allowed to throw in the towel when they became difficult. The agency just couldn't get the hang of simplifying a fairly complex (and illogical) series of rates into simple to understand tables. From the start of design, I liaised with my contacts in the Commercial Office and took on board any feedback from them. I therefore retained the confidence they had in my thinking that I had developed with them. Often they informally asked my opinions on their own projects that were being submitting to the Board for approval. The New Johnston series was used throughout on what developed into a family of posters covering the system-wide fares as well a separate series of local fares posters. Over the years the LT directors of design would view the posters at artwork stage and could never find fault in their appearance. This wasn't through lack of interest – on the contrary, they and the other directors were intensely concerned about the presentation of this sensitive and unpopular information. I was gradually rebuilding my reputation as a reliable problem solver with my tidy graphic and typographic solutions.

At the close of the 1970s the central servicing department, which housed the typing pool and internal printing, decided to set up its own typesetting department. This seemed odd since LT was in the process of disposing of loss making operations. They set up their operation in Bolsover Street next door to the Setting Room's London studio. Nick insisted that we make use of this new facility, but there were very few jobs where we had plenty of time to test them out, so I sent them simple posters to set and produce the artwork for half size to double royal, our standard practice. They made the mistake of trimming the prints containing the type far to close to the lettering, in some cases actually trimming off the tops or bottoms of some of the letters. I took the precaution of sending identical specifications to the Setting Room or one of the other suppliers we were using. The LT Typesetters artwork was always delivered much later than that from commercial typesetters who always delivered the morning after briefing. At least once, the LT Typesetters artwork finally turned up over a week after it had been ordered and after I remonstrated with them to deliver it – they thought we should collect it. Although I am in favour of regular work being produced in house, it must be of better quality and cheaper than that done by outside firms. LT Typesetters matched none of these criteria and duly failed after a very short time.

Paddington escalators

The first of the new escalators is now in service.

Replacing the remaining escalator involves a considerable amount of structural alteration to the surrounding shaft, and will take until 1984 to complete.

Meanwhile, please use the stairs to reach the Bakerloo Line platforms.

We're sorry for the inconvenience.

Attention all children!

You can get your Child Rate Photocard from this station

If you are 5-15 photocards are needed for all tickets valid for seven days or more.

14 and 15 year olds need a Child Rate Photocard if travelling at child rate.

All under 5s travel free on the Underground.

1988 Fares revisions posters
Posters announcing new fares were traditionally designed within the Publicity Office. However, the advertising agency's clamours to be responsible for almost everything was answered by their being handed the fares revision publicity. It was returned to Publicity as being too complicated after a number of failed and rejected attempts. The treatment I devised won the approval of the Director of Design and I continued my association with the Commercial Office and the presentation of the all too regular fares revision packages.

1981 Double Royal poster
Centred heading followed by ranged left text, the whole arrangement being hand set and pasted onto mounting board before being photographed for printing. The ruled backs were designed by Kassa & Steele.

1992 Double Royal poster
Heading and text are set entirely on the keyboard, including any leading and indenting, allowing consistency to letterspacing and attention to leading. The basic layout followed the specification designed by Henrion Ludlow & Schmidt, reverting to a ranged left layout.

1975 Private bus blind

Mock up blind seen fitted to an RM outside Shepherd's Bush Garage and, to the right, mock up attached to rear.

1981 Night bus blinds

Mock ups in position on a Metrobus after dark. The top picture shows existing layout. Below are mock ups displaying route numbers of all one size and revised layouts of intermediate points.

Bus destination blinds

There had apparently been a number of letters sent by intending and frustrated passengers complaining that buses had been driven past them. On investigation it was realised that the passengers had not observed that the errant buses were not in service – understandable when all buses along a stretch of road go to the same point, there is little need to read what is displayed in the destination box. I was therefore asked to design a distinctive blind to be displayed when

buses were not in public service. This project allowed me to visit Aldenham bus overhaul works in Hertfordshire where bus destination blinds were manufactured.

The printing process was by silk screen onto paper which was then mounted onto the transparent canvas roller blind. On each section to be printed, cut out letters were arranged on proofing paper and the organdie in its frame lowered on top. Ink was then dragged across with a squeegee as with normal screen printing. The letters would then form silhouettes and became attached to the underside of the screen by the ink that failed to get through to the paper. Standard size Johnston letters were manufactured in both normal and condensed. The capitals used on RT and RM blinds for ultimate destinations, be they normal Johnston or Johnston condensed, came in one size only which were used for all buses. Whereas the condensed upper and lower case letters used for via points came in two sizes, the smaller versions for RM blinds. Infrequently used letters and punctuation would be cut out of paper by hand by the screen operator.

I concluded that the use of

different colours would be the most eye-catching as had been the use of yellow on Green Line blinds. But there weren't many colours left – red could not be used at night on the fronts of buses and green was not allowed at the back for obvious reasons – blue was already used to denote express services. Which is the reason why I selected purple. The use of the roundel was an innovation too, since this display was also advertising as well as informative. The design has stood the test of time.

When the Night Bus services were re-launched in 1981, I was asked to prepare some mock ups that could be used to ascertain the best display of the route number. Traditionally the operators had used a smaller letter than the number, both for suffixes and prefixes. The New Johnston helped considerably in distinguishing the 1 as being a figure and not a letter, thereby allowing the N to compliment the figures in their own size. I think the bus blind exercise was dreamt up by Michael Cleary who saw an excuse to get into the bowels of a bus garage and play with the vehicles. We went to Willesden Garage and waited for darkness to see the true effect of my work when back illuminated in the destination box, which would be late in the evening because the season was mid-summer. The lateness suited Michael since he intended to spend the rest of the night 'cranking' the existing Night Bus network which

commenced about 23:30. I was eager to leave as soon as I had taken the photographs and removed the mock ups so that I could get to my local, the *Saracen's Head* at Amersham before closing time! While we were waiting for darkness, Michael demonstrated his miming skills my imitating the sounds made by a number of diverse bus types – LT, STL, TF, RF, RT and RM – from the engines starting up and at speed, to gear changing on the earlier types. As a contrast he also showed his prowess by mimicking the crowing and chattering made by chickens – I did not enquire if they were Rhode Island Reds, Plymouth Rocks or Leghorns!

Another range of blinds that I laid out was for the Airbus fleet as part of its re-livery and the re-design of bus stop publicity. I used the same New Johnston extra bold italic style of lettering that formed part of the Airbus identity across the top of the blind, printed out of different background colours to identify the two central London destinations.

Pictogram signing

With the building of the Piccadilly Line extension from Hounslow to the centre of the Heathrow Airport complex, the London Transport Board were considering the possible advantages of including pictograms on direction signs to help non-English speaking passengers find their way around the Underground station and their way into central London.

Since the end of World War II London Transport was a member of two international transport organisations: the U.I.T.P. (Union Internationale des Public Transports) International Union of Public Transport, a forum for the interchange and possible agreement of activities of urban transport operation throughout the world; and U.I.C. (Union International des Chemins de Fer) International Union of Railways, which aimed at standardisation of main line railway equipment and operating methods mainly within Europe. The U.I.C. in particular had made progress with the implementation of a set of pictograms to aid the increasing number of nationals travelling throughout Europe as international travel became easier and cheaper. Pictograms began to appear on railway timetables and on signing, at both stations and on railway cars. Because the U.I.C. had made an early start, their pictograms were fairly rigidly standardised,

both conceptually and graphically. Those of the U.I.T.P. members that had embarked on the use of pictograms showed more diversity, often closely following the treatment of their own countries' road signs.

Because of the physical separation of Britain's railways from those of mainland Europe and its rolling stock size, limiting the use of through international carriages, Britain had not joined the pictogram convention. However, in the mid 1970s British Rail made a start by signing their London terminal and major provincial stations with their generally graphically superior interpretations of the U.I.C. pictograms. Added to the railway signs, and those familiar to motorists alongside roads, signs within international airports throughout Europe were also beginning to be implemented with the addition of pictograms. However, most international airports were usually owned and operated by their countries' government transport ministries, which meant that the design of pictograms usually followed those in use on the national road systems of each country.

When the LT Board decided, in principal, that pictograms on signs would be advantageous to passengers, they were mindful of the physical limitations within many Underground stations to accommodate much more than was already contained on direction signs.

So they decided to experiment on the signs in the Victoria Line booking hall at Victoria Underground Station. This station was chosen for two reasons: firstly, the booking hall possessed very limited floor to ceiling height with a multiplicity of directions; secondly, it was close to the board members at 55 Broadway. Thinking had reached this stage when the job was handed to me. I don't think that the board were aware of the variety of different designs used by the organisations that the Underground would be coming into contact with: British Rail, Ministry of Transport, British Airports.

The layouts used on London Transport's signs had traditionally been centred within their frames. The sizes of many signs depended on the wall or ceiling area that they were to be fixed, which meant that the size of the wording varied between each sign, also depending on the amount of wording. Whilst I was sure that for

clarity, uniformity and modernity, the display at Underground stations should follow a stacked arrangement, the board members could only visualise stacking vertically, whereas I was also envisaging a set of signs placed horizontally where headroom was limited and width was less of a constraint. I therefore devised a layout which accommodated wording, a directional arrow and a pictogram. To allow the elements to range and relate with each other, I redrew the directional arrow to be proportioned within a square, so that it could point upwards, downwards, left or right and always be the same width. Pictograms would also be accommodated within a square for the same reason. Since the signing frames were to be retained within the Victoria station booking hall, for this exercise I standardised the sizes of lettering to that which could be accommodated on the most difficult sign. The main practical

1976 Victoria signing proposals

A manual was prepared to show LT Board members what I had in mind. This showed photographs of every sign that was to be changed, together with the proposed signs retouched onto duplicates of the photographs.

1976 Deutsch Reichsbahn (German Democratic Republic) pictograms

Most European railways showed the range of pictograms that they used within their stations and trains and inside their timetable books. This range from the state railways of the German Democratic Republic is typical of the standardised designs agreed upon by U.I.C. member railway organisations.

1976 London Transport pictograms

The range of pictograms drawn for use on the Victoria Station signing plus others that would come into use if the scheme went system wide. The information italic *i* followed British tourist standards and taking into consideration the proximity of central London Underground stations to tourist street signing instead of the version used by the UIC continental railways. The buffet and restaurant signs were relevant, there being refreshment outlets within the Underground stations at Baker Street, Liverpool Street and King's Cross.

difference between the signs used on the Underground system and those used by other organisations, was that those used by the Underground were generally back illuminated. This not only allowed signs to be seen within dark areas, but also enabled them to be switchable, allowing different messages to be displayed and others to be hidden at different times. Because many signs were still illuminated by rows of separate tungsten bulbs, illuminated lettering on a black background was employed to reduce the effects of pools of brighter light in the areas adjacent to the bulbs that would have been apparent if an overall white background with black lettering had been employed. I was happy to continue with this arrangement, as I also wanted to retain the use of capital lettering. The practical reason for using capitals was their lack of descenders, which was a particularly important consideration, with the limited depths of planks.

As far as the application was concerned, I was able to argue that the traditional method of hand lettering on glass would not be practicable because of the urgency of the scheme – the normal waiting time for any hand lettered back illuminated sign was about 18 months, which was quite satisfactory with the normal planning arrangements. However, I was concerned that the details of some of the pictograms we would be using could take many hours to paint by

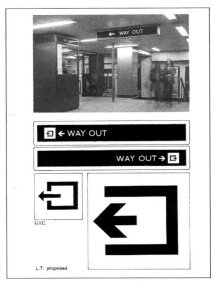

1. No entry/exit
2. Trains
3. Escalators—up
4. Escalators—down
5. No smoking
6. Information
7. Danger
8. Way in
9. Toilets
10. British Rail
11. Way out
12. Air terminal
13. Tickets
14. Buffet
15. Buffet serving alcohol
16. Gentlemens toilet
17. Ladies toilet
18. Bus terminal
19. Coach terminal
20. Restaurant
21. Telephone
22. Taxi
23. Boat trains
24. No luggage trolleys
25. Beware—Pickpockets
26. Exchange Office

KASY BILETOWE ↖
KASA WYMIANY WALUT ←
WYJSCIE ←

DWORZEC KOLEJOWY →
PRZYSTAN KOLEJOWY →
PRZYSTANEK AUTOBUSOVY →

hand. I therefore proposed to produce the artwork to the size of the sign cases myself, by the use of rub down lettering and photoprints of the arrows and pictograms. This arrangement allowed me the flexibility to be able to alter the finer points as the signs were constructed. These artworks would then be shown to the LT Board for approval, before being photographed and same size negatives produced to be sandwiched in the front of the sign case between the back opel

glass and the (new) front clear glass. This method also allowed the use of perfectly reproduced pictograms.

To help the LT Board assimilate the pictograms without the help of descriptions, I asked Michael Kiersnovski, who worked in the

adjoining timetable office, to translate the various directions into his native Polish. The overall effect was to allow the viewers to appreciate the overall layout, individual applications (such as the size and weight of lettering, arrows and pictograms) and to make

them try to understand the meanings of the individual pictograms. It was from these meetings that some of the pictograms became more 'localised' – for instance, the tickets illustration was altered from first and second class to single and return.

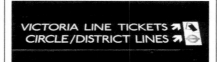

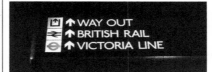

1976 Presentation mock-ups

To concentrate the minds of LT Board members onto the pictograms, the written directions were translated into the Polish language (assuming that it would not be understood). Produced full size, they showed graphically the planking discipline proposed to be adopted.

1976 Victoria booking hall signs

Close ups of some of the signs installed within the existing sign cases.

1976 Victoria booking hall signs

The signs in position within the ticket hall. The sign above the foot of the stairs, in the right hand picture, has not yet been altered.

1976   Heathrow Central
        pictogram signs

The signal engineers had not only planned the layouts and descriptions on each sign, but also specified where the signs were to be installed and ordered the sign cases. The page on the left shows their proposal while the right hand page shows how I adapted the message to be accommodated within the same sign case.

1976   Underground train
        pictogram

I designed this to complement the double decker bus pictogram. This replaced the coloured roundel initially used to indicate dirrerent Lines and was intended to be coloured in the same way.

Having fixed the layouts of the signs, the next task was to sift through the U.I.C. agreed pictograms since British Rail had the most stairwell connections with Victoria Underground station, not just to their main line station or their trains, but also for directions to boat trains and for tickets to boat trains as well as customs (for the international sleeping train). Whereas British Rail were quite happy at their station to accommodate all modes of road public transport within one pictogram, the positions of the separate bus and coach stations at Victoria necessitated, in my view, separate pictograms (additional descriptions using the words bus or coach would have demonstrated a flaw in the system). This consideration led to the perceived requirement that a separate pictogram was needed to describe Underground trains as opposed to main line trains (especially since BR had designed a particularly inter-city looking train to illustrate their services).

For the Victoria experiment the roundel was used to indicate Underground lines, contrasting with the BR symbol which indicated the main line station. The use of coloured roundels to indicate lines was a natural development from the coloured roundels on platform back wall friezes and inside the railway cars either end of the line diagram above the windows. Later, I developed a typically tube looking car end to contrast with the British Rail 'high speed train' front (most unrecognisable to the prototypical trains to be found at Victoria!).

Victoria Station had also been chosen because of its diversity to other transport options. Meanwhile, special notice was being taken of pictograms in use by airlines internationally since Victoria was a rehearsal for Heathrow Central which was to display pictograms throughout. The Heathrow signing coincided with Michael Levey's supersession to Bryce Beaumont as Publicity Officer and therefore the arbiter and driver of the Heathrow signing scheme. Michael had the credentials since he already chaired the U.I.T.P. working group into the standardisation of pictograms on metropolitan railways. But gathering information and collating it as a report and actually making decisions are two very different qualities.

My section was already producing layouts for temporary signs of all types, from directional signs to the large boards at building sites informing of their future purpose. Also, the specifications for signs

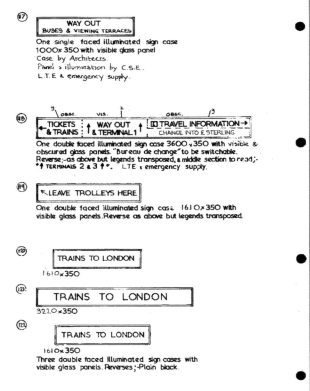

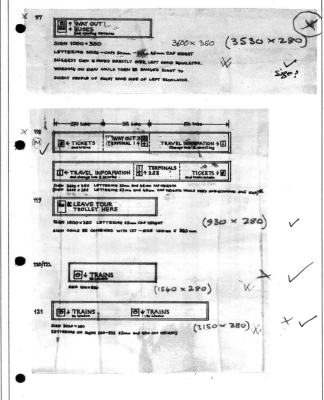

← A1 EXPRESS BUS
to Heathrow Airport
Pay as you enter

BUSES (across the road) ↗
to Cranford Colnbrook Harlington
Hayes Slough Uxbridge

indicating the various engineering projects in connection with the building of the Heathrow extension and regular meetings and the fixing of displays in the site huts at Hounslow. So I was allowed to depart from the official LT sign standards to do further experimental work with pictograms, arrows and stacking on signs to services affected by the building work.

Meanwhile, no one had told the architects or electrical engineers that the signing specifications for Heathrow Central station would be considerably altered. I was envisaging not only different graphic layouts but also different shaped boxes and also positions of signs. So, after asking repeatedly for plans to the station, the first I was shown was a document showing approved signing specifications, all in the traditional layout, boxes to fit the environment instead of the message, different size lettering to fit in the boxes instead of standard sizes. So I was told to fit my system into the boxes which had apparently already been ordered.

Michael went to signing meetings with my layouts using his U.I.T.P.

skills at funnelling differing views into one agreed concept. But at U.I.T.P. he was merely gathering the various opinions and leaving it to others to form the conclusions (usually those with the most self interest, loudest voices and financial clout). He conducted the Heathrow signing meetings in the same way, which meant that all options were considered and I endlessly re-drew the sign layouts to merely prove that many ideas were unworkable. Michael couldn't grasp that directions indicating straight on would still require a ranged left or right layout with an arrow one side or the other – not both sides. Even David Hughes, who was in charge of the project through Publicity's rail development section, ran out of patience with him and told him to come to a decision or the whole scheme would fail.

Once approval for my signing scheme was obtained, progress towards artwork and film positives proceeded swiftly. Perhaps because David wasn't confident that I could complete films in time or to standard, he had glass panels painted in the traditional way, by outside contractors since there was no time for the LT signwriters to complete them. But the result of the hand painted panels was poor Johnston lettering and even worse pictograms. Why hand copy these elements when they are all available in standardised form on film?

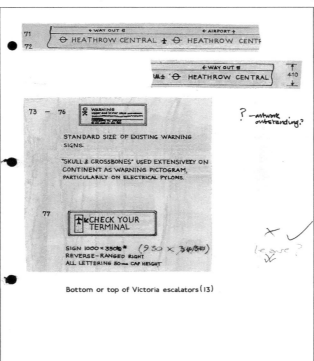

Bottom or top of Victoria escalators (13)

1977   Heathrow Central Station signing

Pictures showing the newly erected signing at the concourse and platform levels. The ranging left or right can be seen. The sign at the foot of the escalator shows how the scheme should not have looked – switchable signs should have be positioned above each escalator indicating precisely which escalator should be used. There should have been a sign at right angles preceding this sign that could be seen on leaving the platform indicating to the escalators.

Trains began regular running into and out of Heathrow Central Station on 16 December, following its official opening by Queen Elizabeth II earlier in the day.

Erection of the signs took place during the week before the opening of the station to reduce the risk of damage to them by the continuing erection ceiling panels and general cleaning up that was also being completed, such was the lateness of the project. Whilst I had all of the film ready for installation, it was found that for some signs the glass had been cut too large – by just a few millimetres. Many sign cases therefore had the hand painted versions installed, which fitted precisely! Some of these hand painted sign layouts differed from my film produced versions, by

having messages centred between pictograms on either side. It seemed that whenever there was a choice of two ways of doing something they always chose the wrong way – why could the people implementing the scheme fail to apply consistency.

I visited Heathrow infrequently following its opening, but have a feeling that the signs had a fairly short life, being replaced by the traditional type. With the retirement of the old guard at the helm of LT within about 18 months of each other, a form of anarchy prevailed while the new intake of management settled in.

London Transport never had a great commitment to a pictogram policy, intending that they would only be installed at important stations likely to be visited by tourists. At the same time, continental systems were proceeding apace and at least one, Netherlands Railways, were using signs displaying pictograms only wherever possible. With all its faults, my scheme was a long overdue update on the traditional signing layouts, but a commitment to plank sign displays would have to wait another 12 years until Henrion Ludlow & Schmidt submitted their scheme.

1977 Heathrow Central Station opening

Eric Wilkins, the Chief Public Relations Officer, studies the hand of Queen Elizabeth II when she came to open Heathrow Central Station on 16 December 1977. Eric Wilkins had provided me with a ticket to the subsequent banquet in one of the airport terminals in recognition of the work I had done signing the station.

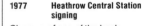

1977 Heathrow Central Station signing

Close up of one of the back-illuminated signs. As with all the signs at Heathrow Central, the plank arrangement was compromised to fit into sign cases designed for signs with traditional centred layouts.

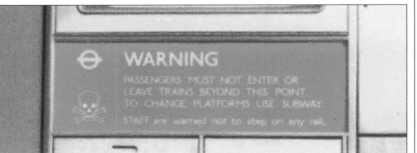

1977 Heathrow Central Station signing

The scull and crossbones illustration is widely used and understood in countries on the continent of Europe, on electrical equipment and pylons especially. This application at the end of the platform next to the tunnel mouth was removed soon after the station opened because it was considered to be too frightening! Surely a testimony to its effectiveness.

1979 London Underground diagrammatic map

My first attempt to design an Underground system map, based on Harry Beck's later map designs and my own design for the London's Railways map, which also owed much to Beck for the style of, especially, interchange stations.

I designed this map as an answer to the two designs, both by Paul Garbutt, that were currently in use for posters and folders and for diaries.

The rectangular Circle Line owed a lot to the final design produced by Harry Beck – there the similarity stops. A kink has been introduced onto the Northern Line to balance the Victoria Line and other lines running through the inside of the Circle Line area.

1972 British Rail Glasgow area diagrammatic map

Opposite page above shows the geographic area covered by the red lines to be redrawn as a diagrammatic map to the proportions below.

Opposite page below is the diagrammatic map drawn to the proportions of the space allowed for in carriage interiors. The focal point is the Glasgow Underground circle line, with Glasgow Central Station in the centre. The lines grow symmetrically from the centre. As on the London Underground diagrammatic map, the river system is represented as being a helpful location point.

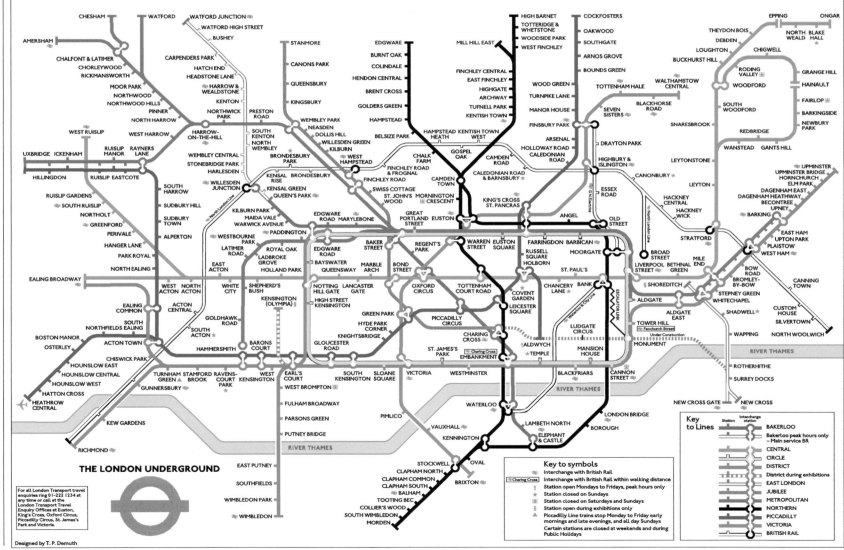

THE LONDON UNDERGROUND

For all London Transport travel enquiries ring 01-222 1234 at any time or call at the London Transport Travel Enquiry Offices at Euston, King's Cross, Oxford Circus, Piccadilly Circus, St. James's Park and Victoria.

Designed by T. P. Demuth

Key to symbols
Interchange with British Rail
Charing Cross — Interchange with British Rail within walking distance
↑ Station open Mondays to Fridays, peak hours only
★ Station closed on Sundays
⊞ Station closed on Saturdays and Sundays
§ Station open during exhibitions only
▲ Piccadilly Line trains stop Monday to Friday early mornings and late evenings, and all day Sundays
Certain stations are closed at weekends and during Public Holidays

Key to Lines
BAKERLOO
Bakerloo peak hours only – Main service BR
CENTRAL
CIRCLE
DISTRICT
District during exhibitions
EAST LONDON
JUBILEE
METROPOLITAN
NORTHERN
PICCADILLY
VICTORIA
BRITISH RAIL

© London Transport Executive 1979

One of the most important duties undertaken by the Publicity Office studio, at the time when I joined London Transport in 1971, was the responsibility for the preperation and supply of artworks of the Underground diagrammatic map to outside printing and publishing organisations for inclusion in their own publications. These maps were known as 'Diary' maps since many appeared in pocket and desk diaries. A small studio staff provided the service of sorting standard maps, constructing special maps to clients requirements or individual proportions by cutting and pasting elements from the stock of artworks. Diary map designs have always been based on the current Underground diagram map and they are still produced, although now, digitally.

Once installed in the studio, one of the first diagrammatic map exercises, entailing the design of a map from scratch, was not for a department of London Transport, but for the Scottish Region of British Railways. The different transport undertakings that had been taken under the national umbrella in 1948, and later joined by a large number of provincial bus companies, enjoyed a considerable degree of co-operation regarding their professional assets. Although British Rail had been producing its own diagrammatic London and South East map (which was drawn by a private studio and purchased through BR's Central Advertising Department) their individual regions still handled localised advertising. An informal relationship then existed between the different nationalised undertakings, often based on personal acquaintances, so the Scottish Region would have felt free to approach London Transport for their known practical experience, also knowing that any financial charges would be for costs only rather than the profits built in by private studios.

The particular map required was aimed to show the suburban rail services operating around Glasgow. The proportion was giving problems since the display area inside trains was landscape, while the actual geographic area covered was upright. This was the most fertile territory for showing the advantages of a diagrammatic format to solve certain space problems. The map submitted was not, in the end, used by the Scottish Region, since the area was subjected to economies which put question marks over some of the lines shown. However, once the system settled down to a more permanent format, they produced their own map based on the design submitted by London Transport's Publicity Office.

Other maps produced for outside organisations came near the close of my career in the Publicity Department. In the 1980s London Transport departments became profit

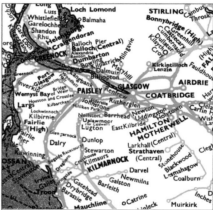

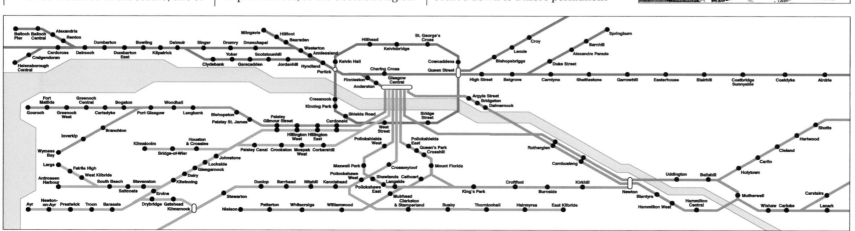

1983   Eurostar map

From a very vague brief (but
in other respects very tight,
concerning the representation
of coastlines) the design was
developed around the italic star
forming part of the Eurostar
logo. Although not winning the
competition, this map had an
influence on later maps that
appeared in Eurostar publicity.

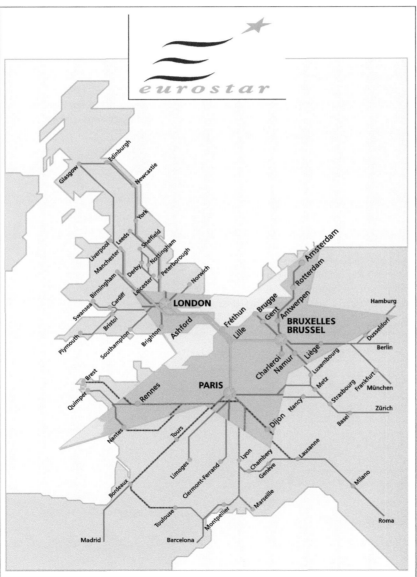

centres, which meant that if they
couldn't produce accounts to show
that they were breaking even, they
would be closed. The other alternative
was that they would be sold or given
to their local management and formed
into separate independent companies.
This was a cynical move by the
government to boost the private sector
which very often led to price increases
to the LT departments that remained.
The Publicity Office was not immune.
From being a service department to
the rest of the organisation, Publicity
found itself having to compete for
work from departments which had
dwindling budgets and were using
outside suppliers. The other side
to this equation (and one that the
government can never have predicted)
was that Publicity was allowed
to compete for work from outside
organisations.

One organisation to require
graphic expertise was the Eurostar
consortium, owned by the Belgian,
British and French nationally owned
railways, which was due to commence
services between Paris, Brussels and
London, via the shortly to be opened
Channel Tunnel. The consortium
was required by European Union
regulations to put out commercial
tenders for the work. They needed a
map of services, which would also
show the proposed extensions and
high speed connections. The brief
was French biassed (which is not
surprising since the French had

invested by far the most on high speed
rail lines and had also built the trains)
but was vague as to which connecting
lines were actually to be shown
– enough trains were being built to
run services through the tunnel from
Edinburgh, Leeds, Manchester and
Birmingham to Paris and Brussels
as well as overnight sleeping trains
from these points to the outer reaches
of France – although I suspected that
the French map designers received
more cooperation that I did by dint of
personally knowing the people they
were dealing with.

A proposal was submitted, in
English and French, with suggested
designs for the map of the system,
backed up by practical considerations
such as black and white reproduction
of the same map and small
reproduction in pocket diaries,
together with costings for the various
types of reproduction envisaged. The
presentation to representatives of the
consortium was intended to be in
their British office at East Croydon.
This had to be cancelled because of
a rail strike meaning that some of
the delegates would have been left
stranded. Their next meeting was at
the Eurostar office in Paris, which
gave our Publicity Manager problems
since he was reluctant to spend the
money on overnight accommodation
or allow two days out of the office.
There is something psychological
about leaving the country – if the
meeting had been changed to an

address in Wigan there would have been no problem. And this parochial attitude manifested itself in other ways too – it was only possible to dial abroad from a single telephone in the boss's office, but calls could be made from any office phone to the far north of Scotland or Ireland, 1000km away. So, after a friendly send off from my comrades in the office my colleague, Helen Henderson, and myself flew from Heathrow to Charles de Gaulle airport in Paris on a day trip. Helen was in command of considerable experience as an account manager as well as speaking fluent French. I had not had much contact with her in the office, since she either dealt with other designers or with other aspects of publicity and advertising. Once the Paris meeting commenced, she conducted the verbal side with a confidence which I thankfully caught from her, as I submitted the

graphics. We withdrew for a short period until being called back to be told, unsurprisingly, that we were not successful. But we left the meeting with the feeling that the consortium had been slightly embarrassed by the high standard of our submission even though they had made up their minds before the meeting even started who would clinch the contract. However, it was with relief that we departed from the precious atmosphere and found our way in Parisian sunshine to a street-side bar to discuss the event. As *madame* brought a succession of *bière á la pression* to relieve a very warm afternoon, conversations between Helen and myself led to a friendship between us that would probably never have had the chance to start had we not been thrown together on this trip. We flew back to Heathrow that evening and made our way to central London and the *Duke of Buckingham*

in Petty France (a coincidental choice of street names), where we were welcomed by some of our colleagues, notably Kim Kavanagh who was one of Helen's fellow account handlers, and Mike Welch my old studio stalwart, who had waited late to hear the result from us. London Transport colleagues were probably more faithful than any others that I have worked with.

Another request from an outside organisation came from a former office colleague, Mike Parker. Mike had used the experience gained from directing London Transport's bus marketing department and its international expertise arm to elevate himself to running the very forward looking Tyne & Wear Transport. Their Metro was being expanded to take over the operation of suburban lines between Newcastle and Sunderland from British Rail, and Mike asked me to construct a diagrammatic map to

show the enlarged system, but within the same image area as the existing maps inside their trains. This was a similar problem to that encountered with the Glasgow map where the geographic shape was at odds with the map area, Sunderland being positioned very much to the south of the existing Tyne & Wear system.

London's Railways

I had been working at London Transport for less than a year, in a position that was regarded as no more than a jobbing designer and artworker, when the Publicity Officer, Bryce Beaumont, asked me if I would attempt to design a diagrammatic map featuring Underground and British Rail suburban lines together within the London area. If it wasn't the first time this challenge had ever been approached, it was certainly the first time a diagrammatic map showing both systems in conjunction with each other had ever been printed. This map was intended to replace a geographic map of greater London showing bus and coach roads as well as all rail lines. Since the loss of the green country buses and Green Line coaches, the map had lost much of its planned function – indeed Bryce believed that its greatest use was when relatives visited each other for Sunday lunch using their cars!

The design for this new diagrammatic railway map was

Key
- ○ Metro interchange
- ⇌ British Rail interchange
- 🚌 Bus interchange
- 🛒 Shopping centre
- ⛴ Ferry
- ✈ Air connections
- 🅿 Station car park

Tyne and Wear Metro

1990   Tyne & Wear Transport

Adaptation of the existing Tyne & Wear Metro car interior diagrammatic map with the addition of the line to Sunderland that was being converted from the British Rail line. For neatness and uniformity, all station names are positioned diagonally. Once again, representation of water is helpful in finding locations on the map.

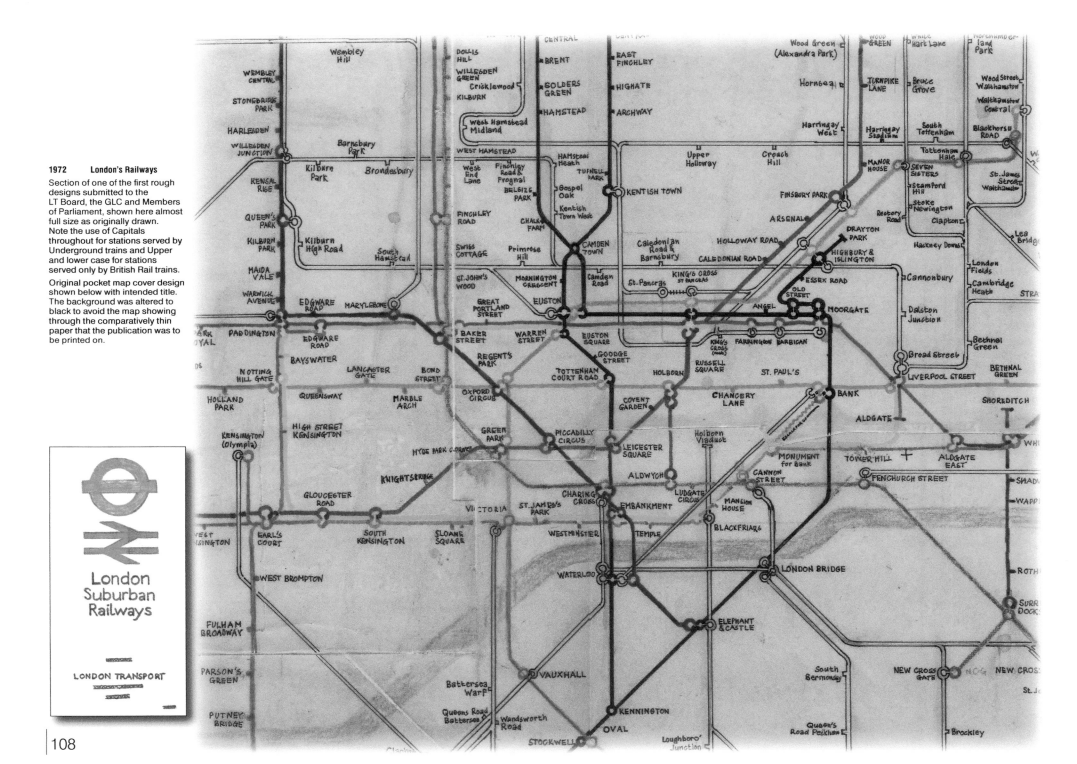

1972   London's Railways

Section of one of the first rough designs submitted to the LT Board, the GLC and Members of Parliament, shown here almost full size as originally drawn. Note the use of Capitals throughout for stations served by Underground trains and Upper and lower case for stations served only by British Rail trains.

Original pocket map cover design shown below with intended title. The background was altered to black to avoid the map showing through the comparatively thin paper that the publication was to be printed on.

London
Suburban
Railways

LONDON TRANSPORT

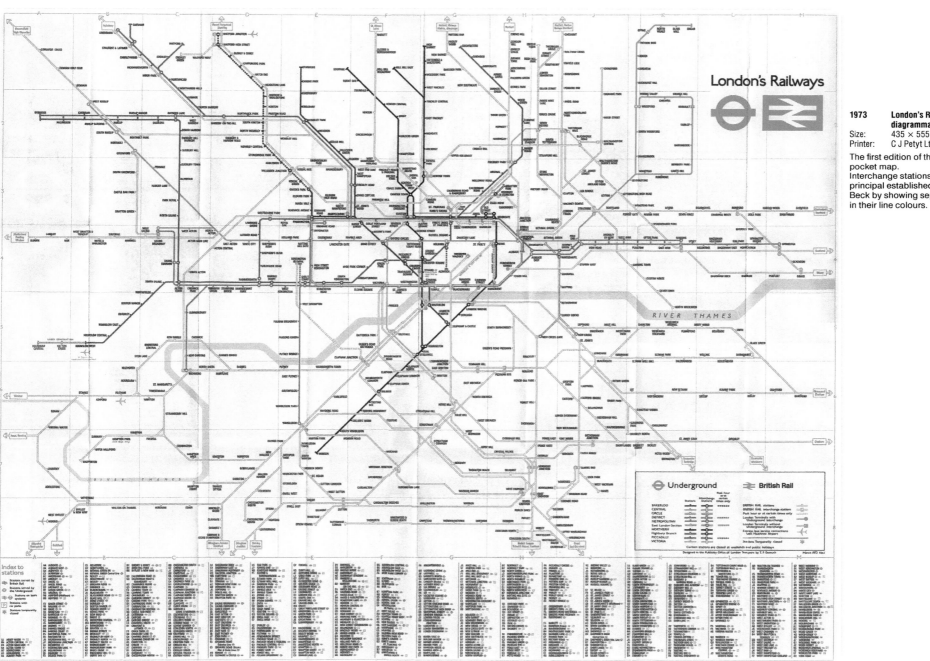

London's Railways

1973   **London's Railways**
diagrammatic map
Size: 435 × 555 mm
Printer: C J Petyt Ltd

The first edition of the folded
pocket map.
Interchange stations follow the
principal established by Harry
Beck by showing separate circles
in their line colours.

1973   London Railways map
          press release

Reproduction of the news item,
introducing the new London's
Railways map, which appeared in
the August 1973 issue of RAILWAY
WORLD magazine,

LT and BR on the map

A new diagrammatic map showing both the Underground and British Rail lines in the London area has been designed by London Transport and is now being issued. It has been produced in two sizes—pocket folder map for passengers and wall-poster map for stations. The map contains more than 600 Underground and British Rail stations, which are listed at the foot of the map in alphabetical order with grid references. London Transport and British Rail symbols are used with this index, so that the 60 stations which are jointly served can be easily identified. All stations with car parking facilities are indicated with a boxed " P " in blue. The new map, designed by Tim Demuth of London Transport's Publicity Office, will replace the geographic *London's Transport Systems* map and will be additional to the existing Underground diagrammatic map, which will continue to be available as a guide exclusively to the London Underground system.

drawn on tracing paper using Rotring rapidograph fine tipped pens for the outlines to lines and lettering, filled in when required by coloured felt tipped pens. I had already taken the decision to use a condensed typeface, Univers bold condensed, for the names of over 400 stations. I didn't know what the final size of my drawing would be until it was finished, since I started drawing from the middle and worked outwards. This drawing took about a year in 1972–3, slotted in between all the other design and artwork projects needed to service this great transport organisation. Whilst the natural boundary to the Underground system was at the ends of the lines, a more vexing question was where to fix the outer limits of British Rail lines. A combination of the outer limits of London Transport's Underground as well as bus systems was the compromise. In the north, Amersham and Ongar were included, even though they were considerably further out than the limit of the red bus network. In the south, Weybridge, Cobham and Leatherhead stations formed the limit since all were served by London's red buses (although some of the intermediate stations closer to London were not). Once the initial drawing had been completed, it was submitted to the LT Board, who submitted it in turn to the Greater London Council and London Members of Parliament. One MP in particular could not understand the

reasoning behind diagrammatic map designs, and insisted on all lines being represented by their correct length in relation to each other (rather like a geographic map drawn with straight lines). This consumed a lot of my time since I had to draw a giant unbalanced map merely to prove that this approach defeated the reason for a diagrammatic map. There have been many instances when I have had to produce designs just to prove to the person insisting on it that their ideas are flawed. But I was now in the spotlight of not only the top people at London Transport, but elected Members in the House too. This wasn't the time to be seen to be digging in my heals on points of principal. Rather, to appear accommodating and co-operative – I was in a position that few graphic designers had enjoyed.

The artwork for this map was produced by David Penrose at Cook Hammond & Kell, cartographers at Mitcham in Surrey. The first proof that David produced, which he showed to me in dyeline form, contained a number of elements, such as junctions and juxtapositions between lines, that had never been on my rough. He had not been aware that I link unconnected lines to form patterns, which also reduces the superiority of one line over another. This is where the design element comes into a diagram map, which isn't necessarily possessed by the skills of a cartographer. He was quite open

about the fact that he thought his version was better, so that was why he had done it that way. This created some animosity and determined me to check his work much more thoroughly than I would normally have done. The reason why cartographic companies were used to produce diagrammatic map artwork rather than commercial studios, was that cartographers drew with tools that scratched onto negative film (rather like engraving). This system produced lines of consistent thickness, now achieved just as successfully by computer.

Car Diagrams

The studio section run by myself was also responsible for the upkeep of car interior line diagrams. When I arrived at London Transport I found that the design of these maps had been allowed to deteriorate to a very messy degree. Amendments to designs were generally made by the printer's studio and only checked for their informational accuracy, rather than their aesthetic quality, at the London Transport end. Maps also appeared in car interiors drawn to different sizes depending on the amount of information that they contained, a practice also prevalent on the typography of bus timetables. I settled on a standard type size on maps that was smaller than some of the more spacious versions, but also larger than at least one congested version. Instead

of making radical changes, which would have required approval at high level with its consequent delay (and compromise), I tidied up the design of each diagram at its next reprint, making further gradual changes at each reprint. I also did a survey of the most convenient stations for interchanging (not necessarily the same as those on the Underground diagrammatic system map which has to cover journeys on all lines from all directions) on each line. Often reprints were implemented to replenish stocks rather than because of actual alterations to the system. I would use these opportunities to make any further improvements which had become feasible since the previous printing. I also entrusted the artwork to a graphic design studio, where greater control could be exercised than the former practice of commissioning each printer to produce artwork for the maps they were printing. The first studio that I used was Bateson Graphics at Vauxhall Bridge Road near Victoria Station, where a budding young artworker called Alan Foale drew each diagram full size. Together with John Slater, one of the reps at Batesons, Alan went on to set up Clockwork Studio near Oxford Circus, where he continued to draw these car diagrams. His Studio has drawn these maps ever since, first with pen, ink and glue, and now digitally by computer.

The new D-Stock trains being

designed in 1978 for the District Line gave me the opportunity to liaise directly with the drawing office staff at Acton Railway Works. Normally, in the days when new railway cars were designed at Acton, the Publicity Office was given the dimensions that they were to work within, but I wanted to take things a stage further by offering suggestions which might result in my map area getting a better showing. I found that got on well with Ron Veness, with his dry cynical humour, who ran the drawing office. The maps inside the D-Stock were to be made from melamine, which was the same material that was being used to form the rest of the interiors – the melamine maps would therefore bridge the area between wall and ceiling. The window seating and door standing bays in which the maps were to span were of basically four different lengths. I devised a system using a combination of a standard width of diagram (the widest that a commercial printer could handle without special equipment) and central area map, and a panel containing a green roundel for line identification. Ron discovered that a space would have to be left, in the areas of the car

diagrams, to access the sliding door mechanisms. Normally, this area would coincide with the position of the car card advertisements, which meant that hinged panels could be exposed by removing one or more of the cardboard mounted car cards. I did not want my maps to be moved to a less visual position, so I suggested that the maps themselves should be manufactured as hinged panels. Ron accepted this idea and designed aluminium framed panels that accommodated and held the different elements of car diagram, central area map and line identification, in position, hinged at the top by a piano hinge and secured at the bottom by about four screws. This to me was the way that different departments should work – each making suggestions to solve common problems.

The next new trains were the 1983-Stock for the Jubilee Line, when I again liaised with Acton Works and

Ron, but these were to be the last. As part of the government's privatisation plans and general smearing of anything produced by the state sector as being old fashioned and inefficient, the designs of subsequent trains were put out to private contractors who, in their turn outworked the designs to consultancies. The areas that suffered most were those containing my car diagrams. Three prototype trains were designed and completed in 1987 by different manufacturers. I was given the dimensions of the diagrams in each which all displayed the Central Line. All were smaller in width and depth than the diagrams inside the existing tube stock, although I was determined that the graphics would be retained to the standard size. When I went to Woodford Station to install the diagrams inside the trains for a special display, I saw why the area for diagrams were so constrained. Inside some of the cars, ventilators occupied

parts of the traditional position. Inside one of the trains, the diagrams had to be applied to panels running across the windows, there being no available space above them. Future trains, all designed by the private sector, repeated the lack of liaison between train and graphic designers, with the result that line diagrams appear to this day on some to be an afterthought.

From time to time the bus departments required route diagrams to publicise individual or small groups of routes which could be conveniently displayed inside buses without creating a straight jacket for the vehicles' availability to work other routes. The justification for these maps was usually to display special features on a particular route, or to highlight routes that had been earmarked as being helpful for shoppers. These small runs of maps which, because of their localised and often short term nature, usually did not require design

1980   Q Stock car diagram
1984   D Stock car diagram

The section illustrated top row left shows the level of scruffiness that had overtaken the design of car diagrams. There is no discipline as to interchange boxes above or below the line, or whether they are shared, to the point that it looks as if it is possible to walk through the BR station connecting Gunnersbury with Wimbledon.

The top row right section of map is that produced for new District Line rolling stock, and follows a style developed in the early 1970s and gradually introduced on maps for all lines as they became due for reprints.

On lines without loops diagrams could be 'handed' as the version below shows. This meant that points on the diagram remained at the same position on both sides of the car.

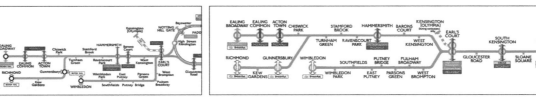

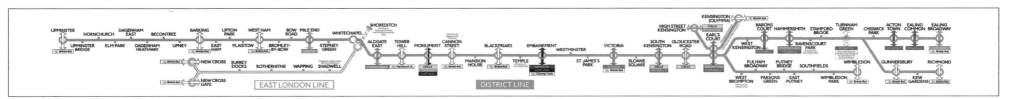

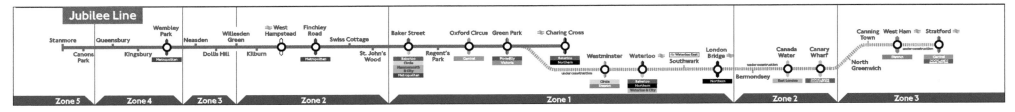

1996 **Jubilee Line car interior diagram**

The Underground has always liked to promote new lines being built although their inclusion is of little use to the person following the diagram for an actual journey. The trains carrying these diagrams were replaced by specially designed stock for the extension.

1988 **Route 207 bus interior diagram**

Map produced to show the overlapping sections of bus route being adapted to give waiting times at bus stops. The opportunity was taken to dispense with arrows running through interchange points on this localised diagram, to test reactions before recommending this simplification in style on reprints of Underground car interior diagrams.

1996 **Northern Line car interior diagram**

The elimination of what had become the meaningless arrows separating interchange stations from their boxes allowed both elements to be moved closer to the interchange circles. On this particular map the space saved was critical for the successful integration of the interchange boxes and station names in the central area.

approval at high level. They therefore gave me the chance to experiment with changes that could later, if successful, be applied to railway car diagrams. One such was to test the feasibility of printing the different line colours from the four process colours, as opposed to using self colours for each line.

Fleet Line

The projected Fleet Line formed only a small amount of additional line, the bulk of it being the transfer of the Stanmore to Baker Street section of the Bakerloo Line, most of which had in 1938 been transferred from the Metropolitan to the Bakerloo.

On the question of the Fleet Line's colour, a lesson was learned from the development of the Victoria Line's colour. In that instance, a lilac shade was intended, but it was not until station signs came to be manufactured that the exact colour proved to be impossible for the enamelling process to reproduce – the resultant shade becoming the present pale blue.

I liaised with the very affable and always practical Howard Butler, who had moved from the Bus Development section to succeeded Tom See as leader of the Rail Development section. The functions of the Bus and Rail Development sections was the measuring and ordering of public information signing, as well as the fixing of all in-house poster and

timetable publicity on bus stops and bus and Underground poster sites.

For the Fleet Line, enamelled iron swatches were produced in shades of grey (the chosen colour) varying from pink and blue hues to one containing a little green. It was this final greeny-grey that proved to be the shade easiest to manufacture in stove enamelled iron, as opposed to a mixture of black and white. Grey formed from black and white pigments only was not particularly practical when it came to printing on paper since the pigments tended to separate after mixing. However, the attraction of a grey containing no other colours was that it could be printed as a tint of black. In practice, when a mix of black and white printing was exposed to sunlight it faded to lime green whereas a tint of black was as colour fast as black. On the enamelled iron side a shade close to the printing tint was aimed for. The original samples

were left on the roof of Griffith House for a number of years to test their colour fastness.

Planning for the insertion of the Fleet Line on the Underground map was made in the Publicity Office by cutting up printed copies of the existing quad royal map and re-positioning the sections. The fact that Baker Street station could be moved to the left to be above Bond Street station made the connection easy. The section from Bond Street to Trafalgar Square presented few difficulties. Beyond Trafalgar Square the trajectory of the route was established to connect with Aldwych Piccadilly Line Station, a new station at Ludgate Circus, Cannon Street District Line Station and a new station connecting Tower Hill but incorporating the name Fenchurch Street. Then the possible connecting link with the southern portion of the East London Line, to New Gross Station. From New Cross a plan

emerged for taking over or sharing all or part of one of the existing British Railways lines towards Dartford, probably that via Barnhurst. But this group of lines were amongst the most profitable sections of BR's Southern Region. So instead, a loss making branch from Lewisham to the back of Croydon at Addiscombe Road and to Hayes was offered by the Southern for transfer to Fleet Line operation.

As part of the work on the Underground diagrammatic map to accommodate the Fleet Line, other amendments were being made to its design. The left end of the Circle Line was deepened to accommodate the Victoria Line between King's Cross St.Pancras and Victoria. The right hand end of the Circle Line was also deepened with the inclusion of the Fleet Line so as to allow a horizontal continuation from the combined Strand and Trafalgar Square stations (which would become Charing

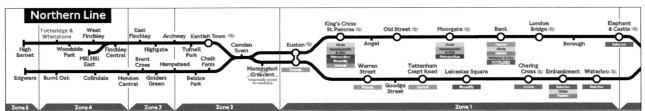

Cross) to Cannon Street and Tower Hill before it curved downwards to join the East London Line. The two other intermediate stations east of Charing Cross were Aldwych which was connected to an elongated Piccadilly Line branch from Holborn and Monument. With this horizontal section dictating the position of the Charing Cross station interchange with the Bakerloo and Northern lines the vertical spacing of Northern Line stations within the Circle Line were balanced by moving the Central Line to a similar position that it held before the inclusion of the Victoria Line.

The section of the Fleet Line from its junction with the Bakerloo Line to a point just east of the Northern Line Strand Station only was authorised in July 1969 – the further section from east of Strand to Fenchurch Street was expected to receive Royal Assent in the next (1968/69 session of Parliament). This gave plenty of time to redraw maps which would include the new line, to be shown by its building stage as well as when it was opened, which was expected to be during 1976.

In the early 1970s artwork for the map was produced by Waterlow & Sons, one of a handful of printers whose experience with London Underground work went back at least 50 years. Since the end of World War II Waterlows generally printed the poster Underground maps while Johnson Riddle & Co had printed folder maps,

and continued to do so until they went into liquidation in the 1980s.

Diary maps

It was during this process of accommodating the Jubilee Line on a poster size map that the size of the station names was reduced. This reduction was not enough to affect the readability of the poster or folder maps. However, the problem with smaller maps was highlighted by Collins Diaries who were so dissatisfied with the reduced name size that they threatened to stop reproducing the Underground map inside their diaries. Collins was one of the more important diary manufacturers and the inclusion of the Underground map provided invaluable publicity for London Transport. LT did not charge clients for artworks of their maps, being worried that this valuable source of advertising might dry up if it did so. Paul Garbutt was approached to redesign the portions of the Underground map which could not accommodate enlarged station names. His solutions in many cases was to hyphenate awkward names – Uxbridge in particular is remembered as being spelt Ux-bridge in two lines, but there were other instances.

The resultant map was definitely not as good as the one that it replaced – the Northern Line City branch made a very long horizontal trajectory from

THE LONDON UNDERGROUND

London Bridge to Kennington. Some of the radii of corners were very suspect (as at Euston) and many angles were replaced with right angled curves losing some of the former flow. It was for this reason that the new design was confined to artworks that were being sent to commercial firms, mainly manufacturers of pocket diaries. Very few colour versions of these maps appeared in London Transport's own publications, the pocket version being preferred, while diary maps with coded lines did appear on LTs own monochrome printed publications since these were the only black and white artworks available. It was for this reason that I saw the solution would be to redesign the Underground map in a way that we could return

to just two artworks, one for colour reproduction and the same design for black and white reproduction.

Because of the needs of diary publishers who required 18 months from reception of artwork to their dates of publication and as a result of the lateness of the opening of the Jubilee Line, I advised that subsequent diary maps should not carry dates of expected changes. But this would not have avoided the Fleet Line appearing on maps long after its name had officially been changed to Jubilee Line – diaries for 1977 appeared with the Fleet Line open when the reality was that the name had already been altered. Keys to diary maps were left generally without station opening and closing times which could be altered

1981   Diagrammatic diary map

This drawing was the result of modifications made to the original design, reducing the number of interchange circles to the fewest possible. This particular artwork was intended for black and white reproduction.

A development of my first design
of 1979. I had been forced to
reduce the number of interchange
circles to as few as possible
making interchange at some
stations, such as Finchley Road
or Woodford, look more compex
than at Green Park or Oxford
Circus, which was far from the
real situation.
The Fleet Line, later to become
the Jubilee Line, is shown in
its planned trajectory between
Charing Cross and the East
London Line.

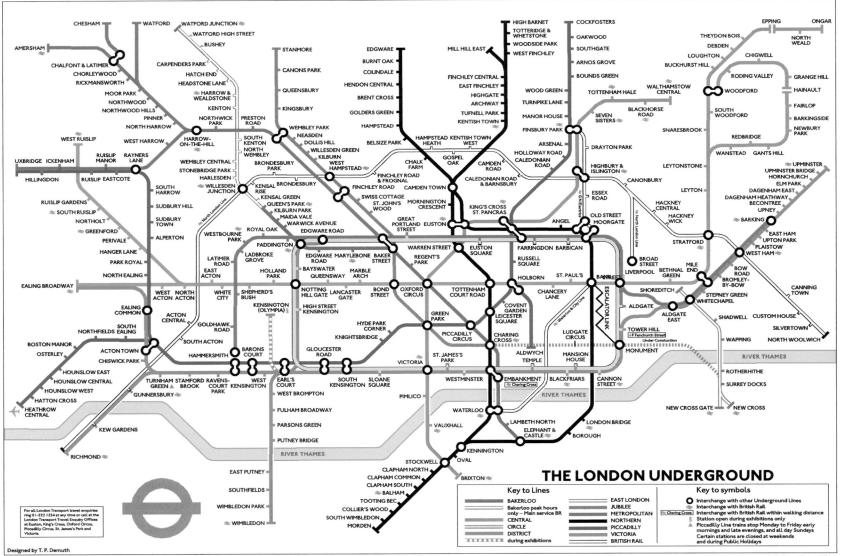

Designed by T. P. Demuth

by the operators quickly (and often were as the Underground's financial situation worsened),

The entire situation was very complicated. Whenever alterations were considered for the main poster/folder designs they had to be ascertained as to their feasibility for the diary designs. They were then sent for approval to Paul Garbutt, which was often a lengthy process. A new design for all needs was urgent.

A new Underground map

I did preliminary work on the design of an Underground map following my own graphic standards adopted for the London's Railways map. The main features revolved around interchange stations. I was keen to return to the principles developed by Harry Beck, using a rectangular Circle Line and separate interchange circles in their own line colours for each interchange. I didn't like the pervading map treatment where interchange stations were represented by one black interchange circle, except where the position of lines meant that two or more circles would be used. This treatment made some insignificant stations, such as Woodford or Finchley Road, look more important than Oxford Circus. A discussion ensued between Paul Garbutt and myself over how many kinks to lines there were on his map compared to mine. While his had more kinks within the Circle

Line, my had more outside the area, so it proved nothing. The design for my map was basically approved in 1979, while Michael Levey was in the process of vacating has short lived post as Publicity Officer following Bryce Beaumont's retirement just a year earlier. The turmoil caused by another change at the top might have helped the approval of my design – there were far bigger problems pressing those at the top. The black and white map appeared in a number of publications, both those of London Transport and some for outside clients, notably within British Rail's national 1982–3 timetable. Artwork for the colour version proceeded at a time when a new poster map was not actually needed. The colour version never appeared in its entirety, but the central section was produced for display inside tube cars. It was also reproduced as a board game called The London Game by Seven Towns Ltd.

Before new posters and folder maps were required there were further changes at the head of publicity, with the departure of Michael Levey and arrival of Nick Lewis. Lewis demanded alterations to the map before he would agree to its printing. He wanted all interchange circles to revert to one per station (something that Garbutt had never achieved). Many treatments were experimented with, including one in the Hutchison style with all lines merging at

interchange stations. The compromise was to adapt the Demuth map to the Garbutt interchange treatment of black circles.

The Underground map was also useful as an aid to recommendations both visually and graphically to departments within the Underground. When the C-Stock took over operation of the Metropolitan's Hammersmith & City section, the Circle Line and District's Wimbledon to Edgware Road section, the latter was left in District Line green. The public couldn't understand why this portion of the District Line was isolated onto another line's map – they weren't aware of the complexities of railway operation.

My proposal was to transfer the portion from Edgware Road to High Street Kensington to Metropolitan Line operation – the staff had always enjoyed Metropolitan Line conditions of service – and show the section from Earl's Court to Wimbledon as dual operation with the District Line, in much the same way as between Aldgate East and Barking. To explain the proposal I adapted the current car interior diagrams and the poster Underground diagrammatic map.

As a separate, but connected study, I proposed that the Metropolitan and Hammersmith & City lines should be shown as separate entities, since they each had dedicated trains running

1981   The London Game
Size: 450 × 630 mm
Producer: Seven Towns Ltd

The concept of this game was loosely based on Monopoly, in that prizes or penalties were awarded according to which point on the board was landed at. Although the map was drawn especially, it was based on the design finding its way onto official London Transport publicity.

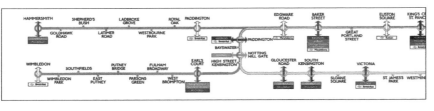

1978 **Wimbledon to Edgware Road section and Metropolitan Line display**

Mock-ups prepared to illustrate how maps might look if the Edgware Road – Wimbledon section was transferred to the Metropolitan Line and the Amersham, Chesham, Watford and Uxbridge branches were transferred to a new line called the Chiltern Line.

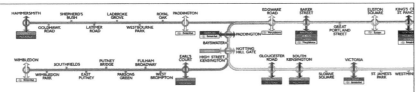

over them. In this case I retained the name Metropolitan and colour for the Hammersmith to Barking section, since within this portion is the original Metropolitan Railway. The line from Aldgate to Amersham, Chesham, Watford and Uxbridge would alter its colour to a dark green and change its name to Chiltern Line.

These proposals were accepted in principal by the Chief Operating Manager of the railways. However, they couldn't be implemented until money could be found to alter the signs on the stations concerned and all stations connecting with those lines. By the time money became available, heads had changed and a different course of action was taken.

The Underground system had settled down to a long period when there were no alterations to it and there was no reason to spend more time and money redrawing and reprinting it, so the Garbutt poster/ folder and diary maps continued in production. This coincided with me being seconded to other duties for a number of months. I returned to find that Lewis had removed the responsibility for the design, updating and artwork of the London's Railways map from me, despite assurances, from his assistant, Thelma Wright, that it was being saved for me to come back to (Beck's history repeating itself). The London's Railways map (renamed London Connections) was sent to a firm called Cooper Thirkell where it was crudely redrawn utilising a particularly undistinguished type face for the display of the station names. During the 1980s the map gradually died, which wasn't surprising since it possessed no

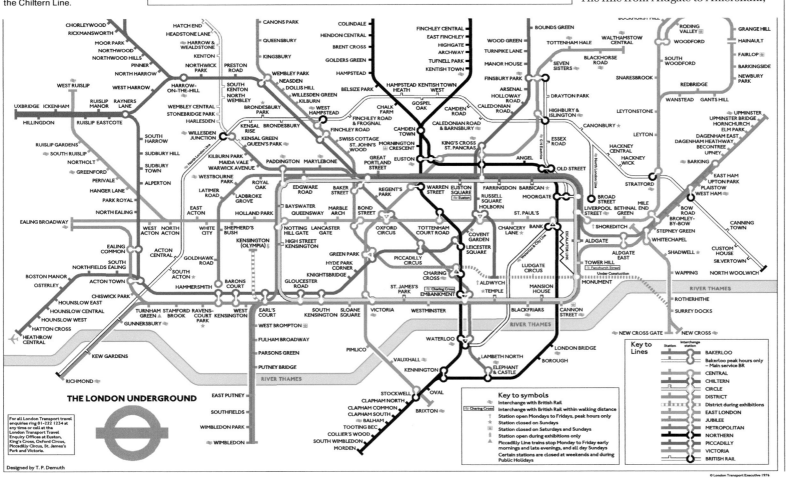

design significance whatever and was difficult to read.

In the early 1980s I was invited by the Commercial Office to prepare rough designs to show the zonal fare structure. They had produced a very crude map with the zonal boundaries weaving around station names and were expecting me to artwork just a neater version. Instead, I managed to formalise the fare zones into a series of concentric roughly octagonally diamond shapes. This was achieved by moving some of the station names up or down their respective lines. This neat solution returned me to the credibility of being recognised as a design expert, not by Nick Lewis since I lacked an advertising agency inspired superficial charisma, but by the Director of Marketing, Basil Hooper. He not only gave me responsibility for the design standards of the map, but also any project which involved the Underground map.

During the 1980s the artwork for the Underground map was drawn by Thames Cartographic at Maidenhead.

Between 1981 and 1985 all lettering was changed to upper and lower case on the recommendation of the Marketing Manager. On his Underground map design of 1968, Harold Hutchison, had retained Capitals to indicate 'important' stations while displaying 'other stations' in Upper and lower case. He also adopted this style of lettering on his new style 'diagonal' track

plates and bifurcation signs. In 1973 I persuaded Bryce Beaumont that we should revert to Upper case throughout – the most important stations on the map are the ones that form the start and finish of any individual journey and they did not necessarily appear in Capitals.

In the early 1990s all Underground publicity was put under the scrutiny of the design consultant Henrion Ludlow & Smith While there were radical changes to the layouts of informational posters and signs, the Underground map was affected by having the colour of its lettering changed from black to a mid blue (not the dark bronze blue of some years earlier). But more serious was their attempt to standardise the line colours based on similarities of tonal values. Over many years, experiments had been conducted in conjunction with printing ink manufacturers as to the most practical hues and shades for each of the line colours, which were then printed and tested for long periods outside, on the roof of Griffith House, to see how they were affected by direct and indirect sun light. All Underground line colours were manufactured by the Coates Printing ink manufacturer. These were then matched by the British Standards Institute to their range of colours, our tests of colour fastness making an important contribution to the work that they conducted in respect of the colours in their entire range.

From the 1987 map the HLS approved colours were used. Some of the colours on posters faded quickly, and still do. Also, in their efforts to arrive at a similar tone for all hues, the differences in line colours became harder to distinguish, especially in shadows or when lighting is not bright, conditions which are regularly encountered on many parts of the Underground. This can be seen to this day, particularly on the Underground map – the company's flagship – and on other posters that are posted outside.

Whilst gradually establishing a reputation for my expertise on the visual and production of diagrammatic maps, and gathered control of most items, a separate Rail Marketing Department was established which would ascertain particular needs which would be bought in from the Advertising & Publicity Department. David Hughes was put in charge of information in this new department and he proceeded to fill it with clerks who would actually attempt to design the items that they were responsible for progressing – the Advertising & Publicity Department being merely employed to produce the artwork. The car diagrams, which I had spent so many years bringing up to a uniformly high standard, were devolved to David Pickles, who had already made an impression on me by altering the typographic specifications that I had devised for bus timetables by the

crude use of bold type. During his tenure, he made no innovations at all to the car diagrams, even allowing some of the design connections between elements to be destroyed and allowing design howlers to re-appear with consistent regularity on each reprint. He annoyed the print buyers and printers by treating the line diagrams as quality fine art productions by refusing to approve anything but complete perfection. Pickles next tried to take over the Underground map, but had to accept that neither he nor the new assistant, Judy, possessed the professionalism when they jointly passed a map for printing in my absence which had to be reprinted because they had allowed so many mistakes to go uncorrected.

Once I had gained full control of the Underground map, I was then consulted, as a matter of course, over any reprints that were required. The artwork was a gift for production by computer, and it meant that a reprint made necessary by a small alteration to a piece of information in the key gave me the chance to make any design improvements – and improvements always came to mind in the weeks following a new printing when I was just musing in front of the poster map whilst waiting for a train. I was also helped in the late 1980s by a request from the Underground planning office to design a map showing the system of the future. There were many lines that the

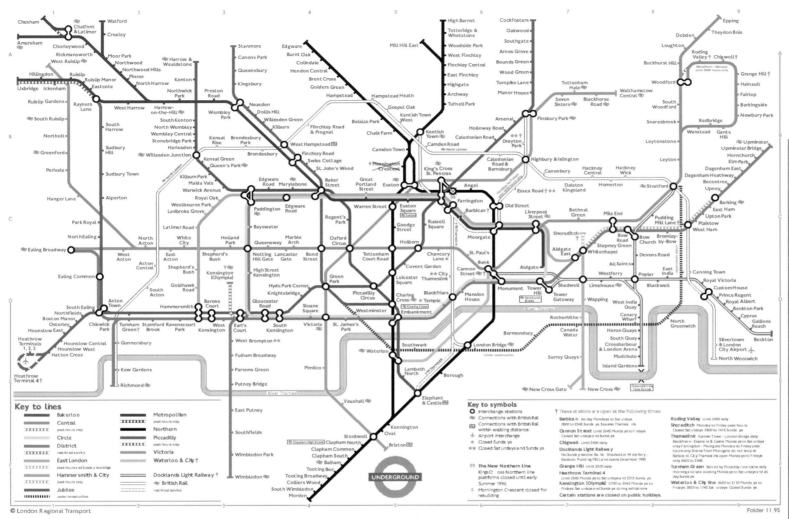

Key to lines

Bakerloo	Metropolitan
Central	peak hours only
peak hours only	
Circle	Piccadilly
District	Victoria
restricted service	Waterloo & City
East London	Docklands Light Railway †
peak hours and Sundays mornings	British Rail
Hammersmith & City	restricted service
peak hours only	
Jubilee	
under construction	

© London Regional Transport

Key to symbols

○ Interchange stations
⊛ Connections with British Rail
▣ Connections with British Rail within walking distance
✈ Airport interchange
✢ Closed Sundays
✳✳ Closed Saturdays and Sundays

† These stations are open at the following times:

Barbican † All day Mondays to Saturdays
0800 to 2345 Sundays. See also Thameslink.
Cannon Street Until 2045 Mondays to Fridays.
Closed Saturdays and Sundays.
Chigwell Until 2000 daily.
Docklands Light Railway
No Sunday service; Bank – Shadwell or West ferry –
Beckton. Pudding Mill Lane opens December 1995.
Grange Hill Until 2000 daily.
Heathrow Terminal 4
Until 2345 Mondays to Saturdays and 2315 Sundays.
Mornington Crescent closed during exhibitions.
Certain stations are closed on public holidays.

Roding Valley Until 2000 daily.
Shoreditch Monday to Friday peak hours.
Closed Saturdays. 0800 to 1415 Sundays.
Thameslink Kentish Town – London Bridge daily.
Blackfriars – Elephant & Castle Mondays to Saturdays
only. Farringdon – Moorgate Mondays to Fridays peak
hours only (trains from Moorgate do not stop at
Barbican). City Thameslink open Mondays to Fridays
only 0600 to 2045.
Turnham Green Served by Piccadilly line trains early
mornings and late evening Mondays to Saturdays and all
day Sundays.
Waterloo & City line 0630 to 21.50 Mondays to
Fridays 0800 to 1745 Saturdays. Closed Sundays.

◊◊ The New Northern Line
King's Cross Northern line
platforms closed until early
Summer 1996
◊ Mornington Crescent closed for
rebuilding

UNDERGROUND

Folder 11.95

1995 London Underground diagrammatic map

The ultimate development of the map that I had worked on for 25 years and been entirely responsible for its design since 1980.

planners had reached various stages, from looking for 'traffic objectives' to trajectories where buildings along the line of route were already being compulsorily purchased. This map gave me an excellent chance to design a blueprint that could be used to experiment on for the regular production map. It also gave me a chance to establish a new studio to produce the artwork. The computer stage had commenced with the

artwork being transferred to Lovell Johns at their cartographic office at Long Handborough, one stop on the train past Oxford. Lovell Johns at first produced their artwork by way of the syquest system, which was incredibly inflexible, the drawing then being copied onto a high resolution disc and transferred to an establishment in Putney who generated the films required by the printer. This system was entirely satisfactory for the

production of cartography, when the lie of the land doesn't change once the checking of spelling etc has been completed. The Underground map is a flexible design and needs checking for alignments as well as spelling. This meant that I had to travel to Lovell Johns and spend a day looking at the map on their computer screen before the long winded production concluded when printing films were made (sometimes, the process had

to be repeated if late alterations were made to running patterns affecting information on the map or its key). In those days the rail lines were shown on the computer screen as thin black lines between crosses which were the plots indicating a change of trajectory. Equally, lettering did not have the style of the selected typeface, but appeared as spindly outline. The sacrifices and mental wear and tear that were made by me in those early days of the computer in the quest to keep up with the march of time are unbelievable, when compared with today's convenience of an Apple Mac! However, their quality and service was second to none once they invested in Apple Macs. I dealt day to day with Peter Markley who had learnt his cartography with the army. He always dressed immaculately and stood at his desk to attention when speaking on the phone if it was to the boss. The Lovell Johns rep would pop in to my office to see me occasionally – he didn't really need to since he knew that there was no other work that I could hand to him – but following trips abroad to cartography fairs he would dump plain envelopes containing pornography on my desk. Who did he think I was!

Travelcard fare zone map

Once the London's Railways diagrammatic map showing the Underground and British Rail lines, had been wrenched from my stewardship during my most unhappy period working within this great organization, it was allowed to flounder through lack of attention and understanding by the clique that had taken control of the Advertising & Publicity Office. It finally died during the early 1980s.

Towards the end of that same decade so much had changed. The Advertising & Publicity Office had become a service department to those other departments within London Transport that required its expertise. But there were two factors that were around to foil this notion: firstly, a revitalised Marketing Department was to all intents a new Publicity Office; secondly Nick Lewis, the Advertising & Publicity Officer, had filled his office with people with no sympathy or experience in the need for design to communicate and portray the organisation in the best light to an increasingly sceptical public. The country was in the grip of Thatcherism, which rejected state ownership (whether profitable or not) or its employees' sensitivities of aesthetics (unless they were profitable). Lewis had handed over the running of the Advertising & Publicity studio to Chris Knowles, whose acumen for gimmicks was matched by his ignorance of design or the production of artwork and printing. The suits that he wore, looking as though they had been purchased

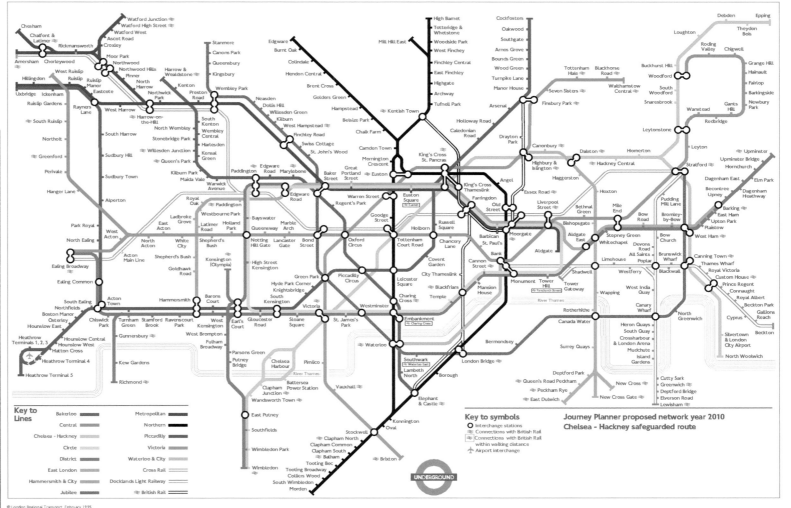

Key to Lines

Bakerloo
Central
Chelsea – Hackney
Circle
District
East London
Hammersmith & City
Jubilee
Metropolitan
Northern
Piccadilly
Victoria
Waterloo & City
Cross Rail
Docklands Light Railway
British Rail

Key to symbols
○ Interchange stations
Connections with British Rail
Connections with British Rail within walking distance
✈ Airport interchange

Journey Planner proposed network year 2010
Chelsea - Hackney safeguarded route

from a charity shop, were generally matched with white trainer shoes – it might have been cool in a spiv sense but it definitely wasn't in any other.

The need for a new map showing both Underground and British Rail lines was entwined with the need to show the fare zones within the London area, since the newly introduced Travelcards could be used on both systems. First of all, David Brant, an operative from the Rail Marketing department (and possibly the blueprint for David Brent in the BBC series *The Office*), arrived at the Publicity Office with a poster size quad royal board upon which had been applied a plain border, a heading entitled London Connections and a diagrammatic representation of the River Thames two thirds of the way down the board. In Chris Knowles' office, Brant gathered a representative following of Advertising & Publicity Office professionals, including Bernie the print buyer and myself and aggressively barked "Artwork this!". When I asked if he meant it literally he hissed back "No stupid: the map as well!". What map? There was no map. What were they to do? The Rail Marketing department had made a commitment to produce this map, but had made no provision to budget for its complete design and artwork (it was rumoured that over £2,000 was paid

1995   Future projects map

This design provided a pointer to the future look of the map. It was briefed to me by Kim Kavannagh who liaised with the New Works department dreaming up these schemes.

It was updated regularly and many of the developments that appeared on the official Underground map germinated here. While some projects are now actually being served by trains, others such as the Chelsea – Hackney link, have been sent to back of the filing cabinet.

1994   Travelcard zonal map

The zonal boundaries indicated
by vignettes were portrayed in
this way at the insistence of the
Advertising & Publicity Officer.
They were difficult to draw and
maintain and were changed to
simpler coloured zones as soon
as the Advertising & Publicity
Officer was replaced.

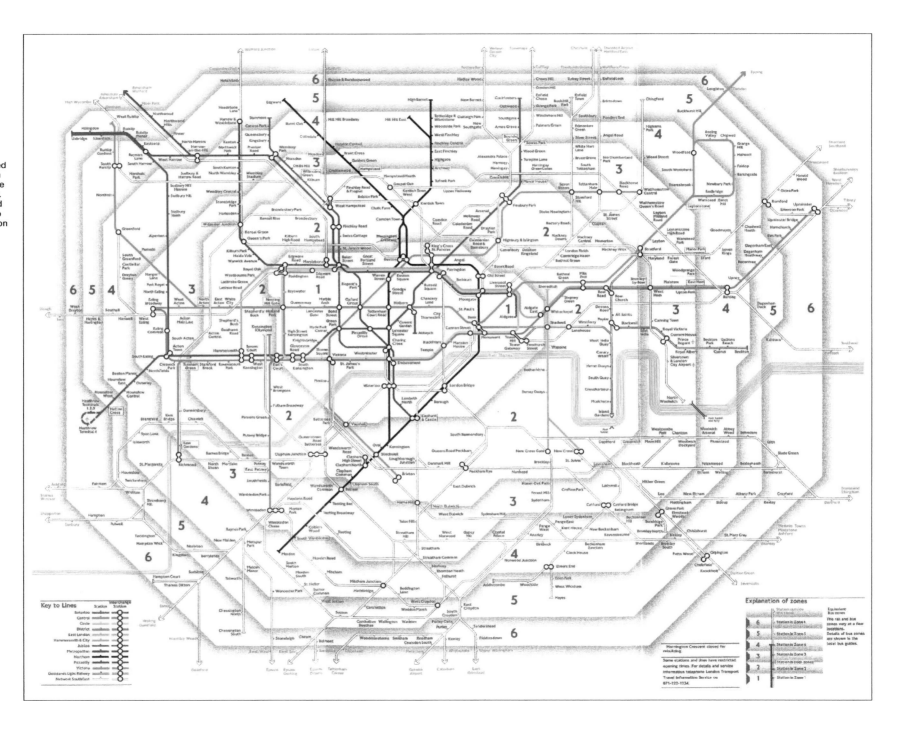

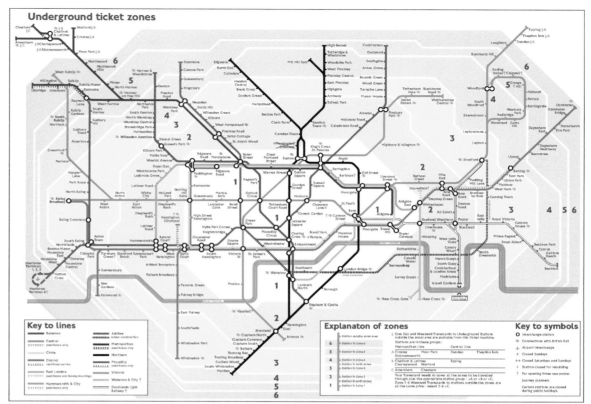

Underground ticket zones

to the design consultancy that had dreamed up the almost blank quad royal display board). No one, except Bernie, in the office was aware that I used to draw the map – indeed, I had originated it, and Bernie didn't let on. So I volunteered to 'have a go at it' during a week off as leave, so that if it didn't work there would be nothing lost, or Chris Knowles would have to look for someone else to design it.

I had kept my tracings from ten or more years earlier and adapted them for the central area of the map to be more similar to that of the Underground map, which by then I was in full control. By working almost throughout the days and nights, I had completed tracings of the entire map in about four days. On this map the outer boundary related to the outside of Zone 6, and adapted the style to that prevailing on the current Underground map. Zonal boundaries were no problem since I had invented the treatment on the Underground map, which I adapted.

When I delivered the map to Chris Knowles, he summoned his Advertising & Publicity cronies and the two Davids, Brant and Hughes, from Rail Marketing. Once Knowles had received general approval, he craned his head around the door of the studio and shouted "Right Tim, we'll 'ave it – get it artworked". I explained to him that it wasn't their's to have. It had been designed by me in my own time – but I might be

prepared to sell it to them. Knowles returned to the meeting to relay the ridiculous proposition advanced by me (in fact he was probably the only one to understand my action since he would had done exactly the same). He returned to the studio with the offer of £1,000 which I turned down. He then returned some minutes later – all these delicate and confidential negotiations were conducted with just his head showing through the doorway to a fairly well populated studio with me sitting at the far end – upping the 'generous' offer to £1,500 which I accepted (in those days my wage was about £15,000 per year).

Production was by Lovell Johns, who already had experience with the drawing of the Underground diagram. The Travelcard fare zones formed the reason for this map, and while their portrayal in different pastel colours posed no problem with the people in charge of bus publicity – or the Commercial Office responsible for ticket security and ordering stocks to be printed – for some unknown reason the Rail Marketing department would have nothing to do with colours. In charge of Rail Marketing was Jeff Mills, who insisted on showing the concentric fares zones as a series as grey vignettes. There was the visual impracticality of showing the very precise boundaries in this way, when some station names had, because of their closeness to borders, to be shown almost on them. Other stations were

situated on the zonal boundaries, with ticket availabilities covering two adjoining zones, and had to be shown in a special way to explain their dual position. The mechanical constraint was that the computer system just couldn't cope with vignettes of the size and complexity required on this map. So each vignette had to be built up with increasing percentages of black, to give the effect of graduation, but using an enormous amount of computer memory.

This was the first of a number of my encounters with Jeff Mills' approach to design, which rarely worked in my favour since he believed that an in house designer could not possibly be a serious professional, but just a clerk

without the standard of expertise required. His own vacuity of design credentials occasionally landed London Transport with massive bills for dubious design solutions, when he had opted entirely for the advice of poorly qualified designers working within the consultancies he was relying upon.

The person immediately in charge of the Travelcard map was the unpredictable and irascible Richard Sharpe. Whilst Sharpe insisted on writing text within leaflets in his own peculiar combination of belt and braces fares talk and modified English – any opposition generated foul mouthed shouting punctuated by spitting – he was surprisingly

1994 Ticket zonal map
The Underground Marketing department were very hesitant to accept colours to identify the different fare zones compared to Bus Marketing who realised their value since the inception of fare zones.

A chance to deviate from the LT style was a series of maps produced for the state owned British Airports Authority, showing all road services from the main bus station. The lettering style is the Transport series as used on Ministry of Transport road signs.

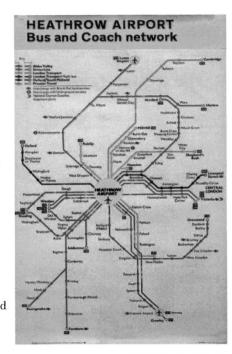

HEATHROW AIRPORT
Bus and Coach network

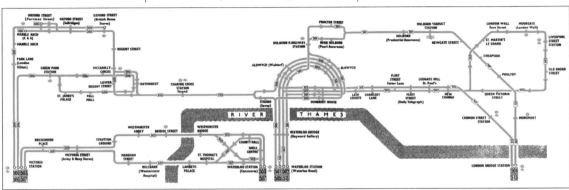

receptive to design propositions put to him during has relatively docile

around the corner, or past the common or the town hall or cross roads. All

these benchmarks and more would be missing from a diagrammatic map. Corners, road junctions and the perceived distance between stops might be shown in different places from where they were in reality.

However, I was prepared to countenance the use of diagram maps in certain situations. One such was the portrayal of single routes on posters usually to be found above the windows within bus interiors. Another was the expression of the Red Arrow express bus network. Firstly, it was a flat fare system so there

1974   **Red Arrow diagram map**
Size: 150 × 225 mm (pocket)

To revitalise the system of inner central area express single deck buses, a diagrammatic approach to the map of routes was thought to give a clearer solution. Lessons have been learned from work on the Underground and London's Railways maps, especially, treating the whole as a balanced abstract layout and including the River Thames as an anchor point for users of the map to get their bearings.

1988   **Red Arrow diagram map**
Size: 150 × 300 mm (pocket)

When new buses (and a new logo) were introduced the opportunity was taken to extend the Red Arrow network, while the basic approach to the design was retained. Details included: illustrations to give an informal look aimed at casual travellers; route numbers reversed out of diagonal panels to indicate terminals; the use of tints on this 2-colour printing to give the effect of four different 'colours'.

periods, usually during fag breaks at the entrance to Albany House in Petty France. It was during one of these *sojourns* – and when he was nursing the wounds of yet another dressing down from one of his superiors – that I was able to persuade him to use coloured zonal representations on the Travelcard map. He accepted that this treatment not only considerably eased production, but also allowed maps to be reproduced in smaller sizes in brochures than had been possible with the zones constructed as vignettes.

Bus maps

I was never generally in favour of diagrammatic maps showing bus routes. With a geographic map, the passenger could see that the stop required to alight at might be just

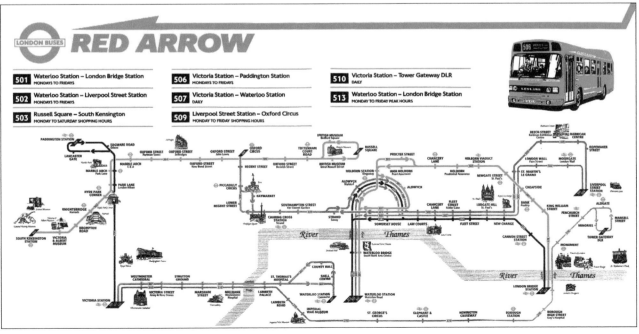

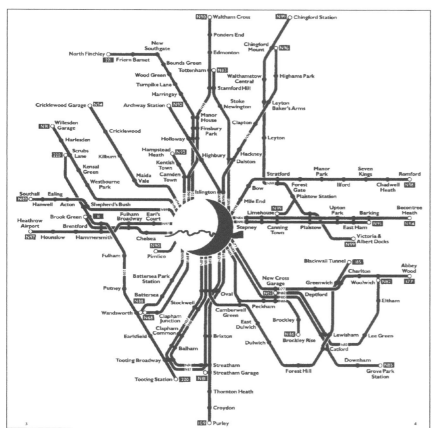

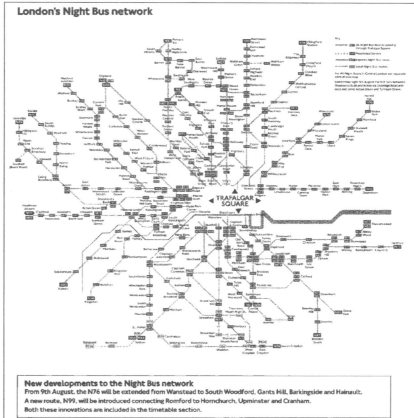

1979 Night Bus map

The designer's input starts right at the beginning by specifying the angle of the diagonal lines. They don't have to be 45 degrees to the horizontal, or 60 degrees. But they must be consistent.

1986 Night Bus map

To avoid the map appearing as a diagrammatic spiders web, the roads were reduced tonally. Route numbers were shown at place names, saving the need to trace along routes to their outer terminals for the route numbers.

New developments to the Night Bus network

From 9th August, the N76 will be extended from Wanstead to South Woodford, Gants Hill, Barkingside and Hainault. A new route, N99, will be introduced connecting Romford to Hornchurch, Upminster and Cranham. Both these innovations are included in the timetable section.

was no penalty for overrunning the required stop, except a long walk back. Secondly, the network was at that time designed mainly for commuters from the main line terminal stations. This meant that the map performed an introductory function to a way of travelling that would become so routine for commuters that memories of individual journeys would become merged and often forgotten altogether. The map also gave me the excuse to devise another pocket folder, to a similar size as the Underground map folder, that would provide me with an additional cover for the range of pocket maps that I was designing. Initially, the network was allowed to

contract, as can be seen by the maps illustrated which were produced without much time separating them.

Then in the late 1980s, with the replacement of the dwindling fleet of very unreliable buses by a brand new fleet of Leyland Nationals, the opportunity was taken by the Bus Marketing department to re-vitalise the network and aim it also at shoppers and other more casual passengers. Just as the first maps had coincided with the introduction of new cover designs, this renewal of the map came at the same time as a new bus livery that I was designing to cover all of London Transport's varied range of red buses.

A similar story of promotion, followed by stagnation and promotion again can be related regarding London's Night Bus network. But, in this case, my maps came in at the beginning of the re-vitalisation and helped to develop the 'N' routes into the busy system of nocturnal buses that they are today.

In the case of Night Buses, I was prepared to go along with a diagrammatic representation of the system, since it would never be traversed during daytime which meant that the geography of the routes could not be appreciated.

Since the 1960s Night Bus passengers had diminished as the

army of night workers – cleaners, printers, gas and electrical engineers, night watchmen, market porters – transferred to their own cars for commuting. But they were gradually replaced in increasing numbers by that up and coming breed of late night revellers whose regularity appreciated the cheapness of a bus to take them home (at daytime rates) in preference to the expense of a mini cab. Night bus journey times were also far quicker to those of daytime buses. So, as with the Red Arrow map, the map that was produced to promote the Night Buses formed an introduction to the network to people who may not have been aware of it before.

1971   **Escalator panel**
Size: 509 × 318 mm
Printer: The Baynard Press

Following my arrival in London Transport's Publicity Office the first design that I produced in the studio was for an escalator panel advertising the Country Walks book. The brief stipulated the use of the drawing with a bullseye head, of which a large stock was held covering every conceivable subject. The typography was a toe in the water use of the venerable Johnston display type (measured in lines rather than points) which was confined to the heading, the text being set in the equally prestigious (but more universally available) Bembo italic. The continuity of the use of the linear bullseye would not see out the end of that year.

COUNTRY WALKS

The new edition of 'Country Walks (Book One)', London Transport's 1971 collection of walks in London's countryside, is now on sale at London Transport Travel Enquiry Offices and at most Underground station ticket offices. Price 30p.

Designing posters for what was still considered in the 1970s to be the world's most respected public transport organisation was regarded by most people to be the icing on the cake. My training and experience so far was in the intricacies of typography using text size faces which were printed on some of the finest quality papers.

By comparison, the printing of posters appeared to me to be crude, as could be witnessed by close inspection of the large dots and the spaces separating them to express halftone pictures. So I approached poster design as a relaxation in comparison to the typographic working out of a timetable or the text side of a *concertina* folded map.

London Transport's poster production policy in the 1970s allowed for the design and printing of six pictorials per year. These six were the pinnacles of good design and were what maintained the notion of the organisation's leadership in design inspired by Frank Pick, its Managing Director until the 1940s and whose name was still revered with a messianic respect. This was a true enough assumption but needed the backing of all the other products, from the vast range of other posters, leaflets and booklets to station and bus shelter design and the buses and trains themselves. A selection of artists and designers were commissioned and paid to design this small number of specialised posters, all of which were 25 inch by 40 inch upright 'double royal' size. Some designers prepared their entire posters as camera ready artworks. Other posters were conceived by artists who submitted their paintings which were scanned by the printers who positioned them on the paper leaving a space at the base for the overprinting of some promotional text. This text was written in the Publicity Office copy section and typographically laid out by myself or one of my colleagues.

I was against using artists who could not design the entire poster, while I was completely in favour of poster designers commissioning artists to enhance parts of their own work as they might with photographers or typographers. Designers who were used regularly were Hans Unger and Abram Games. Three designers, William Fenton, Peter Roberson and Harry Stevens were retained by the Publicity Office to work on general poster designs as well as book, leaflet and ticket designs. I think their retainments amounted, in 1980, to £1,500 each per year to be always available to design for LT, while additionally charging their normal fee for each piece of work. They would usually be given one pictorial poster per year each to design. The annual pictorial posters were commissioned by Bryce Beaumont although Michael Levey often briefed the designers. All other poster designs were commissioned and briefed by Michael Levey. And there was Foote Colne & Belding (FCB), the advertising agency, who had recently succeeded S. H. Benson, whose long association with London Transport had began in the 1930s, who designed the occasional poster as part of a particular advertising campaign.

One of FCB's first poster campaigns for London Transport was to persuade passengers to tender exact fares to drivers of one man buses then being rapidly introduced. But the agency were usually left with little else to do than design press advertising, so that they could earn their commission by booking space in publications.

The situation that I came into on joining the Publicity Office was that I would design events posters and some others, while members of the poster print buying section designed others, especially those advertising the LT Theatre and Operatic groups' productions at Wimbledon Theatre. Many were poorly designed and artworked in such a way that self colours were required for the printing, sometimes amounting to up to 10 impressions, which often exceeded the printing costs of the prestigious pictorial posters. I felt that the bad designs were an insult to the many art students who would have given their eye teeth to design just one poster each and for nothing. So I got Michael to agree that all in-house design briefs should be sent through to me. He would, of course, continue to brief his retained designers on any projects that he thought they were most suited to work on. Briefs were usually in the form of internal memos sent from the departments requiring posters, often merely one sentence long, such as 'this year's production is ………… – please submit poster designs'. I continued to brief specific members of the print buying section, usually Bernie, but insisted on a number of designs to be submitted from which I would judge the one to go through to Michael for approval. I also offered the help of professional studios to produce the artworks. Bernie told me he appreciated the assistance I was giving him, and as a result the standard of his designs rose considerably.

A number of posters were designed as fillers for escalator panel and (20in × 30in) 'double crown' sites that Commercial Advertising had not sold. The first poster layout I was given was for an escalator panel promoting *Country Walks* booklets. The brief specified that it was to be printed letterpress on an existing pre-printed coloured paper and make use of a particular cartoon illustration from a series that had been in existence for about 20 years – a somewhat frightening introduction to poster design. I chose to use the revered Johnston poster type, together with Bembo and the outline bullseye – both the latter of which proved to be favourites of Bryce.

The icing on the cake?

1971   **Chelsea Flower Show poster**

Size: 25 × 40 ins
Printer: Leonard Ripley & Co Ltd

My first attempt at designing a double royal poster might have been my last if my superiors had been more design literate. However, this design actually lived to be repeated the following year. Printed silk screen.

1971   **Farewell to Steam poster**

Size: 25 × 40 ins
Printer: Leonard Ripley & Co Ltd

A later silk screen printed poster demonstrated that bold simple motifs were far more successful at commanding attention, especially when there was so much text to be read.

The same design was reprinted with text specifically directed towards the Open Day.

initial brief and designs to printing and posting. However, this design was repeated the following year, confirming my view – later expressed by me to Michael – that anything produced for and by London Transport is (misguidedly) assumed by those in charge to be top quality. This observation was later impressed on me when I was waiting for a train at Aldgate East and overheard a middle aged working class women comment to her friend that she didn't think much of a particular poster displayed on the platform wall, "but it must be alright because it's LT's". She had a point, for the poster was a particularly bad production, both in its design and

I was left on my own to design the next poster, which was the announcement of the annual Chelsea Flower Show. It was almost a repetition of my elevation from the first year basic design course at Kingston Art School to the second year specialising in graphic design. I took leave of my graphic education, and instead produced a rather poor representational drawing in ink of a flower display. By the time the poster was displayed at stations many of the flowers illustrated were out of season and no longer alive, reflecting the long lead times in those days from

artwork. Her conclusion confirmed my impression that London Transport was regarded as the practitioner and projector of good design, a very heavy responsibility. LT's publicity might not have been as exciting as that displayed by commercial advertisers but it was regarded as being reliable. Reliability was central to the organisation, not only in the timekeeping of its buses and trains, but also in safety, which was generally taken for granted by passengers. This accolade was later stretched to breaking point by the replacement of design standards by Nick Lewis's pursuance of the

advertising agency philosophy of consumer research being the arbiter of all. Henry Fitzhugh tried to rescue the tradition with his series of *Art on the Underground* posters reproducing paintings by fine artists, but it never brought back the general well being of being surrounded by functional graphic design.

The next poster project was considered important enough to be earmarked to be designed by William Fenton. Of the three maintained designers he was rightly considered to be the transport expert, numerous bus and train books going to him for page layouts and cover designs. So the publicity commemorating the withdrawal of steam locomotives on the Underground was a natural for William to work on. But he was on holiday when the designs were required to be done, so the brief was (apologetically) given to me. The convenience of the Publicity photographic library became apparent to me, in that I could wander round and pore over albums (covering every imaginable subject and therefore very easy for me to be sidetracked) until I found a suitable photograph of the type of locomotive to be used on the last commemorative run, which I converted to a bleached out image. Michael sent my rough design through to Bryce, who forwarded it to Eric Wilkins the Chief Public Relations Officer, who ultimately approved all poster designs and to whom Bryce

reported. When I submitted the design I stressed the economy of production and suggested that for a modest increase in cost extra copies could be printed that could be sold at the event. My suggestions were not only accepted but, when printed, copies were fly posted on station buildings and hoardings along the Metropolitan Line, a rare break with LT's normal posting disciplines. I was then given the job of producing captions for every item of rolling stock on display at the Neasden Works open day on 6 June 1971. I had not only gained the confidence of Bryce and Michael (Michael admitted that he had never before heard of or seen a bleached out photograph – *bless him*). I had re-discovered my design skills, which lay in the use of clear bold expressions.

Poster designs covered a wide range of subjects: recruitment, safety, bank holidays, events, openings, withdrawals. These were fitted into a routine of diary tube maps, letterpress poster specifications, one-man bus leaflet designs, tube line car diagrams and meetings around the system with bus garage managers and tube station masters over the layouts and siting of special signs that were peculiar to their specific environments, as well as layouts for signwriters for hoardings around building works. I had also been selected as the local trade union representative of the TSSA (Transport Salaried Staffs Association). This mainly involved resolving staff

complaints about their treatment at work – the solution was usually to calm down tempers, but the process was time consuming.

In preparation for the opening of the southern section of the Victoria Line between Victoria and Brixton in June 1971, I was briefed to re-design the cover of the existing leaflet describing the line. Michael was always generous to me by attributing any of my designs to 'the in-house artist' or 'staff designer' when sending rough designs to the officers or chief officers who had commissioned the work. Most of the work emanated from Eric (F. E.) Wilkins, the Chief Public Relations Officer. When he approved the Victoria Line leaflet cover he

**1971   Victoria Line
         Brixton extension leaflet**
Size: 178 × 108 mm
Printer: Frederick Printing Co Ltd

This was the latest of a number of reprints of this 8-page folder following the progress of the Victoria Line up to its opening in 1968. Previous covers had been designed by Abram Games, whilst the insides were designed by Peter Robeson. I designed this cover but left the inside intact, which I re-designed for a later reprint. When Eric Wilkins approved the design he asked for the designer's name to appear, which I modestly put on the back – the first time my name had appeared in print!

1971   New Type buses leaflets
Size: 178 × 108 mm
Printer: various

This was a new cover design for leaflets which were delivered to households along routes that were being converted to driver only buses. Bus stop timetables were reduced in size and printed inside.

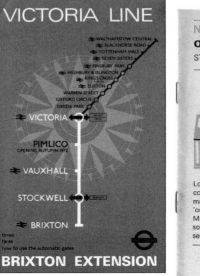

1972 Don't drop litter roof panel
Size: 11 × 24 in
Printer: Johnson Riddle & Co

The posters designed for the bus environment used bus tickets cut to form the letters of the message. Rather surprisingly it was printed litho using opaque inks, onto brown wrapping paper to give a utilitarian look. The brown wrapping paper cost far more than normal poster paper.

1972 Don't drop litter poster
Size: Double Crown 30 × 20 in
Printer: Johnson Riddle & Co

This poster was printed in the same way as the bus roof panel, but utilised cut up newspapers to form the letters of the message. My unbiassed selection of newspapers is illustrated in the detail below – the MORNING STAR was the only newspaper to hand! This poster was designed as a filler for spare commercial sites, but is shown here mounted on a Double Royal back which made it suitable for posting on LT sites.

returned it with a note asking for the designer's name to be included on it. In my modesty I had it put on the back cover next to the printers imprint, a practice that had pertained at the printing and design establishments I had previously worked at. This leaflet also introduced me to Ron Pigram who ran the copy section which, in addition to writing the text for all posters, leaflets and booklets, also bought the design and printing for leaflets and booklets. Ron was very much his own man, dealing with his own range of printers and two of the maintained designers, William Fenton and Peter Robeson, who designed most of his publications. I left the interior of the Victoria Line leaflet in the form of the previous edition: I hadn't been asked to re-design it and didn't want to push my luck with Ron who I hardly knew. I had already discovered that there was no love lost between Frank, who ran the poster printing section, and Ron who might therefore see me as part of the enemy. I later found out that Ron could be very offhand in his independence. He might alter an artwork or order a reprint when I could easily have given him an updated layout or artwork.

However, I gradually demonstrated to Ron that I could make his life easier if he involved me more with the printing process without upsetting the intimate relationship he had with his suppliers – and what suppliers some of them were too! One rep, who regularly

visited Ron from a major national printer, was also an active freemason and member of a lodge in which I had to endure the tenacity of him and his friends when he took me to lunch at his favourite restaurant in the City. Another printer that Ron used issued a fascinating type catalogue composed of a range of unusual and ancient type faces. When I visited this printer with Ron at their Wanstead premises I observed that their equipment was pretty elderly too. I also saw the other reason why we were visiting: the owner had died and left the entire outfit to his daughter who was struggling to keep it going and was considering selling it – Ron was determined to keep the printer open – the daughter was very attractive!

Ron made considerable use of the London, Rochester and St.Albans factories of Staples Printers. Their rep, Norman Furness, was regularly in the office always looking dapper and at least 20 years younger than his real age. Staples shared the hard bound book runs with Aylesbury based Hazel Watson & Vyney. Ron also used a number of smaller printers, especially if they could do him favours in return.

Frank used a greater number of printers, each with their distinctly different reps, partly through the variety of different printing methods employed for poster, timetable and map printing: letterpress, litho and silk screen. Vauxhall based Leonard Ripley was represented by the shy,

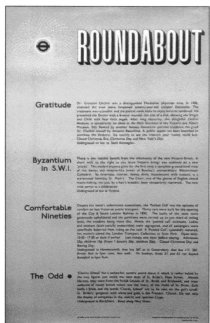

middle aged Stan Gasson who bought a fruit cake into the office every Monday, which he claimed his wife had cooked, and loved fast cars and inviting the young women from the office to ride with him in his coupé, sometimes apparently down to the south coast! Bill Armager represented Whiteman in Lewes Sussex, which was part of the Burrups Group – indeed I had produced faretable artwork for them when I worked in the Burrups studio. On one occasion Bill reported that his dust bin had been filled with leaflets informing of local bus changes which should have

been posted through letter boxes. The ultimate insult was that they had been printed by his printer! The mighty Waterlow & Sons was represented by the elderly dignified cockney Alfie Hobbs, who allowed his loyalty to slip when he uttered some home truths to Frank on a farewell visit following his retirement. The affable Percy Seymour fronted the venerable Baynard Press, renowned for their high quality poster printing. There was also the litho only C. J. Petyt and silk screen only Walter Brian. Johnson Riddle printed the pocket Underground maps, as well as pictorial posters where they benefited

from one the last of the litho artists who copied them onto litho plates – in their classy *art deco* 1930s factory at St.Mary Cray in Kent and who sadly folded in the late '70s.

There was only one printer that spanned both Ron's and Frank's sections and that was Bournehall Press at Welwyn Garden City. When I joined LT Robin Brooke was the managing director and had succeeded his dad who had been a great friend of Ron. Frank used them mainly for the printing of bus stop timetables, but they often won more prestigious poster work because their Johnston

type was less worn than that held by the other printers. The arrangement with Bournehall changed when Baynard Press folded, their rep Percy being taken on by Bournehall as well as Baynard's Johnston display type to supplement Bournehall's own. Percy was a go getter and got much poster work as well as increasing the timetable production for Bournehall. He worked beyond retirement age, but eventually left in his late 60s – to get married! Bob Sansom of mainly letterpress equipped London based Kelly & Kelly regularly took me for a beer at the *Beehive*. He assumed that I was a Tory such as himself, as he made outrageous classist and racist statements – I had to change my drinking partner.

Bryce and Michael wished to update the designs of some of their regular posters and publications. Some items needed re-design following the ruling on the use of the roundel, especially when the former wording across the bar (which now had to be empty) formed part of the title. *How To Get There* was a pocket publication listing places of interest and the buses and trains

1974 Roundabout booklet
Size: 172 × 102 mm
Printer: Staples Printers

Booklet cover and inside spread showing typography.

1971 Roundabout poster
Size: 25 × 40 ins
Printer: Baynard Press

The type was hand and machine set and printed letterpress on a litho printed background.

1972 A London Diary poster
Size: 25 × 40 ins
Printer: Baynard Press

This poster appeared every month and was by far the most useful of the three posters – it also appeared in a reduced size for display on notice boards (particularly in London hospitals). The type was hand set in Johnston with text machine set in Univers and printed letterpress on a litho printed background.

1972 A Music Diary poster
Size: 25 × 40 ins
Printer: Leonard Ripley, Vauxhall

Appearing quarterly, it covered mainly classical music venues. The type was printed letterpress on a silk screen printed background.

1973   **The London Transport Collection poster**

Size: 25 × 40 ins
Printer: Johnson Riddle & Co Ltd

This was one of three designs that I submitted and was the one chosen as the first to be printed since it was considered to best reflect the historical aspect of the LT Collection. For the official opening I also designed invitation cards reflecting the style of the poster. The type face used on the poster is Richmond Old Style, one in a family which includes the more well known Windsor. The different transport operators' symbols on the right hand side were all drawn as original artwork for the poster.

Part of Bryce Beaumont's research into the expression of animal noises in different languages.

	English	French
Dog:	woof woof	waf waf; wouf wouf,
Sheep:	baa	bêêêê
Cat:	meeow	miaou
Cow:	moo	meuh
Pig:	snort	grouik grouik
Donkey:	he haw	hi han
Lion:	arrw	graoooo
Duck:	quack quack	coin coin
Fish:	glug glug	gloup gloup

---

that served them, for which I re-designed the cover. *Roundabout* was a booklet containing essays, written by members of the copy section, describing items of curiosity to be found in odd corners of London. The cover and inside were re-designed by me, as was the accompanying double royal poster. My re-design for *A London Diary* poster was accepted early in 1972. This was followed by *A Music Diary* about a year later, listing mainly classical concerts. These three posters contained a very middle class approach to research and copy preparation, as was most other literature produced at that time, reflecting the intellectual level of conversation normally conducted between Bryce and Michael and to which they were quite content to include me if I was in their company. On one of my visits to Bryce's office he asked for my help in compiling a list of animal noises as expressed in different languages. Some are shown in the table in the margin. I don't think it was ever published!

The London Transport Collection

A space was found in west London at Syon Park to accommodate the LT-owned vehicles that had been homeless since the demise of the fabulous Transport Museum in the former bus garage at Clapham. Bryce asked me to design a poster

to publicise the London Transport Collection at its new venue. The description *Collection* was specifically used since there would be no reference library or other study facilities normally attached to a museum – just a small shop selling souvenirs.

From the three alternative and very diverse rough designs that I submitted, initially the most traditional, featuring a sepia and vignetted photograph of Aldgate High Street, was chosen. Designs for invitation cards to the opening were also asked for.

Later, and somewhat surprisingly, Bryce asked for the other two designs to be taken to artwork. The version featuring type flowers and a B-type bus was also adapted to form the background to a short film featuring the LT Collection at Syon Park. The design was also used as a cover for

Letraset instant rub down dry transfer lettering,

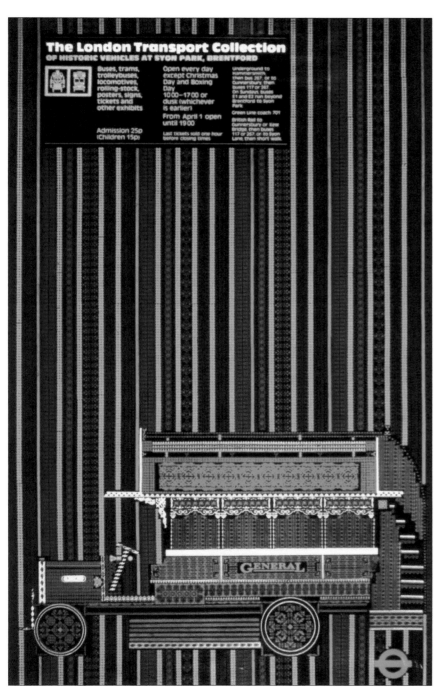

even though most of the ornaments I had used to form the poster were typesetters' repros, and not those of Letraset! And the poster design also found a place amongst other best considered graphic designs in MODERN PUBLICITY 44, published in 1975.

In a very short time I gained confidence in the creative work that I was producing. What I couldn't produce myself I would brief commercial studios, from pure artwork to the more creative, depending on the tightness of the brief that I was giving them. There were still a number of large studios around which existed to service advertising agencies and whose staff were mainly ex-agency people who had grown too old (in their late 30s) to give the right image to their former agencies by staying with them. I could therefore draw on a broad range of artists, photographers, retouchers and art directors, but not usually designers which is why I briefed thoroughly at the start of projects, since I was acting as art director. At the same time I think I gained respect from the staff around me as the standard of design coming from our studio was rising to equal or even surpass that briefed out by Michael Levey to the LT-retained freelance designers.

In my first ten years at London Transport our little studio handled any type of graphic work thrown at us. On the strength of the displays that I mounted to update the progress

being made on the construction of the Piccadilly Line Heathrow extension, I was asked by Michael Levey to step in to design an exhibition at the Victoria & Albert Museum at South Kensington. The display was to celebrate the centenary of the birth of Frank Pick in 1878 and was to be called *Teaspoons to Trains*. Work by the museum had stalled so I stepped in to produce an overall design of panels to fit in with the display cabinets they already had. I used Kevin Danes of City Display to produce the panels which were basically cream painted 2-metre high hardboard panels with horizontal blue strips at the heads and feet, reflecting the tiled walls of 1930s Charles Holden designed station platforms. While these were being erected and fitted with shelves and graphic images, a team of middle aged and elderly ladies, resembling a Womens' Institute team as portrayed by the Boulting Brothers, were arranging, cataloguing and typing out captions for the various objects ranging from the cutlery to curtain material to posters to large photographs of buses, trains and buildings whose designers Prank Pick had patronised and promoted. I had brought a slice of cake from the museum café on their 1950s cottage style plate which I lazily left in an empty display cabinet. I noted later that the plate had been left and given a caption associating it with Pick!

I had kept in touch with Maggie

1975   **London Transport Collection poster**

Size: 25 × 40 in
Printer: C. J. Petyt

The London Transport Collection was situated in Syon Park, known for its flowering plants and bushes. This poster uses a play on the word flower, which is also used by typesetters to describe what are otherwise known as type ornaments, used for borders and backgrounds. The artwork was produced in black and white only, using strips of ornaments printed as repros by a variety of typesetters. Once photographed to double royal size an overlay was marked in the colours that the printer would reproduce the ornaments in – no problem with registration since the black final printing would hold it all together.

1976   **Gala Day poster**

Size: 25 × 40 in
Printer: —

Another opportunity to apply period graphics and styles on a basically very cheaply produced poster.

1972/3   **Vintage Bus Service poster**

Size: 25 × 40 in
Printer: C. J. Petyt

The bus enthusiast, Prince Marshall, had acquired a semi-derelict ex-Tilling ST-type London bus of 1930, which he had renovated and reconditioned to carry passengers once again.

Both posters owe their style partly to the fact that colour photographs were not available. Both also gave the opportunity to revive period typefaces and graphic styles.

The 4-page leaflet supporting the Double Royal poster was also printed in 2-colours only.

Huscroft from Kingston Art School having seen a lot of her when living in Kingston when she was with Roger Bristow. She had taken charge of the graphics section at Harrow Art School. I spent occasional afternoons there in the early 1970s, setting projects for the students and telling them how I went about my work.

About ten years later, in 1984, I did a similar exercise at Canterbury School of Art, where Chris Steele from Kassa & Steele who was doing work for LT, taught graphics part time. When his students visited London I briefed them to design a leaflet promoting the Round London Sightseeing open top bus Tour. I then when to Canterbury on three separate occasions to view their progress, give advice and finally join in the criticism when they submitted their completed designs.

The social life in the 1970s was also pretty furious. Christmas parties comprised the entire compliment of Publicity Office staff and their guests, standing around in the main office area or attempting to boogie to a background of a crackly and fuzzy Radio 1 playing through a battery powered *trannie* radio. Following the 1972 party I arranged for candidates to put their names forward for a future committee to take over the organisation of the next one. I cleared this move with Kathy McDicken, the staff clerk, who had been running the party for the previous decade. I think she was quite relieved, being quietly

confident that future events would not come up to her standard! Obviously my name had to go on the voting slip, and so did Kathy's. I won 100 per cent of the votes cast and the percentage of votes cast was far higher that at any general election! From amongst the staff I found volunteers who would cook food, produce decorations and, of course, Chris Leadbeater who was a disc jockey at weekends to supplement his weekly wage. I went round the office every week with a raffle of goods donated by the staff – I used to donate a bottle of beer each week which was worth considerably less than the price I was asking for a raffle ticket – it was all conducted in good humour. The 1973 party was to be fancy dress.

Following my joining the newly formed Campaign for Real Ale (CAMRA) in the early '70s, together with Peter Sims of the timetable section, my studio assistant Kate Murphy set up the LT Real Ale Society, which was mainly concerned with arranging visits to breweries. Kate accommodated these additional duties with enthusiasm and designed a letterhead for the purpose of writing to breweries, but omitted to include our address as part of the design. Harvey's Brewery of Lewes were worldly enough to piece together the initials 'LT' and the roundel and duly replied to 55 Broadway, London SW1 'care of the chairman'. Their letter found its way to me with 'try Demuth in Publicity' scrawled across one

1974 **Hatton Cross poster**
Size: 25 × 40 inches
Printer: Walter Brian

Printed silk screen using transparent inks, this is a good example of the use of two colours overprinted to form a third colour, as can be seen on the underside of the aircraft and Heathrow extension of the diagram map. Below is shown the cover of the litho printed accompanying leaflet. The inside opened up to show the full Piccadilly Line diagram map stretching across the middle.

133

1974/5   Chelsea Flower Show posters

Size: 25 × 40 in
Printer: Leonard Ripley, Vauhall

These posters make use of huge enlargements of type ornaments – or flowers – which are normally repeated about 6 to 12 mm high as typographic borders to book pages or advertisements. The red and blue poster shows what can be achieved by using transparent inks, giving an additional colour when overprinted. Both were printed silk screen.

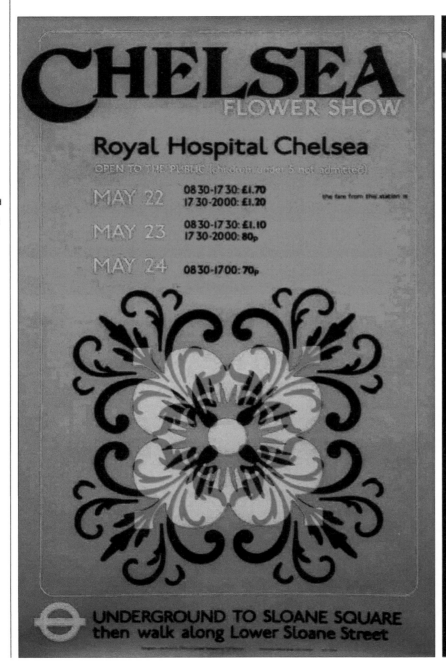

Philbeach

CONVALESCENT HOME, HYTHE, KENT

*London Transport Benevolent Fund's
Home for women and children*

TWO NEW TRANSPORT BOOKS

LONDON'S TRAMS & TROLLEYBUSES

BUSES OF LONDON

Price £4·95 each from bookstalls and London Transport shops

LONDON'S LAST RT BUSES

This bus is one of the last of a great fleet of about 7,000, the first of which ran in 1929. The buses formed one of the largest standardized fleets ever built and were the mainstay of London's bus service in the 1950s and early 1960s. They take their final bow on Route 62 on 7 April.
Throughout the world, the RT bus was a symbol of London and all that was best in British bus design.
Watch for the farewell cavalcade of RT buses over Route 62 in the late afternoon on Saturday, April 7. It will leave Barking Garage at about 16.00 and return about dusk. For more details, please ring 222 1234 any time.

ROUTE 62   SATURDAY 7 APRIL

1972/77   Bus roof panels
Size: 8 × 26 and 11 × 24 in
Printers: various

Posters intended to be positioned above the windows inside buses were often designed to be trimmed to two different sizes using just one printing, the wider for posting in RFs and RTs and the deeper on all newer buses.

corner by the chairman – such was the interaction between individuals of all levels in those days! Once our letterhead was corrected we did enjoy visits to a number of breweries, most of which are sadly no more.

During the working day – and often quite late into the evenings – I combined a social lunchtime with colleagues and suppliers (and quite a lot of ale) with routine management of a small department producing anything from simple artwork to the design of complete maps, booklets and posters ranging from staff recruitment to pictorials. At weekends I found time to design invitation cards for weddings of members of staff as well as headed stationary for friends who owned businesses locally to Amersham where I lived with my wife, Jan, and daughter, Alice, together with a menagerie of dogs and cats. I also designed, painted and installed fascias and signs for local shops and the pub across the road from my home.

When I had a poster to design I usually took the brief home to think about where I could have complete peace. I often worked well into the night until content that I had ideas that I could develop myself or brief out to studios to produce rough designs for presentation.

Another organisation that I helped initiate, this time with Chris Godbold who was then a staff clerk in Publicity, was the LT branch of the Communist Party. We met monthly in a hall in one of the blocks of council flats on the other side of Marylebone Road from Griffith House – ideal for us but a treck for some of the 16 members who came from outlying rail depots and bus garages. I was also a member of the South Bucks CP branch which met in High Wycombe. During a spot check of party cards they found mine filled with Courage brewery's spot the ball competition stamps in place of official CP stamps. My penance was selling MORNING STAR newspapers on High Wycombe High Street every Saturday. I took Alice with me and she sat patiently in her pushchair for an hour while I dispensed a few papers.

Mention must be made of Harry Marion who was in charge of the road development section in the Publicity Office. The section really ran itself with a small staff of Howard Butler, Dianna Strickland and Michael Walton within the office and outdoor roadside publicity inspectors, which included Albert McCall who was credited with possessing the world's largest collection of bus, tram and trolleybus tickets. They looked after the installation of timetables and other publicity into bus stop frames and poster frames in bus shelters, as well as the measurement and installation of any enamel signs required at bus stations or at sites along bus routes. Dianna was often required to drive the office car to pick up Harry from one of his venues. Harry had started his career on the buses before World War II, had volunteered to join the army for the duration the war and returned to join Publicity once peace returned. With his department possessing a fleet of cars and vans to enable his staff to cover the entire LT system, which then included the green country bus

1974   Philbeach folder
Size: 210 × 98 mm
Printer: Staples Printers Ltd,
           Rochester
A 6-page folder giving details of the London Transport Benevolent Fund's convalescent home on the Kent coast. An opportunity to design in a style other than the official one.

**1974   South Kensington
           Dining Club poster**
Size: 297 × 210 mm
Printer: Leonard Ripley, Vauxhall

Designed for office notice boards and employing an illustration produced by myself.

Join your own **Dining Club** at **South Kensington**

1973 **Clearway to a career**
Size: 152 × 96 mm
Printer: —

A 4-page leaflet aimed at school leavers for trainee jobs on the Underground. Using stock photographs of signals indicating a clear way ahead. Printed in one colour only.

1974/5 **Recruitment posters**
Size: various
Printer: various

Issued regularly during the early 1970s as staff left LT to beat the wage freeze, they were pasted to lower deck windows on buses and to windscreen panels inside tube car interiors either side of the sliding doors.

1974/5 **Defined Area booklets**
Size: 148 × 102 mm
Printer: Strange the Printer and others

These 12-page booklets were issued to staff prior to sections of line being handed over by the civil engineers to the operators, ready for energising the live rail. The Piccadilly Line covers are set in Johnston, while the Fleet Line cover is set in Granby, making an interesting comparison.

network he extended his own job by chauffeuring Harold Hutchison, the Publicity Officer from 1947 to 1966, to meetings at the various diverse office locations around the system, including *The Spaniards* on the edge of Hampstead Heath! When Hutchison retired in the early 1960s, his successor Bryce Beaumont had no need for a car or a driver, being quite happy with the service provided by the tubes and buses, or making his own occasional use of a publicity van. So Harry successfully delegated the operation of his department to his staff, making brief appearances in the mornings before 11:00 pub opening time. Unless I could avoid him, he

collected me for an eleven o'clock 'meeting' at the *Beehive*, a tiny one bar pub half way down the equally tiny Homer Street, off Old Marylebone Road opposite Griffith House. Harry was a mine of information on what could be done and what might be

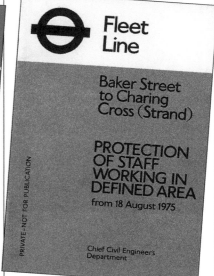

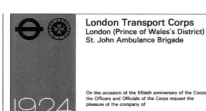

1973/4   **St.John's Ambulance**
Size: 150 × 207 mm
Printer: Bournehall Press

Items were designed for the
LT Corps, which attended LT
sporting functions as well as a
number of public ceremonial
events with trained first aid staff.

inappropriate regarding my ideas for publicity, including my redesign of the bus stop. While sipping glasses of Whitbread *Final Selection* extra strong ale interspersed with an occasional 'Small Harry', his name for Crawford's Scotch Whisky, he would tell me of his latest activities with Mimi, his conquest who lived in South Kensington and who would often breeze into the pub to join us. Her daughter was my age and more to my liking. She would today be described as a dissident (a word not in regular use in the 1970s), having taken the ongoing plight of the Palestinians to her heart. She invited me to go with her to a little private cinema off Oxford Street which was showing films of the prevailing situation in Palestine, most of which was not being mentioned by the mainstream media. The police welcoming party outside the cinema outweighed the size of the audience within, which was entirely peaceful, a situation which invariably persists to this day. When Harry's age necessitated his retirement he

1974   **The Ten Best poster**
Size: 20 × 30 in
Printer: Leonard Ripley, Vauxhall

Printed letterpress on a pre-
printed paper. A poster promoting
the Central Line Photographic
Club film competition.

1975   **London Transport Players
poster**
Size: 20 × 30 in
Printer: Leonard Ripley, Vauxhall

Wimbledon Theatre was a regular
venue for amateur productions
of musicals by the London
Transport Players and operas by
the London Transport Operatic
Group. Posters were designed
within the Publicity Office. This
poster utilised an illustration
taken from an LT leaflet published
in the same year in the 1930s that
the production is set.

1974/8   **Art Group poster**
Size: 25 × 40 in
Printer: Leonard Ripley, Vauxhall

Posters were designed for a
number of LT societies and then
posted on spare LT sites. They
gave a chance to experiment
with various techniques that, if
successful could be developed
for other graphic projects.

1973 Round London Sightseeing Tour bus interior roof panel

Size: 8 × 27 ins
Printer: Leonard Ripley, Vauxhall
Bus interior panels, bus sides, bus double crowns and bus lower rears, all of different proportions called for a very flexible design.

1973 Tourist leaflets

Size: 99 × 210 mm
Printer: various
Leaflets were produced in the major European languages and Japanese for display in their relevant countries. These show the compromises that were necessary to a standard layout to accommodate varying volumes of text, something I had learned at Kynoch Press. The colours of the leaflet heads match those of the different language tourist map covers that I was working on at the same time to primarily aid the storeroom.

1972–74 How to get there booklets

Size: 169 × 98 mm
Printer: Staples Printers, Rochester
The cover of the public and staff editions of 1972 and 1974. The style of the staff edition follows that adopted for staff timetables. The inside of both was identical.

1977 How to get there booklet

Size: 170 × 101 mm
Printer: Staples Printers, Rochester
A replacement for the cover designed by me in 1972. I art directed the photograph which was taken in Trafalgar Square. The models were Richard Fagge, who ran the Publicity Office accounts section, together with his daughter and Dianna Strickland who was the clerk in charge of the road development section.

lasted no more than six months before boredom ended his life.

The state of adrenaline in the office was to last only for the first half of the 1970s. During the same period, outside the office the world and me were being constantly recharged with inspiration from The Doors, The Who, T.Rex, Delaney + Bonnie and Friends, Three Dog Night, Dr Hook, Alice Cooper, Deep Purple, Pink Floyd, Joe Cocker, Queen and ... Led Zeppelin!

In 1974, Bryce decided to retire the following year after his 62nd birthday, possibly because his boss, the Chief Public Relations Officer Eric Wilkins, was also taking retirement.

During the

1974 fancy dress Christmas party I expressed my concern to Eric Wilkins, with my midriff enclosed within a barrel made of cardboard, at Bryce's future replacement by Michael Levey (odd how some of the most serious and ground breaking discussions are conducted when – at least one of – the parties are made up to look very silly). Eric assured me of Michael's tenacity, which had impressed him at controlling and overcoming the paralysis that had so weakened his legs that he needed clamps to aid his standing and walking.

Michael Levey was duly elevated to the post of Publicity Officer and his place, as my immediate boss, was taken by the classy and ex-advertising agency Bill Oswald. The Marketing

job was also up for grabs, which was going to effect us in Publicity since we would in future be under the wing of the Director of Marketing. The easy going and friendly Sandy Brown was the front runner, but that was not to be. Instead, the new regime at the top chose Basil Hooper. We were indeed in for a shake up.

A shake up we needed too. Life had become exceedingly tiring under Michael's leadership – never making decisions while being pushed around by all that he sought approval of my, and others, work. The Heathrow Airport signing scheme was being continuously and repeatedly re-planned, each stage requiring hefty re-draws and new layouts. Meanwhile FCB, the advertising agency, were

London Transport Shops CATALOGUE

plight and falling revenues. Nick Lewis had been an account handler at an advertising agency (an account handler is the agency insider liaising between the agency machine and the account executive who deals with the client). Nick tried hard to get me on his side by taking me to the pub to express his excitement at his latest challenge. He had mixed with creative people at the agency and he knew that it was mainly them who could make the success of any campaign. Of the creative people in the Publicity Office there were only myself as the designer and Ron Pigram leading Lea and Jeff, his two junior copywriters.

I was in the happy position in the Publicity Office studio of having a

flexing their muscles and reporting to the LT Board that LT's financial future would improve by replacing the Johnston typeface. So Michael was turning to me for alternative strategies, such as revised poster layouts and colours. These are recorded in the Johnston chapter.

I was tired, and relieved when Michael was released from the post to which he was clearly not suited. The office was rudderless, with Basil Hooper at the ultimate top but out of touch with day to day running. I now realise that he may have been subjecting us to what has become

known as *shock therapy* where an upheaval is created so that other measures can be introduced without being noticed or objected to. A fragile relationship developed between Basil and myself – others were vocal regarding the spats they were having with him – I kept my judgement to myself. I met him regularly since I was now reporting directly to him to seek approval for my work. He was supportive of what I was achieving and continued to be.

The next appointment of Publicity Officer reflected the new thinking that was designed to remedy LT's financial

1976   London Transport Shops Catalogue
Size: 148 × 210 mm
Printer: Bournehall Press

The cover of an extensive fold-out catalogue of everything that could be bought at the LT Shop which was then situated at Griffith House in Old Marylebone Road. The posed photograph features two of the staff who worked in the shop: Ruth Austin and Michael Walton who managed it, as he still does at the LT Museum at Covent Garden amongst his other duties.

1977   London Transport Shops Catalogue
Size: 148 × 210 mm
Printer: Bournehall Press

The reprint two years later features Michael Walton again, looking even younger, showing a poster to Dianna Strickland of the road development section, with Maggie Jones on the far right. On the far left, thumbing through the poster rack are Kate Murphy, my studio assistant, and Peter Sims who ran the timetable section. Kate and Peter were later married and have a family in Sussex.

1978   Season Sense
Size: 179 × 108 mm
Printer: —

A 4-page leaflet promoting season tickets on the Underground. The tickets illustrated were ordered through the Commercial Office and printed at BR's ticket printing works at Derby.

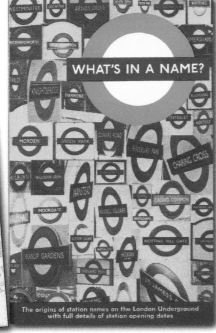

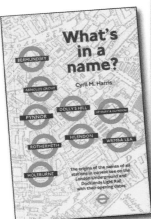

1977   What's in a name?
Size: 170 × 102 mm
Publisher: LT/Midas Books Ltd
Printer: Chapel River Press

The larger of the two cover designs is formed from a collage of station name bullseys cut from photographs from the LT photographic library. I have designed every cover to this publication through different publishers, the inset above showing the 2002 edition published by Capital Transport.

1979   Easter Bus Rally
Size: 210 × 99 mm
Printer:

A 2-colour litho folder containing lists of all the vehicles taking part in the procession. The use of the Clarendon typeface followed the style of all London General Omnibus celebratory material.

Ugggh! The standard of graphics that Nick Lewis commissioned from his choice of studios and required me to aim for, a level that I found impossible to attain!

stream of phone calls from artwork and design studios, as well as individuals performing the same type of work. Each had their particular *forte* and my skill was to attempt to allocate projects to the appropriate contractor taking into account the standard required, their ability to work to time and their price for doing so.

One studio I took with me to LT, who I had used when I worked in the Burrups studio, was Knighton Studios whose stock in trade was quickly produced hand drawn illustrations and artworks mainly for the mail order catalogue sector of advertising. Knighton's front man was Roland Taylor, a polite, disciplined gentleman in his 50s. When Nick Lewis decreed that headings on bus stop timetables would be replaced by diagrammatic maps I recommended that Knighton Studios would be the perfect answer. Their standard was not particularly

high but they could churn out artwork quickly and cheaply.

Nick was rejecting my designs as being too stodgy. I tried to design in the carefree way that the agency was producing work to his satisfaction – I came to really believe that I had been left behind in a design bubble which resulted in my completely losing confidence in myself.

One work that I remember, that was produced by the advertising agency, showed a cartoon-like Kenny Everett climbing the clock tower of Big Ben to advertise a travel ticket. I don't think other people have any reason to remember this poster at all for it had nothing whatsoever to recommended it graphically, except I believed that it was done in the semi-cartoon style that Nick expected me to be following. Nick liked to be in the company of the famous – he kept a framed photograph of himself and Spike Milligan on the shelf behind his desk.

Meanwhile, I was descending into a depression that I had never known before, trapped in the only profession

that I knew. I wanted to go, but I had a family to support and my mental state left me completely unsuitable to do any other job. Our family visited pubs at weekends in Hampshire and Wiltshire with a view to buying one to work in full time. But they tended to be very run down which was the reason why they were for sale. But at least those weekend expeditions took my mind off my desperate situation, until Monday dawned all too soon. I reflected later that I had been suffering from overwork, burn out and depression and discovered that the brain has mental limitations in much the same way that the body has physical limitations. But it did have an unintentional upside, as setbacks often do. Some years later, in 1993, when my father suffered a stroke which left him with severe depression and the first stages of altzeimers I was able to channel to him the right kind

of sympathy that left his wife, Nancy, aghast at my understanding of his situation – first hand experience is an invaluable teacher.

Nick took over the running of a regular design meeting that I had chaired since the departure of Michael Levey. But since the meetings developed into his seeking

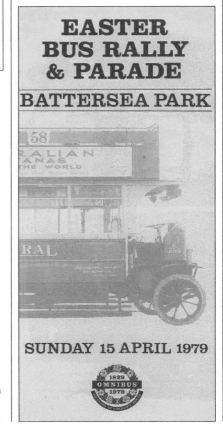

general approval for work he was commissioning, I invariably had to disassociate myself from the discussions. I decided to say nothing, since whatever I was thinking was negative which would have been reflected in any comments I might have made. So Nick reacted by excusing me from further meetings.

Nick's next move was to employ Thelma, probably for sensible motives because she was a systems person, which he was definitely not. Thelma introduced job numbers and job sheets and weekly progress meetings, on the basis that work was being produced behind schedule. I was not aware that any work coming from my section had been completed late, unless I had already warned those concerned of the reasons why. However, she supplied some very spurious information to Nick, implying that my work was not being completed on time, who used it to threaten me with the sack. He then had his secretary type out our conversation at that meeting which I refused to sign, since it was a far from truthful account of what had actually been discussed. I immediately informed my TSSA rep who wrote to Nick reminding him of the agreed procedure when disciplining staff, requiring a third neutral person to be present at the meeting.

I only ever told one office colleague about my increasingly depressing relationship with Nick. Ruth Austin, who worked in the poster shop, was

not only sympathetic but also kept an eye on him. On one occasion she scolded him to his face when he accused me of letting him down over preparations for a meeting which he had never in fact advised me of beforehand.

Thelma then reorganised the office and seemed surprised that I accepted it without a murmur. She had disbanded the design, poster and copy sections and replaced them with two creative teams, a print buying section and a timetable section. Lee Ginger, as the copywriter, and me, as the designer formed Team A and Jeff Levy and Mike Welch, as copywriter and designer respectively, became Team B, the arrangement following advertising agency practice. Ron Pigram headed the print buying section with Bernie Hawes as his assistant. The timetable section was headed by Frank Mussett with Margaret Lambert and Shiela Hole as his assistants.

Frank took the reshuffle badly, to the extent that he failed to come in to work. So I deliberately took time off to visit him at his home to see if he was alright: no one in the office, from Thelma down to the staff clerk had made any effort to contact him. I didn't report back to Thelma immediately but waited a few days until she asked me, which was probably only because timetables were not being processed while the standoff persisted.

In Team A it was me who dreamed up most of the creative ideas. I usually

Gone but not forgotten...

London's trams died in 1952. Read their story in London Transport's new book 'London's Trams and Trolleybuses', £4.95 at the London Transport Shops at St. James's Park Underground Station, at Griffith House (near Edgware Road Circle Line Station) and at the London Transport Collection, Syon Park. Also at bookshops

1977   Gone but not forgotten poster

Size: 25 by 40 inches
Printer: Bournehall Press

The illustration was originally produced as a lino cut and printed on A4-size paper which formed the rough design for approval. It was then photographically enlarged to the final poster size, thereby emphasising the lino cut marks. The ticket type was also enlarged from an original ticket from the route that the subject of the tram illustration which was one LT's preserved trams, used to operate.

got my way with Lee, leaving him to write his wordy copy, which I often later reduced to its salient points, especially the headlines. Basil had demanded that, in the main, posters be produced photographically – possibly to reduce the risk of Nick repeating the use of Kenny Everett climbing Big Ben – so I did far more briefing to outside design and photographic studios. I suspected that Lee was providing regular reports to Thelma as to my behaviour, so I involved him closely with the studios that I employed so that we would share collective accountability should Thelma wish to criticise my choice of,

or relationship with, any of them.

I have already mentioned Bateson Graphics who I met since I joined LT. Their studio was situated in Vauxhall Bridge Road at Victoria. Their reps were Jonathan Sunderland and John Slater. It transpired later in conversation with Jonathan, that his wife was the daughter of Wallace Heath, the managing director of Kynoch Press. When Jonathan moved on, he was replaced by Sarah Dungate, a rather beautiful, highly strung and temperamental dresden doll from the posher part of Essex. She later went to Bill Mariner Associates (BMA), one of the last of the large all-embracing

studios servicing advertising agencies. BMA produced artwork for a number of posters and leaflets for me as well as art directing photographers. When Sarah and I had lunch together we normally went to cafés or wine bars. But lunch with her boss Bill Mariner was usually in Simpsons-in-the-Strand, a very traditionally English restaurant. Roast beef was carved and served straight from the trolley by a dedicated waiter who filled my plate with scraps from the edge of the carving tray until Bill advised that I needed to be holding a ten pound note as I indicated the cuts that I desired. Neck-ties were compulsory as I found

to my financial hardship when I was required to hire one from them before I could enter. The tie had, over time, become impregnated rigid with previous meals. On one occasion, as I made my way through the dining room, I was accosted by two elderly ladies who thought I was a waiter. When I offered to find a genuine waiter they threatened to report me for shirking at my job! On another visit Bill's false teeth broke as he gnawed his way through a pork chop, which meant that I was at last left alone with Sarah, as he returned to his studio and later to a dentist. Sarah left BMA to form her own design consultancy by

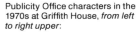

employing freelance designers to work on particular projects. She produced a number of pictorial posters for LT.

In 1981 I was asked by Paul Mijksenaar, one of the design tutors at Technische Hogeschool van Delft (Delft Technical College) in the Netherlands, to give a lecture tracing the development of the London Underground map. I showed a number of slides illustrating the development of the design of buses, trains, stations and publicity to connect the mood of change to the introduction of a new graphic rendition of London's Underground lines. It was followed by a discussion and my comments

to their own design of the Tube map following a visit they had made to London. Sarah travelled to Delft with me and gave welcome moral support. Whilst at the college I met Professor (Ootje) Oxenaar, head of the design department. He was also design consultant to the Dutch Post Office and the designer of the beautiful Dutch bank notes of the 1960s–2000. Siep Wijsenbeek, the corporate design manager of Netherlands Railways (NS) was also there. He arranged visits for later that week to observe rolling stock and stations of the main line railways. Paul Mijksenaar arranged similar visits to Den Haag

tramways and Amsterdam tramways and metro for whom he had given design advice. I got on particularly well with Siep. He was aware of much of the work I had done up to then for London Transport, observing it on his frequent trips to London for meetings with his counterparts at British Rail. His compliments helped to lift my confidence. This was during the time that my relationship with Nick Lewis was at rock bottom. I suppose Nick knew about this trip since I spent a lot of time in his outer office using his secretary's phone which was the only one that was enabled to make calls to countries beyond Great Britain. I

booked time as annual leave to make the trip and paid for myself and Sarah, claiming nothing for any part of it.

The very upper middle class Mercedes Palfrey-Rogers fronted Amperand, another large studio also staffed by ex-agency artists. It was their lettering artist who drew up the New Johnston extrabold italic for display on Red Arrow buses, Airbuses and others. I was lunching with Mercedes in a restaurant in Victoria Street, when I mentioned to her that I had received an invitation from Sid Sharman to his wedding reception which was to be at Claridges in Mayfair on the following Saturday.

Tim's pearly king outfit decorated with beer bottle tops drilled and sewn on for his 1975 Christmas party entry.

Deni Potter (Miss Kettle) on the rocks at St.Ives, Cornwall.

left Bill (Gwylim) Thomas and his assistant Sylvia James supplied graphic design to the Publicity Office from the early 1970s. They are seen here in the studio at Griffith House.

below Christmas office parties at Griffith House used to be quite lavish fancy dress affairs. Here is Una Rabbitt at the 1975 party. She also posed in the Night Bus publicity.

Kate Murphy, who worked in the studio, acting out her social dream at the 1975 party.

Robin Brooke, in the sun glasses, was already printing posters and booklets at the Bournehall Press for the Publicity Office when I arrived at LT, as had his father since before World War II. He kept his yacht at Lymington on which I occasionally sailed in the Solent, together Bernie at the helm.

Sid ran his own litho printing company, having gained experience at C. J. Petyt. When I told Mercedes that I had no one to accompany me (except the other staff who had been invited and always kept together for safety), she called the waitress over and proposed that she join me at the wedding reception, to which, to our surprise, she accepted. The waitress was called Deni and agreed to meet me on the Saturday outside Green Park Station. On that day her boy friend delivered her and she looked stunning in a red dress together with her very long naturally blond hair slightly crinkled. She had adapted a chrome plated electric kettle into a handbag to which she had attached a leather belt to form a shoulder strap – she later became known as Miss Kettle. When we arrived at the reception, more

heads turned in our direction than for Sid and his new wife. Deni took it very well considering she neither knew me nor any of the other people at the reception. She later worked at Rough Trade Records off Pentonville Road, was unwell and was moving from one squat to another. I spoke to her mother who lived in Cornwall and we arranged that I would accompany Deni home. She did not want to go, so I virtually kidnapped her onto the train

from Paddington ostensibly to visit my home in Reading. I already had rail tickets for us to Cornwall and so kept her on the train until we reached St.Erth, one stop short of Penzance, where her family welcomed her and over time coaxed her back to health. I took the train to Cornwall to see her every other weekend for about a year, often repatriating possessions from her various squats. On one occasion I collected her base guitar and two large speakers from her friend's house in Manor House – my first visit to that area since riding there on one of London's last trams 30 years before. Deni's recovery was helped by joining the Prince's Trust for 18 months where she partook in outward bound treks and dry stone wall building.

Redgrave Graphics was a studio I used since moving to 55 Broadway.

They were conveniently situated nearby in Denbigh Mews, off Denbigh Street in Pimlico. The studio was run by Cliff Redgrave, who later dabbled in finding cheap holidays on the internet. Cliff's rep was Carolyn Reeve who was pushy, efficient and funny. Redgraves later employed another rep called Katherine Lunt, whose ambition was to find a husband so that she could change her unfortunate surname. The studio did a lot of work for me, especially artwork for leaflets explaining new bus routes or changes to existing routes. They also produced all the mock-ups for the bus livery scheme that I presented to the LT Board in the 1980s.

Cliff took his staff to Majorca during the week before one Christmas and invited me along, so I took Deni. We missed the flight from Gatwick

because she didn't have a passport, so we bought a temporary one and we were put on a flight the following day.

During one summer Cliff organised a trip to France for myself and Lee and some of his other clients to France. A coach took us from Calais to a restaurant that he had booked near Le Touquet, an accomplishment for him since he was an anglophile with no great love of French cuisine. All went well until our return, when some members of the party discovered their partners getting far too familiar with others who had become separated at the back of the coach!

On the printing side I continued to keep in touch with the printers that Bernie and his staff in the print buying section were selecting for particular jobs. A familiarity with the printer often saved time briefing. There were also occasions when the printing process could help the look of a job or make it considerably cheaper – I have already mentioned the overprinting of two transparent colours to form a third. I never ceased to be amazed at the ignorance of some studios of the purpose of artwork and of printing methods – usually studios working for advertising agencies. The

reason for overlays on artwork was to separate colours or photographic processes such as line from halftone. And yet, some artworks turned up with no overlays or some that were totally meaningless to the process.

In the 1980s Thelma persisted with requiring members of every section to attend her progress meetings, despite there being very few cases when she actually caught people out who had failed to complete their part of current projects in time. After all, she had introduced a progress department in the capable hands of the flamboyant Perry, who offered practical solutions

if alerted that an individual job was floundering. Entire afternoons were devoted to the weekly progress meetings, through which I generally lethargically awaited my job numbers to be called to which I would confirm that each job was on schedule or completed. During one meeting I was awakened by Mike Harris's elbow jabbing my side causing me to bark out the situation of the first of my jobs that were on the list, to which Thelma told me to be quiet and await my job to be called. I whispered to Mike to explain my confusion and he replied that he had nudged me because I was snoring!

1979   Last RT Souvenir ticket
Size: 148 × 81 mm
Printer: Bemrose & Co, Derby

The front and back were based on a Bell Punch ticket and was typeset by Wace & Co, one of the foremost type setters regarding quality. The ticket opened out to display a side view of an RT-type bus overprinted with a short history.

1974   Tourist tickets

Designs were developed to standardise and make rover and go-as-you-please tickets more attractive and different looking to tube season tickets.

1978   Visitor's Pass
Size: 73 × 89 mm
Printer: —

Passes to allow visitors to enter LT offices.

1975/82   Travel Permits
Size: 8 × 26 in
Printer: Glasgow Numerical
             Printing

At the top is the original rough design followed by two printed proofs. At the bottom is the first to be issued with space for a passport size photograph.

1979   Last RF Buses invitation
Size: 105 × 148 mm
Printer: —

Printed in just two colours using offside and nearside views of an RF coach and bus.

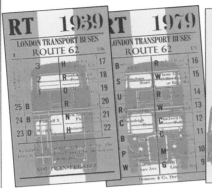

Ticket designs

At the time when I joined the Publicity Office in 1971, the only tickets it was responsible for the design and production of were confined to special events and farewell tours. Their production came under Ron Pigram's copy section wing and were designed either by the retained designers or the printers of the items. The design of most featured text describing the event and a bullseye. With the photographic section so close, I was able to get reference very quickly for illustrations that I wished feature on

tickets commemorating final journeys of particular wehicles. The production of these special tickets brought me into contact with the Commercial Office who gradually came to Publicity for assistance with designs of their regular tickets. They needed to be confident that any designs would be practical over the entire range of tickets within a batch – daily, weekly, monthly, annual, adult, child, as well as (in those days) male and female for added security. My contact was Terry Morgan, always impeccably dressed, affable and practical.

A successful range of Go-As-You-Please ticket designs led, in 1976, to my designing the first elderly persons' Travel Permits. Free travel was being introduced on the buses for old age pensioners, handicapped and blind people between 09:30 and 16:30 It was funded by the Greater London Council at the time when Ken Livingstone was its leader. A run of over a million annual passes were

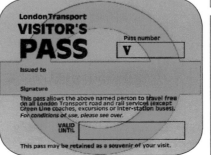

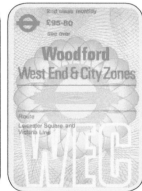

required which would be produced by Glasgow Numerical Printing who also manufactured the automatic numbering machines to individualise each ticket. Their printing and numbering machinery appeared to be extremely cranky and noisy, but it produced the required results on a roll of card which was sliced up at the end of the process to form the individual tickets. Background colours were changed each year for added security.

On a subsequent visit to Glasgow I took the artwork for the tickets' background on the overnight train as usual. This time I consumed far too much whisky with some Scottish lads who were celebrating going home and I awoke with a massive hangover. Terry had asked me to also brief the printer with the colours for the student half fare identity cards. But I briefed the student colours for Travel Permits and vice versa – a million Travel Permits appeared in Student colours! Terry was ecstatic at the bold colour changes, but requested that I warn him in future if I planned to make other unilateral decisions!

New tickets were required for use in the fare zones that were being introduced, first in central London and later throughout the LT system. Printing had become more sophisticated allowing very fine backgrounds to be reproduced. I visited the Bank of England printing works at Loughton in Essex. They were endeavouring to supplement their income by producing security backgrounds for sale to outside organisations. The studio manager showed me an album of security backgrounds to choose from – for recognition of his rank and profession he was equipped with a large paintbrush in the top pocket of his white knee length coat. The backgrounds had been created in the darkroom by placing a piece of photographic film on a record player turntable and fixing a laser light to the stylus in place of the needle. As the turntable spun the stylus would be moved randomly by the operator.

I chose about ten backgrounds to cover the different combinations of Underground fare zones, expecting to pay about £100 each for them. When I was quoted £20 each I failed to stifle a gasp which led the Bank's artist to reduce the price including a quantity discount to £50 for all ten!

Basil decided that Terry and me should go to Bemrose's printing works in Derby to discuss ticket designs and printing methods for the new range of zonal travelcards. Terry had been many times but this would be my first visit. It was Basil's loyalty test, entailing taking the train from London on Sunday afternoon and staying overnight in a Derby hotel for an early Monday start. Most of the day was spent on the factory floor with Bemrose's rep, Andrew Linsey, while their craftsmen and machine minders demonstrated different printing

Terry Morgan and Trevor Brooks looked after the production and ordering of all tickets for use on the London Underground and bus systems.

1980   Upright tickets designs

Tickets were redesigned and standardised to be viewed upright.
The Leytonstone to Gower Street ticket is a rough design aiming to make annual seasons look more prestigious than the weekly and monthly ticket treatments seen to its right.

1980/85   Zonal Season tickets

Fare zones on the Underground started with the central area divided into two zones. Later, when the entire system was converted to fare zones, tickets were given differing background designs and colours to aid security and checking.

The Saracen's Head

1976   Pub and antique shop hand painted signs

The style of the fascia that I designed and painted for the *Saracen's Head* when it was owned by the Kelly family (*inset above*) and later style with additional signs, including the illustrated pub sign that I designed and painted for the pub's subsequent owner, Dave Short (*right*).
Fascia and window signs on an antique arcade (*centre right*). These establishments are situated in Amersham's Whielden Street. The *Saracen's Head* pub (*right*) is directly opposite Tim's, Jan's and Alice's former family home (*below*).

Alice and Jan (*below right*).

methods using water and non water based inks and split duct printing where two or more colours would merge and separate across the ticket.

It was during a meeting in the Commercial Office, with Basil Hooper, Terry Morgan, myself and Nick Lewis present, that the question arose as to how newsagents could keep a large variety of stocks of different combinations of bus passes. I suggested that they could hold the basic background shell tickets for 1-day, 1-week, 1-month and annual passes. Separate self adhesive zone-coloured stickers could be affixed on the space provided and then be stamped with the expiry date. Basil thought this idea was a winner, but he also admonished Nick for his own lack of enterprise and failing to promote his staffs' creativity. As Nick and I waited on the platform for a Circle Line train back to our office at Edgware Road, Nick smouldered and growled about the treatment he had suffered from Basil – as I inwardly glowed! Newsagents were subsequently supplied with their packs of blank bus passes, stocks of different coloured zone stickers, which were all accounted for, and date stamps with ink pads. To my knowledge there were never any complaints from them – a simple solution, even if not state of the art. Indeed, I had suggested that newsagents would have fun with the system and would like to feel involved.

Back to the posters and leaflets

Gradually the style of graphics that I had introduced using bold simple images on a disciplined grid was making itself apparent as more posters and leaflets, be they informational or promotional, were to be seen side by side. The lives of posters varied generally from one to six months, giving an idea of how long the introduction of a scheme needed to become familiar as a style. Rough designs for every item of graphic work and usually artworks too were approved before printing by Basil, who gave his blessing, support and constructive criticism. In the gap between Michael Levey going and his successor, Nick Lewis, arriving a year later I was the direct link between the LT Board, Basil, myself and getting jobs produced. One of the last tasks demanded of the long suffering Michael before his departure in 1978 was to terminate the contracts of the retained designers, Peter Roberson, William Fenton and Harry Stevens.

Shortly into the new scheme Basil required the by-line *Let's make the most of London* to be seen in conjunction with the roundel. He later amended it to *Going places*. The grid treatment demonstrated the importance of a creative layout, which can do as much to enhance the interest in the subject matter as the image appearing. The grid was also

indicating half way across with an arrow across to the centre. I knew what she was trying to do, but she did not have the diplomatic skills to be able to explain to me why. So she brought in a studio, Kassa & Steele, to design a centred poster grid. So, at least she recognised that some sort of discipline was necessary, instead of the untidiness with different sized roundels in different positions that Nick, and his predecessor Michael Levey, were comfortable with.

But Nick was still determined to have me removed permanently from the office if he could. He dreamed

seen to be very adaptable, in the right hands, and by no means compromised promotional poster and leaflet layouts.

Nick played little part in the development of this innovative poster style, mainly because it had been approved before his arrival. The advertising agencies he was dealing with preferred simplified centred layouts. So, once again, the project was not allowed to be developed fully before being rejected and superseded.

With the arrival of Thelma, Nick used her to order a return to centred layouts, which she readily agreed with. Initially, she crudely encircled the roundel on the artwork – not even on the overlay – with a ballpoint pen,

up a proposal that I would benefit from working in a commercial studio for a time to catch up with the latest developments in advertising and design. He allowed me to chose where I went so I selected Lloyd Northover who were a design consultancy that Nick and Thelma knew and apparently liked and I believed that I might actually benefit from. My place sitting opposite Lee would be filled by Mike McMann, a very agreeable refugee from the failed LT Typesetting disaster. I found Lloyd Northover to be dull and I had nothing in common with the people there – they were in

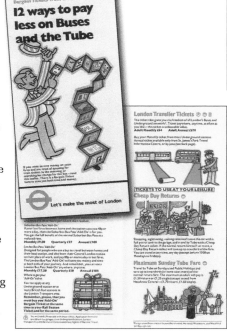

1979   **Bus change leaflets**
Size: 104 × 146 mm
Printer: Kelly & Kelly and others

I had designed the bus change leaflets since my first days at LT. Short introductions describing the changes, were followed by reproductions of bus stop timetables reduced in size to fit the leaflets, the timetable type becoming 6pt, common to most timetable booklets.
For the covers I asked Gwylim Thomas, who was also drawing the maps inside, to go out with his camera and photograph some recognisable points along the routes concerned, which was often difficult to achieve since many routes ran through similar looking estates. These designs persisted for about two years.

1979   **12 ways to pay less folder**
Size: 99 × 210 mm
Printer: —

The folder was illustrated by Gwylim Thomas.

1979   **Bus stop panels**
Size: '12inch' and '24inch'
Printers: various

Panels informing of local events were as professionally designed as was all other publicity.
The Free Family Show layout, illustrated by Gwylim Thomas was one of an ever changing series conceived to announce shows at bus garages throughout the bus system.
I designed the Harrow Bus Station panel to publicise the bringing together of all bus routes in the new venue adjacent to Harrow-on-the-Hill Station.
A humorous approach was employed for the request stop panel. The scenes were shot in Tudor Drive Kingston. The model (person) was again Una with an immaculately turned out model RM (bus) from Kingston Garage.

1979–81   Night Bus posters
Size: 25 × 40 ins
Printer: Impact Lith (Woking) Ltd

Bus interior roof panels and double royal posters were used to promote the revamped Night Bus network. The model is Una Rabbitt, with Jim Lovatt who ran one of the printers to LT.

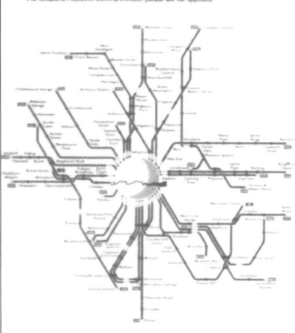

their early 20s, I was in my late 30s and therefore close to the scrapyard in their graphic design environment. They gave me a few unimportant projects to stop me getting totally bored. However, they did ask me to submit a series of page layouts for the DESIGN & ART DIRECTORS (D&AD) ANNUAL which were also being worked on by two of their own designers. The couple of weeks of lead time allowed me to formulate my ideas and produce very detailed layouts with type drawn in and pictures added which were portions of black and white photographs to give an abstract effect, as I had done at Burrups when mocking up designs for company annual reports. A few days before the deadline for submissions, and after I had completed my designs, the two in house designers had made very little progress. So I helped them develop their sparse ideas to some sort of conclusion and took on some of their mock up page layouts so that they could meet the deadline. It was not until I had been back at the Publicity Office for some time that Nick took the latest D&AD Annual from the shelf to show me examples of good design, that he was greeted with an exclamation from me that the book's page layouts had been produced from my specifications. Of course he didn't believe me, but admitted some years later that he had spoken to Lloyd Northover who had confirmed that D&AD had indeed chosen my layouts.

Nick was keen to move the Publicity Office to LT's headquarters at 55 Broadway. This came about in 1980, having divested itself of the shop and photographic sections, both of which had become part of the LT Museum at Covent Garden, successor to the LT Collection at Syon Park. The road and rail publicity sections, which in the past had initiated many marketing schemes, had been disbanded, most of their tasks and some of their staff being incorporated into the respective bus or rail marketing departments. What was left was re-named the Advertising & Publicity Department to become a service section to the various departments it had spawned.

Following these reorganisations, Gill Cork took over the hiring of professional photographers for shoots and, if necessary, models too. This coincided with the tv presenter, Michael Aspel, appearing in some ticket promotions. Gill organised the taking of the pictures of Michael, who showed a natural interest in what Gill and myself did at LT. When I met him again some weeks later when he was filming a sequence in the bus control centre above Baker Street station, he remembered me and continued to ask more questions of myself.

The regular posters continued to be produced, but the lines of command were blurred. Someone on my level but in a different department now had the power to alter or even reject any piece of work that I had produced.

1979   **London Transport Museum**
Size: various
Printers: various

An Underground car and a General bus were used to highlight the new museum. Double royal posters (*left*) and press advertisements (*above*) were produced.

1979–81 Events posters
Size: 25 × 40 ins
Printers: various

These posters were conceived by myself and developed by studios.

David Anderson Designs artworked the cricket poster. The Centenary Test logo was a requirement by Lord's.

Turner Associates artworked the red London Marathon poster, with its requirement of the small sponsor's lettering above the roundel.

Turner Associates also produced the *Everyone's a winner* poster design following my brief stipulating that I wanted a connection between the participants and the audience. The runner and the little girl were separately photographed and superimposed on a stock picture of the Marathon taken the previous year – hence the absence of their shadows on the road surface!

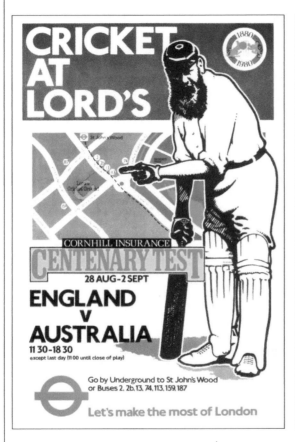

Indeed, that person could even go directly to an outside agency for the production of their publicity work or even design it themselves – hardly a professional approach in a world class public organisation. Much of this was the result of Nick getting Basil's authorisation that the department become a profit centre. Advertising

& Publicity would stand of fall by its ability to produce enough work to pay the staff wages and central London (prime site) rent. It was rumoured that Basil hoped that A&P would fail.

The new office was on the 5th floor Wing-over-Station, situated in Petty France and physically connected to 55 Broadway and to Albany House,

slightly further down Petty France. Nick went on a spending spree by commissioning an interior designer to turn the main office into a semi-open plan area with a footpath down the middle, which was also used by people with no connection with A&P taking a short cut between other offices within the organisation, many

of whom continued their meetings loudly as they traversed the open office. The studio was in a long narrow room off the main open office. My desk was closest to the door facing Gail Everett, Mike McMann who later left to go freelance and whose place was filled by Les Hayes was further down and, at the furthest end,

New management team for this station

London's Tube Management has been decentralised to keep more closely aware of local needs.

Mr Michael Fish, Divisional General Manager, is now responsible for the Metropolitan and the Jubilee Lines, and his duties include the overall day-to-day running of this station.

It is his job to keep in touch with you – the passenger.

You can contact him at,
Divisional Office
Baker Street Underground Station
Baker Street
LONDON
NW1 5LJ
Tel 01 935 6688

Let's make the most of London

New management team for this station

London's Tube Management has been decentralised to keep more closely aware of local needs.

Mr Walter Matthews, Divisional General Manager, is now responsible for the Northern and Victoria Lines, and his duties include the overall day-to-day running of this station.

It is his job to keep in touch with you – the passenger.

You can contact him at,
Divisional Office
72 Euston Street
LONDON
NW1 2HA

Let's make the most of London

New management team for this station

London's Tube Management has been decentralised to keep more closely aware of local needs.

Mr William Clarke, Divisional General Manager, is now responsible for the District and Piccadilly Lines, and his duties include the overall day-to-day running of this station.

It is his job to keep in touch with you – the passenger.

You can contact him at,
Divisional Office
Earl's Court Station
Warwick Road
LONDON
SW5 9QA

Let's make the most of London

1980–81 Informational posters
Size: 25 × 40 ins
Printers: various

The Underground requested that the actual area managers be shown, giving a human touch to the divisional offices. This treatment also illustrated the problems of using real people as models – some looked good, others not so. Whilst the Elderly persons publicity (shown overleaf) makes use of professional models who are more responsive to the art director's instructions. All posters were art directed by myself.

was Mike Welch. I sat by a window through which I had a perfect view of the flagpole topping Buckingham Palace. I therefore knew exactly when Her Majesty was in residence or was arriving or leaving as indicated by the flying of her Royal Standard or its raising or lowering. She usually departed to one of her weekend

retreats on Friday early afternoons, returning during Monday mornings. Heads of states were honoured with an enlarged Standard flying for the duration of their visits to the Palace.

My view also overlooked the backs of some flats fronting Petty France, one of which was occupied by a couple in their 20s and wealthy enough to afford

the central London rent. Obviously relishing each other's company, they often canoodled naked in the kitchen as they prepared breakfast. This regular performance was abruptly terminated by Mike Welch whose excitement led to him lean out of the office window and cheer raucously!

Our studio was later moved to

the end of the building, in a swap with Nick Lewis's office involving more building work. My view of Her Majesty's movements was replaced by the prospect of the roof of the London branch of GCHQ (Government Communications Headquarters) agency for intelligence activities – a building which didn't officially exist!

The publicity posters, car cards and leaflets made use of professional models who were not only more responsive to the photographic director's instructions but wore appropriate clothing. They were photographed at the Bill Mariner Associates studio.

Elderly?
Now you can travel on London's Underground with your British Rail Senior Citizen's Railcard

Now a British Rail Senior Citizen's Railcard is an even better bargain! You can use it to travel in London between any two Underground stations* for the London OAP Concessionary fare (currently 20p) at any time after 9.30 a.m. on Mondays to Fridays. And there's absolutely no time restriction at weekends or on Public Holidays.

Tickets to Baker Street and other Underground stations may also be used via Marylebone (B.R.).

*Except north of Queen's Park.

Let's make the most of London

1980   D-stock door buttons
Size: 415 × 263 mm
Printer: C. J. Petyt

The D-stock was originally built with passenger operated sliding doors, which allowed only those required for use to be opened, enabling warmth to be kept inside cars more effectively. It was also hoped that wear and tear would be minimised to door opening motors if they were used less often.

At the end of the 1980s Alice came to work at London Transport Pensions Office, just three floors below me. I had seen little of her since she had gone with her mother to live in Wendover and I'd moved to Reading. So she often came to my office. But it did mean that I had to control my regular outbursts of frustration at the system that was stifling me.

Before our move to 55 Broadway, a series of posters were required to inform tube passengers that their monthly or weekly season tickets could be renewed over the phone instead of by personal visits to station ticket offices. I thought we should show some slightly extreme circumstances precluding Sunday afternoon visits to local stations prior to new tickets becoming valid the following Monday. Three possible venues came into my imagination. One was a hiking trip miles from London, another a holiday trip by the swimming pool and the third an all-day stay in bed. I had met a studio who were connected with Ray Gething, an agency art director that I knew and had done some work for at his home, close to mine in Amersham. This studio produced roughs from my ideas and, initially, the hiking scene was accepted by Basil.

We needed first to find a site in the country with a telephone box, so Lee picked me up about 4:30 in the morning and we drove to the Peak District of Derbyshire where we meandered around looking for a suitably placed phone box. As we were ready to give up looking we came across a red telephone box by the side of the road in a perfect position – except that it was partially derelict and without a phone. Once back in the office I contacted the GPO telephone region in charge of the particular box and they promised to spruce it up ready for our visit about a week later. Following another very early start, Lee and I met the studio representative, photographer and models at the telephone box. The GPO had been true to their word. They had re-painted the red and added a telephone. However, the fog was so thick that neither the box nor the background scenery could be seen through the murk. We had no choice but to abandon the site and search for a better one. Our budget could not possibly stretch to another day for photography and Thelma would never have allowed an extra day for what she considered to be an unnecessary day out anyway. We

drove up above the fog and found a site where a temporary box, which the photographer had brought in kit form as just such a precaution, could be erected. Time was passing. It was now the afternoon and the models had to be back in London at a particular time in the early evening or we would have to pay them for another day's modelling. All was achieved, including a sheep which strayed onto the set and joined the models, for nothing!

Back in the studio, I selected the most suitable of the many photographs taken and then turned Lee's lengthy poster title into a question that the man was asking down the phone. The same type of direction was done for the next poster, the couple in bed. This time the picture was shot entirely within a studio so it went closer to plan. The third poster never materialised, probably because Nick and Thelma could not bring themselves to authorise visits by me and a photographer to the continent. It could have been done in this country in a health spa with locally hired models. This was one of a number of double standards being set – the agency could have travelled to the continent with all their hangers-on without any questions being asked.

I was keen that design students visited for short periods to gain experience of working in a design studio. Normally I selected them, but one young person was directed to me. Whilst being public school and

1980   **Tube Season posters**
Size: 25 × 40 ins
Printers: C. J. Petyt

Regular commuters used to have to visit their local stations to renew their season tickets, usually on a Sunday. These posters were designed to imply the alternative activities that could be taken once renewing by telephone replaced the need to visit stations in person.

1979–82 Wimbledon Tennis posters
Size: 25 × 40 ins
Printers: various

Different posters were designed and printed every year since London Transport had a special interest in publicising the bus service they ran to the tennis courts from Wimbledon and Southfields stations. These are some of the clever ideas combining directions for travelling to the event as well as publicising the event itself. They do not show the strain of developing a different idea every year, which I did with the help of Kate Murphy and Mike Welch, the studio assistant at Griffith House.

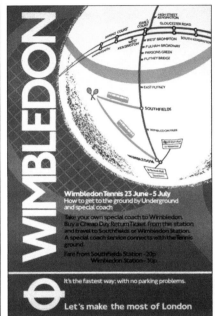

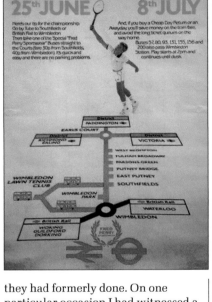

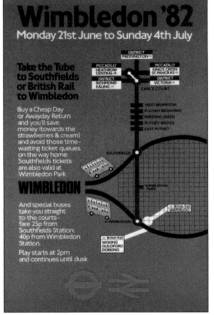

university educated she possessed a very limited design understanding, so I set her to work on copy editing to which she seemed more at home. But I was uneasy, so I was very careful how I expressed my feelings towards the management whilst in her presence. During the 1984 Christmas season I invited her to accompany me to a reception at the London Transport Museum at Covent Garden. I stayed with her and when the LT Chairman, Keith Bright, approached us felt able to introduce her to him. However she countered by introducing me to him as her being part of his family!

I had already met Keith Bright a few weeks earlier at a reception he was hosting at 55 Broadway for LT fire wardens. This was shortly after the fire at Oxford Circus Underground Station on 23 November 1984 which was traced to a paint store off a connecting passageway between the Bakerloo and Victoria line platforms. I commented to Keith Bright that, since smoking had been banned from trains from July 1984, I had noticed more passengers discarding their still lit cigarettes on platforms when trains came in, instead of waiting to light up once inside the train which

they had formerly done. On one particular occasion I had witnessed a cigarette being tossed into the air and landing on the channel conduit above head level carrying wiring along the length of the platform. At my regular meetings with the LT Permanent Way Safety Committee, they made me extremely aware of the fire hazards in tunnels caused by dust, most of which consists of human tissues and hair. So I suggested to him that the Oxford Circus fire might have been more likely as a result of more people smoking on platforms since they were no longer allowed to do so on trains.

He moved on to socialise with other people that he felt more at ease with.

On the 18 November 1987, 31 people died inside King's Cross Underground Station which it is thought was caused by a fire started by a lighted cigarette or match spreading through accumulated dust.

After the move, I had retained my position of fire warden which I had gained at Griffith House. With a spate of bombs being detonated inside buses and trains and with London being alerted with the help of the posters that I was designing, my training was extended to the

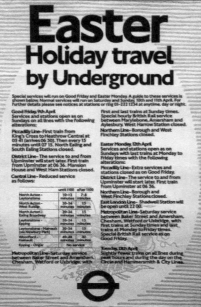

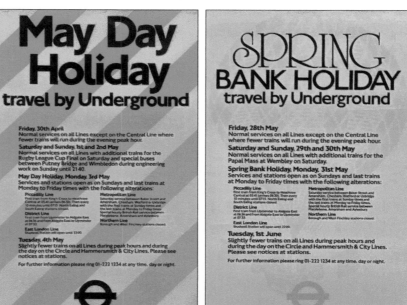

1979–82   Holiday posters
Size: 25 × 40 ins
Printers: various

The annual statutory holidays created a challenge to imagine new idear and images. These three posters were amongst the first to be produced as filmset artwork instead of letterpress using simple images in limited areas. This explanation goes a little way to these posters being rather over set typographically.

marshalling and protection of my colleagues should a genuine bomb threat need to be addressed. Evacuations were practised about every two months for which I was as ignorant as everyone else beforehand as to their authenticity. The only genuine fire I attended was caused by the unfortunate Chris Knowles whose cigarette stub caused the waste paper in the bin under his desk to set off the fire alarms as it smouldered. Having ordered one of the secretarial staff to handle the evacuation of the staff to the pre-arranged St.James's Park assembly point (and reminded

Lee Ginger that it also applied to him), I set about extinguishing the still smoking bin. I had never tackled a fire with carbon dioxide before. But I held the nozzle much to close to the bin, causing an explosion of paper ash to engulf me when I pressed the handle – the fire was already virtually out – I had created a scene of drama from one of order. The fire brigade arrived and sat me down and congratulated me for containing the inferno, forwarded my name to the Chairman who later sent me a congratulatory note! On the strength of my bravery the office manager made me an environmental

safety warden, giving me the power to conduct inspections of offices and corridors regarding their tidiness, condition of floor surfaces, electrical wiring and office machinery. I used my powers to have offending areas closed until being rectified, so the management must have been relieved when I resigned the post as being too time consuming. The job passed to Andy Byles who conducted it with a relish that he had failed to perform in any of his official appointments!

Bernie's printing section was moved from the centre of the open plan office to right down to the

extreme end from the office. He had gained a clutch of assistants: young and helpful Natalie, Kate, the guttural central european Margaret Lambert and the survivor Frank Mussett who had reverted to despatching bus stop timetables for printing. While Frank was replenishing his coffee from the machine at the other end of the office – an area that encapsulated the office's social life – Bernie's assistants, with the encouragement of Stacey in the adjacent section, regularly dialled Frank's phone number, prompting him to run back to his desk, usually showering coffee over him and anyone

1987   Covent Garden poster
Size: 25 × 40 ins
Printer: —
Photo: Michael Lloyd

We were given very little time to arrive at an idea and produce a poster announcing the forthcoming opening of Covent Garden Station on Sundays. I sent Michael to the area to take a range of photos that I could build a design around. Having chosen this picture as being the most dramatic, I devised a quote attributed to the performer which seemed to be a better solution than the usual heading and text toward the head of the layout. (I also cleared with the acrobat that he did actually work on Sundays – and he was rewarded to his satisfaction).

1989   The Royal Wedding poster
Size: 25 × 40 ins
Printer: Bournehall Press
Artist: Martin Handford
Artwork: Redgrave Graphics

The function of this poster was primarily to show the route of the pageant in relation to Underground stations and bus stops. Martin was already known for his humorous detailed illustrative work in childrens' books. His final artwork had to be thoroughly checked with a magnifying glass that none of his characters were indulging in inappropriate activities! The overall layout was conceived by myself and the artwork and hand lettering by an outside studio. The photograph Prince Andrew and Sarah Ferguson was supplied by Buckingham Palace. The Palace were shown rough designs of the poster at progressive stages up to completion.

nearby. They would ring off as Frank picked up his receiver, yelling "Thank you very muchly … now I'm soused in coffee!" into the unresponsive equipment, followed by a lengthy sniff that only Frank's nose could inhale. The centre of the office was occupied by the progress section led by the outrageous Perry and his assistant Les, before he moved into the studio.

Thelma decided to marry one of the printers who handled LT's work, meaning that ethically she could

not remain in the office while her husband's firm continued dealing with us – I have a lot to thank him for! She was replaced by Jennifer Cousins who was a breath of fresh air and very cuddly. She possessed little technical knowledge of buying work from studios who often ran circles round her with badly produced artwork which was near impossible to reproduce from. Her claim to fame was that she was one of the highest graded females within the London Transport

organisation and unique in being afro-caribbean too. Channel 4 television made a documentary of her at work featuring our progress meeting, the camera following her voice around the table as she ascertained the situations of the jobs we were handling and waited for our answers. Her presence made a welcome break from the pseudo culture that had dominated the Lewis/Wright regime.

That wasn't the first time I had appeared on national television.

Some years earlier the BBC invented a game show, hosted by Terry Wogan, where competing teams would guess the correct purposes of objects that were placed in front of them. I was part of the team called 'the Unders' representing the Underground, opposing 'the Overs' from bus operating. Terry punctuated the show by asking team members what they did in their respective departments. Christine Holland, who worked in my studio, replied that she designed the posters apologising to passengers for cock-ups on the Underground. The intake of breath amongst us could be heard as a hiss, which was replaced for transmission by hilarious laughter and clapping! A future edition featured opposing banks; the series lasted for a very short season only.

My other broadcasting appearance was on a Radio 4's Saturday evening *Loose Ends* show, hosted by Ned Sherrin, where I explained the art of coal hole and drain cover rubbings using a stick of black waxy 'healball' on wall lining paper.

Meanwhile back at work, Jeff Mills was remorselessly increasing the staff of his Rail Marketing department to have the capacity to remove all informational work from A&P, who were still handling the production of posters, leaflets and maps. He was briefing a design consultancy to overhaul every Underground associated visual image emanating from his department – and further.

This was achieved in conjunction with Jeremy Rewse-Davies, the Design Director since the early 1990s, who would have recommended Henrion Ludlow & Schmidt to analyse the existing visual situation and come up with recommendations.

The HLS proposals were sprung on us as a complete surprise – I don't think even Nick Lewis knew about it.

No doubt, discussions were held between the heads of departments over the future production of work, should the A&P staff who were affected by the changes chose not to co-operate. I am sure that Jeff Mills expected, and hoped, that the changes would lead to a transfer of all production work, including print buying, to his department, leaving Nick solely in charge of dealings with the advertising agency and day to day work for other departments including what was left of bus publicity.

Chris Ludlow, of HLS, presented the series of poster layouts that his firm had devised to a silent audience of A&P staff. I was regarded as the leader of a possible revolt, but instead I asked a series of, what I was told later and congratulated upon, very practical and constructive questions. The HLS proposals were very close to the layouts I had devised and developed some years previously – I felt vindicated. Indeed, at that presentation and later, I was accused of jumping the gun and flagging problems before they were actually

seen to exist. One such regarded the flexible position of the roundel in relation to poster headlines, necessitating the printing of posters in 2-colours, whereas a standard position for the roundel next to the first line of headlines would allow information posters, which formed the majority of printing output, to be overprinted in one colour on pre-printed roundel backs. This suggestion was a re-assertion of what had always been done for economic reasons and Bernie thanked me for making the point, which I was able to express in designer terms rather than office terms.

My old mate Chris (Basher) Leadbeater became the Underground's marketing design supremo (self appointed?) and proceeded to dictate to me what was good, bad, acceptable or unacceptable design. He also insisted that nothing but New Johnston type could be used on all posters, leaflets and booklets whatever the circumstances.

In the late 1980s the Design Director, Jeremy Rewse-Davies had a vacancy looking after and buying in corporate design throughout the LT organisation and reporting to Paul Moss of his small department. I had

met Jeremy on a number of occasions, particularly when designing items of interest to the LT Board, such as fares revision posters and vehicle liveries. I was told later, by Paul Moss, that they had decided not to fill the post at the present but I was the first candidate when they decided to go ahead. Shortly after, the post was filled by Corynne Bredin. She later had the task of steering any designs of a corporate nature through Henrion Ludlow & Schmidt. Neither Corynne nor HLS could quite keep up with my continuing developments of diagrammatic maps and other items of a corporate nature – they seemed to think that once a particular style of design had been approved it should remain as such as if framed in a museum. Bernie, in particular, supported my case and helped me to persuade Corynne, perhaps less than the designers at HLS. At our regular meetings we would sit around a very wide table, me opposite the amply bosomed designer representing HLS. I would submit my design proposals by placing them immediately in front of me, so that she had to climb across the table to see them clearly! In future Corynne not only trusted

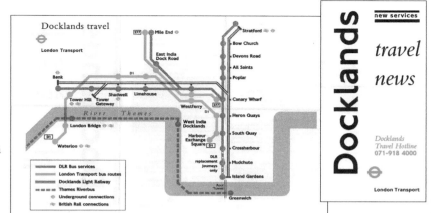

1990   Docklands Travel News
Size: 159 × 75 mm
Printers: Cullum Litho, Chigwell

The Docklands Light Railway was in trouble by breakdowns and rebuilding. Following mounting public complains that went as far as Parliament, the DLR came to Publicity for a solution. All the important people had gone home, but myself, Bernie from the print and Ivor Godfrey-Davis from Public Relations were still around to plan the type of publicity required to keep the public informed of day to day changes and to indicate the alternative bus services. From text written by Ivor, I produced overnight the design for a folder, including the map, while Bernie obtained printing prices. It was all printed and DLR benefited. But, alas, too late to keep it with London Transport – privatisation was too good for the Tory government to miss.
Designed following the latest LRT corporate style it uses the specified type faces of (New) Johnston and Bembo – haven't we been here before?

1983   London Bus Sales
Size: 297 × 210 mm
Printer: Staples Printers, St.Albans

Chiswick Bus Works turned to Advertising & Publicity Office help sell its rapidly growing fleet of supernumerary buses. The majority were DMSs and I had one photographed on the forecourt of Fulwell Depot, where tramlines still existed set within granite cobbles – the impression implied that the buses were well equipped to drive on uneven surfaces as might be found in the third world. Within the cover, separate specification sheets for each type of bus for sale could be stored in a pocket.

me to continue designing without continually submitting new projects for approval, but also allowed me to approve other designers' work.

I had already unwittingly gained a relationship with Corynne. In November 1990, as I walked down the corridor to my office with Corynne, we were discussing the resignation of Margaret Thatcher as Prime Minister the previous day. Corynne became emotionally tearful to the extent that I had to take her in my arms until she regained her composure – a less sympathetic ally she could not have found, if only she had known!

During the early 1980s, I designed one of my last memorable posters. It was intended to be no more than a message to advise tube passengers to keep their personal stereo players turned down to a level that adjacent people could not hear. Most existing – and subsequent – graphic representations show the user looking happy and content while the characters either side are seen to be expressing annoyance and aggression. Since the action was in the hands of the stereo wearer, it was that person that had to be persuaded to play their equipment at a reasonable level.

So I focused on the individual by showing the head of a shop display dummy and positioned parts of the stereo player to emphasise some of the face, with the intention of making the user look characterless. Because the message was directed to the user I needed to emphasise this in the title, which therefore had to be *personal*. Script lettering assisted this direction, implying an invitation. However, this treatment incited the wrath of Chris Leadbeater, the self-styled corporate design commissar, for not rigidly following his house style rules over the use of New Johnston type.

Thanks to Jennifer who gained the support of Jeff Mills, Chris's boss, my design went through unscathed. The poster was displayed at the ends of tube car interiors and acquired some recognition by being reproduced in TIME OUT magazine before most posters were slid out of their frames by collectors and taken home to adorn bedroom walls. It was also reproduced in London Transport's own publication, *Underground Art* by Oliver Green, together with a caption crediting – yes – me! The anonymous in-house designer was again given public recognition! Neither Nick Lewis or any other higher members of the Publicity or Marketing offices made any mention of the poster to me – good or bad!

In this fairly unhappy time my life was made more tolerable by serving drinks from behind the bar at two pubs in old Amersham – the *Saracen's Head* directly opposite my family home and the *Nag's Head* just along Whielden Street. Working in the *Nag's Head* usually covered long weekends while the landlord, Brian Murphy, took his family away for breaks. I slept in the pub overnight to frighten any intruders and during the days cleaned the pipes to the beer engines and changed barrels in the cellar. At the *Saracen's Head* I worked regularly three nights a week and often at weekends. The owner, Dave Short, was usually never to be seen, especially if there was trouble that I had to handle

If your stereo annoys other passengers you are contravening the bye-laws.

on my own and sometimes resulting in the barring of customers and clearing up the mess created by them. A relationship developed between me and the regular customers. Some would be especially obliging after closing time if they thought they could stay for more drinks. Others came to sample the snowballs that I mixed myself instead of serving them from a bottle (possibly because gin or vodka formed part of my recipe) – very time consuming which irritated the other waiting customers. There were also the young lads, just old enough to drink alcohol legally, with their girlfriends who had definitely not yet reached the legal age since some even brought their homework to complete for handing in the next day at school. One of the girls, called Kim, was more individual than the others and often sat at the bar for a chat.

In the mid '80s, after Jan had gone with Alice to live in Wendover and I had moved to a terraced house in Reading, Kim phoned me at work out of the blue. By then she was about 20 years old. She visited me at weekends for about two years, during which time we caught up with the 'metal' aspect of the current music scene by visiting gigs featuring Ossie Osborne and Black Sabbath, Saxon, Magnum and others at London and Reading venues – a very positive tonic when my domestic and work lives were in danger of fracturing simultaneously.

My house in Reading was

convenient during the Reading Festival at the end of each August for some office youngers in which to spend nights to recuperate and wash. Julii, who worked in the Tourism Office brought her friends for a number of years in the late 1980s. I sometimes went to the festival with her and was grateful for her protection when I was verbally attacked and addressed as 'grandad'! We often got in for nothing by using the complimentary tickets that had been passed on to me by the LT Press Office. There was one band in particular that we made sure not to miss: Fields of the Nephilim – gothic rock, fronted by the growling voice of Carl McCoy. One evening, they had a practice run at the Majestic, a local cinema converted to a club. I stood at the front close to the speakers as the sound actually deflected my face and hair. They performed as The Preachermen, so as not to overfill the hall, before appearing on the Reading Festival stage the next day.

Julii later introduced me to her boyfriend's mother, Marion, who was looking for somewhere to live in Northumberland, so we toured the windswept desolate and inhospitable countryside between villages until finding a terraced cottage to rent in Rothbury. I spent alternate weekends in Rothbury, travelling by train on Friday after work from London's King's Cross and reaching nearby Morpeth, where Marion collected me by car

1987   **Keep you personal stereo personal!**
Size: 415 × 263 mm
Printer: Cullum Litho, Chigwell

Only ever printed in one size for display inside tube cars, it was later reproduced in London Transport official poster books, TIME OUT magazine and as a postcard. It was also displayed in the Design Museum on London's South Bank.

Kim Haswell

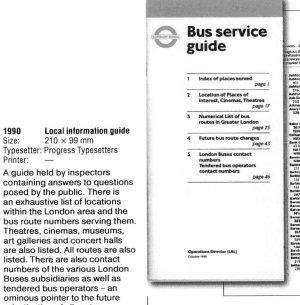

1990　Local information guide

Size:　　210 × 99 mm
Typesetter: Progress Typesetters
Printer:　—

A guide held by inspectors containing answers to questions posed by the public. There is an exhaustive list of locations within the London area and the bus route numbers serving them. Theatres, cinemas, museums, art galleries and concert halls are also listed. All routes are also listed. There are also contact numbers of the various London Buses subsidiaries as well as tendered bus operators – an ominous pointer to the future privatisation of all routes.

This was a typographer's dream and challenge, of how to get a lot of information into a confined space and in a readable form bearing in mind that it may be read in less than ideal lighting conditions

1986　Green Park mugs

These were commissioned by the manager of the Piccadilly Line, responsible for the operation of Green Park Station. The leaves came from St.James's Park, but were probably very similar to those to be found in Green Park and were photocopied in the office to form the artwork.

---

about 3½ hours later, returning to my Reading home on Sunday evening.

The tranquillity of a sleepy village and long walks through unpopulated moors and forests were an irresistible tonic – my weekday and weekend lives supplemented each other. This encounter lasted about 18 months. I never embraced the country life completely by not buying the correct clothes for hiking across water laden fields and rocky climbs, but it brought me far closer to the environment than if I had just visited as a tourist.

In 1989 a further re-organisation resulted in a takeover by Advertising & Publicity of the separate rail and bus marketing departments, but in name only. In reality, the rail marketing department, headed by Jeff Mills absorbed the rump of A&P that was left, by ousting Nick and some of his staff. Also shown the door was Chris Knowles, our frilly-shirted trainer-shoe wearing studio manager employed a few years before by Nick

to be the creative catalyst who would propel LT's publicity to new heights!

Most of the existing staff were made to apply for jobs that were slightly different to what they were currently performing. Those of us left in the studio – Mike Welch, Les Hayes, Gale Everett and myself were excused interviews since our jobs were staying basically the same. But we had to fight for our continued grades – we were being compared with drawing office staff, not that they don't possess particular skills, but we also had their skills plus creative imaginations.

Shortly before this reorganisation,

a former colleague from my earliest years in the Publicity Office, Jeff Levy who had started his LT career in the copy section, was suffering from nerves while struggling to hold onto his job as a publicity rep. This was a resurgence of a complaint that first became apparent when he was moved in with Mike as the copywriting half of their creative team. His latest plight was considered serious enough that his superiors were looking to let him retire on medical grounds. I suggested to Lee that a place could be created in our studio for a copywriter which Jeff could fill so that we could look

after him while he helped us out by writing. My idea was snapped up – it solved the problem of possibly making Jeff's condition worse should he not have wished to go at that time. Later, as part of the reorganisation, a studio manager's job was advertised which I applied for. I never received a reply, let alone an invitation to an interview. No interviews were conducted, it was given to Jeff. Within a very short time Jeff had totally recovered, until he found that he couldn't handle his new appointment and was glad for a later transfer to an easier post.

Staff were offered the chance to discuss the possibility of voluntary severance with Dr Henry Fitzhugh, who had succeeded Basil Hooper as the overall office director. When I phoned Fitzhugh for an appointment, he was so vague about the scheme that nothing transpired. I would have to wait a few more years before leaving.

My work settled down to learning how to operate an Apple Macintosh computer and co-operating with the rail information section to produce posters and leaflets from the copy they had written. This section was led by Richard Sharp, whom I had some dealings with but kept them to a minimum since he was prone to let his emotions get the better of him, with resulting expressive and aggressive language. My main colleague was Lucinda Harridge, who dealt with the operating departments concerned, then wrote the copy from which I

produced layouts and artworks. Luci was a pleasure to work with, her air of confidence inspiring me to give of my best on the jobs that we were working on together, with results that rarely failed to succeed. She presented herself as slightly bohemian, with orange hair and floppy clothes which could have masked her well endowed proportions had they not swayed erotically as she approached me walking, reminiscent of, and answering my teenage fascination with, those electric express trains to Portsmouth! As my confidence with the computer increased I would tap in the text and design the layout around it. I then transferred the layout onto a floppy disc which was given to a typesetting house to produce artwork for the poster ready for the printer.

Once Jeff Mills completed his takeover from Nick, I had another physical office move into the main open plan area where I realised how little work was conducted, replaced by a constant echoing banter. The central walkway also formed a short cut to other offices for people unconnected with publicity matters. Their voices, as they walked past, competed with the banter and shouting up and down the office to save phoning, while I was trying to mentally solve graphic problems. I bought a personal stereo which exhausted batteries in no time fuelling the full volume entering my ears. Sometimes I had to leave the office, almost in tears through

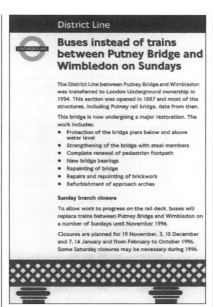

frustration, to go for solitary walks through Parliament Square and alongside the Thames until I had calmed down.

Design problems were referred to the sectional heads, who had no design experience whatsoever. I was usually given designs to do that had been concocted by these people in their meetings. If I attempted to offer a creative input I was quietly dismissed and reminded that I was employed to produce the ideas that they had hatched at their brain-storming meetings. I did develop some creative ideas during this period, which was in the first half of the '90s. But much of my time was spent fine tuning the

diagrammatic Underground map, taking in amendments to the system and adding new lines – the story is covered in other chapters.

It was during this period that the people from London Buses marketing were transferred from their premises in Buckingham Palace Road to our office in Petty France. We were warned that they were very good and that we should make way for them to express their efficiency. I don't know who put that story about – it was probably the higher ups at London Buses who were bent on getting rid of them (it was usual to move unwanted people to other sections by giving them glowing references).

1990   **Underground engineering works information**

Size: A6 (148 × 105 mm)
Printers: various

The prevailing style was utilised on a series of leaflets incorporating a recognisable graphic or map to identify the location of the subject of the text.

1990   **Jubilee Line Open day**

Size: A6 (148 × 105 mm)
Printer: Waterside Press, St.Albans

An open day was held to mark the 60th anniversary of the opening of the Stanmore branch by the Metropolitan Railway in 1933.
The leaflet opened out to display a potted history of the development of the line and its trains and stations.
Printed in two colours, Underground blue and black.

Natalie at the Nice Film Festival.

Had I continued to be in charge of the design updates of the London Underground map, it may have looked something like this today. The refinement of styles continues – what was once seen to be an ultimate solution can later be improved – notably the treatment of fare zone boundaries – to accommodate an increasing amount of information into the present area without compromising the size of the lettering.
This map continues to be designed to fit the pocket map, which remains folded to the same size since the early 1930s.

After a very short time another reorganisation emerged which was more ruthless than previous ones. The three 'designers' remaining were to be reduced to just one. I spoke to Mike King, who was one of the ex-bus marketers and who had already passed his interview to be a higher manager in the new regime, to find out what duties this designer would have and how much the job holder's opinions and suggestions would be respected. The answer was that the job holder would perform any menial tasks that couldn't be done by outside agencies. The holder would not even be allowed to brief outside agencies – I had already had the power to sign orders to suppliers removed from me during Jeff Mill's regime.

This was therefore the time for me to exit the organisation – severance money was still apparently on offer. I had to apply for one of the jobs on offer or I could be accused of apathy, so I opted for a vacancy as a representative to develop signing strategies. On the evening before the interviews, Mike expressed surprise that I had not applied for the 'designer' vacancy. I think he had, in fact, written the job description around me – I was considered to be the 'heavyweight' of the design section, mainly because I always came up with solutions and on time. So I wrote an application by hand which qualified me for an interview the next day. I could have easily answered the questions and

secured the job. Instead, when asked to explain what a corporate identity was I accused the interviewers of concocting corporate identities themselves instead of handing them over to people such as myself.

The ploy had worked so far, but I was still in the organisation and was being sent for retraining. I demanded to see a representative in the human resources office where I said I needed some time off to gather myself together to consider my future. When asked if I wished to take it as annual leave I retorted that they owed me some time after all they had put me through. My friend Natalie from the print buying section had also failed her interview, for the same reason as I had. So I told her to see the human resources people quickly and demand some time off, which she accomplished successfully. I then phoned Cliff Redgrave, who found a holiday available in Menton on the Mediterranean coast of southern France. Bernie joined us in the hotel restaurant at Gatwick, where we had a surprisingly good *fruits de mer*, before bidding goodbye to him and prepared ourselves for the flight early the following morning. The trip coincided with the Cannes Film Festival which was being held along the coast by train from Menton, as was Monte Carlo, where we walked along part of the Formula 1 *grand prix* circuit. We also took the train from Ventimiglia, on the French-Italian border, ascending the Col de Tenda to

Limone Piemonte. Construction of this line necessitated numerous viaducts and tunnels as it crossed from one side to the other of the narrow valley of the fast flowing River Roya. The line had opened shortly before World War I but some of the viaducts were destroyed by retreating armies. Reconstruction was completed in 1928, only for a repeat of the destruction during World War II. The damage was severe and the line remained untouched and isolated, with decaying electrical pylons and rolling stock lying on mountain sides where they had rolled from the line, until work was undertaken on its second restoration in the 1960s with re-opening throughout in 1978.

On returning, Natalie and I reported to Griffith House, where David Southwood was in charge of the redeployment centre. It was on the second floor, one floor below where I had started my career in the London Transport Publicity Office just short of 25 years previously. I already knew David from when he worked in the Commercial Office, often joining Terry and myself at meetings over new ticket designs. With much apology David admitted that he had no records of us coming to the section and asked if we would mind withdrawing for a week while he made enquiries. A week later he asked us to take more time off until our records could be located. Eventually they were found and Nat and I formally entered Griffith House a month after leaving 55 Broadway

– our longest vacation on full pay since entering the organisation and non of it coming out of our annual leave!

While the other refugees were busily learning new trades, writing and rewriting their CVs and attending interviews, Nat and myself were making representations to David for us to be made redundant. I spent most mornings in the public library at Marylebone Road. I was gathering information for a book analysing the typography of timetables, a project I intended to develop once I had left London Transport. I regularly met Nat for lunch in nearby pubs or we tried local restaurants – one was an excellent Swedish restaurant with a full *smörgåsbord*. If we had consumed drinks with our lunch, which we usually did, we couldn't return to Griffith House since the ban on drinking whilst at work had come into force – had we returned and been breathalysed we could have faced dismissal with no compensation – I needed redundancy pay which would finance establishing an office at home.

I checked my account at a bank cash machine. It showed an awful lot extra in my account – I read and re-read the noughts – my redundancy pay had come through, exactly a quarter of a century after my entry to London Transport, to the day! I celebrated my departure with a small gathering in the *Beehive* in Homer Street, the pub where I had spent so many lunchtimes and evenings in the 1970s.

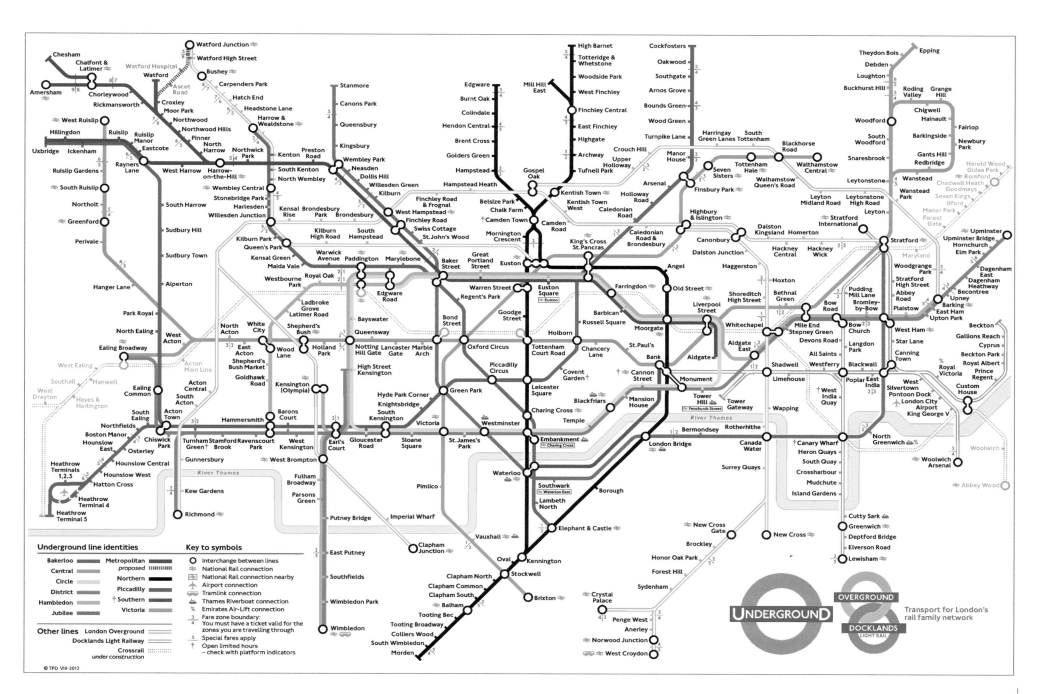

165

Roman figures refer to text pages;
figures in *italics* refer to captions.

167